9th Edition

British Bu

Notable I

British Bus Publishing

Body codes used in the Bus Handbook series:

Type:

A Articulated vehicle
B Bus, either single-deck or double-deck
C Coach
M Minibus with design capacity of 16 seats or less
N Low-floor bus (Niederflur), either single-deck or double-deck
NC Interurban - high-back seated bus
O Open-top bus (CO = convertible - PO = partial open-top)

Seating capacity is then shown. For double-decks the upper deck quantity is followed by the lower deck.

Please note that seating capacities shown are generally those provided by the operator. It is common practice, however, for some vehicles to operate at different capacities when on certain duties.

Door position:-

C Centre entrance/exit
D Dual doorway.
F Front entrance/exit
R Rear entrance/exit (no distinction between doored and open)
T Three or more access points

Equipment:-

T Toilet
M Mail compartment
TV Training vehicle.
RV Used as tow bus or engineers' vehicle.

Allocation:-

s Ancillary vehicle
t Training bus
u out of service or strategic reserve; refurbishment or seasonal requirement
w Vehicle is withdrawn and awaiting disposal.

e.g. - B32/28F is a double-deck bus with thirty-two seats upstairs, twenty-eight down and a front entrance/exit., N43D is a low-floor bus with two or more doorways.

Re-registrations:-

Where a vehicle has gained new index marks the details are listed at the end of each fleet showing the current mark, followed in sequence by those previously carried starting with the original mark.

Annual books are produced for the major groups:

The Stagecoach Bus Handbook
The First Bus Handbook
The Arriva Bus Handbook
The Go-Ahead Bus Handbook
The National Express Coach Handbook

Regional books in the series:

British Bus Handbook: Smaller Groups
British Bus Handbook: Notable Independents
British Bus Handbook: Coaches
The London Bus Handbook

British Bus Handbook: Notable Independents

This ninth edition of our Notable Independents book is one of a trio of books which details the fleets of certain bus and express coach operators throughout Britain. A list of current editions is shown on page 2. The operators included here are more of those which provide tendered and commercial services, primarily in England. The Smaller Groups book comprises those operators that so far have not featured in their own dedicated volume. Quality photographs for inclusion in the series are welcome, for which a fee is payable. High-resolution digital images of six megapixels or higher are also welcome on a memory stick which we will return.
To keep the fleet information up-to-date, the publishers recommend the Key Publishing's magazine Buses published monthly, or for more detailed information, the PSV Circle monthly news sheets.
The writer and publisher would be glad to hear from readers should any information be available which corrects or enhances that given in this publication.

Principal Editor: Stuart Martin; Series Editor: Bill Potter.

Acknowledgments:
We are grateful to the operating companies and Tom Johnson for their assistance in the compilation of this book. The front cover photograph is by Richard Godfrey, while the rear cover views are by Mark Lyons. The frontispiece is also by Mark Lyons.

ISBN 978-1-912063-67-3
Published by British Bus Publishing Ltd
16 St Margaret's Drive, Wellington, Telford, TF1 3PH
Telephone: 01952 255669 - www.britishbuspublishing.co.uk

Operators

Aintree Coaches	5
Atlantic Travel	7
Beeston's	8
Blackpool Transport	9
Brylaine	12
Bus Vannin	14
Cardiff Bus	17
Compass Travel	20
Connexions Buses	22
DRM	24
Delaine	25
Eastern Transport Holdings (Stephensons/NIBS/Galloway)	27
Falcon	31
Faresaver	33
Globe	35
Go Coach/Hulleys of Baslow	36
Grant Palmer	38
Hornsby Travel	39
Houstons	40
Ipswich Buses	42
JMB Travel	44
Land Flight	46
Lloyds Coaches	47
Lynx	49
Marshalls	50
Minsterley Motors	52
Moffat & Williamson	53
Newport Bus	56
Nottingham City Transport	60
Nottingham Community Transport	63
Nottingham LRT	64
Pilkingtonbus	65
Redline	66
Reliance	68
Roberts Travel	69
Safeguard	71
Sanders	73
Sargeants	76
Stotts	77
Tanat Valley Coaches	78
Townlynx	80
Travelmasters	81
Tyrers	82
UNO	84
Vectare/Central Connect/Simonds	86
Vision	91
Warrington	93
Weardale	95
Whippet	97
White Bus Services	98
Whitelaws	100
Xelabus	101
Yeoman	102
Index to vehicles	105

Since the last edition of this book there has been a notable start to the transition towards the ambitious 2030 goal for electric vehicle, though parts of the country struggle with the funding for rural routes. Meanwhile, operators do as best they can to brighten their buses. Remembering the days North Western travelled around Glossop, Go Coach 15, MX63XAU, which is part of the Hulleys operation, carries its 1960's colours as it passes through Chunal. *John Young*

AINTREE COACHES

Aintree Coaches (International) Ltd; J Cherry, Hooton Park Stables, Hooton Lane, Ellsmere Port, CH66 1NH

	M	GB03ACL	Volvo B12B	Plaxton Panther	C53F	2003	
142	H	X111ACL	ADL Trident 2 10.2m	ADL Enviro 400	N41/26D	2005	Candy, Cobham, 2020
147	H	K100ACL	ADL E20D 10.2m	ADL Enviro 200	N29D	2006	Ensignbus, 2021
	H	CX55EAP	Volvo B7TL	ADL ALX400	N45/24F	2006	Presidential, Bootle, 2023
	H	CX55EAY	Volvo B7TL	ADL ALX400	N45/24F	2006	Presidential, Bootle, 2023
	H	CX55EBC	Volvo B7TL	ADL ALX400	N45/24F	2006	Presidential, Bootle, 2023
	H	CX55EBF	Volvo B7TL	ADL ALX400	N45/24F	2006	Presidential, Bootle, 2023
	H	CX06EAK	Volvo B7TL	ADL ALX400	N45/24F	2006	Presidential, Bootle, 2023
152	H	YJ06YRU	Optare Solo M780 SL	Optare	N21F	2006	Otley Coaches, 2024
150	H	CN07KZM	Optare Solo M950 SL	Optare	N31F	2007	First, 2023
145	M	SK07CFU	Volvo B7RLE	Wrightbus Eclipse Urban	N38F	2007	Lothian Buses, 2021
150	H	CN07KZM	Optare Solo M950 SL	Optare	N31F	2007	First, 2023
	H	YJ58VCE	Optare Solo M950	Optare	N33F	2009	Express, Bangor, 2023
	M	YJ09CXD	Temsa Opalin	Temsa	C35F	2009	A1, Methil, 2023
	M	LK58KHE	ADL Trident 2 10.2m	ADL Enviro 400	N41/24D	2009	Metroline, 2023
	M	LK58KHO	ADL Trident 2 10.2m	ADL Enviro 400	N41/24D	2009	Ensignbus, 2021
	M	LK58KHR	ADL Trident 2 10.2m	ADL Enviro 400	N41/24D	2009	Ensignbus, 2021
	M	LK59DYY	ADL Trident 2 10.2m	ADL Enviro 400	N41/24D	2009	Metroline, 2023
	M	LK59DZL	ADL Trident 2 10.2m	ADL Enviro 400	N41/24D	2009	Metroline, 2023
151	H	XOI2520	Volvo B12R 15m	Plaxton Panther	C65FT	2009	Stagecoach, 2021
	M	JFZ9036	Scania K320 IB4	Irizar i4	C51F	2012	Ulsterbus, 2022
	M	LFZ8051	Scania K320 IB4	Irizar i4	C51F	2012	Ulsterbus, 2022
	M	MV12YYL	Ford Transit	Ford	M16	2012	Marchant, Crosby, 2024
	M	MV62HTX	Ford Transit	Ford	M16	2012	Marchant, Crosby, 2024
100	H	W100ACL	ADL E40H	ADL Enviro 400	N45/30F	2013	ADL demonstrator, 2022

Operating in Merseyside, including Sefton, Maghull and surrounding areas, Aintree Coachlines also continues to supply services into Chester which is where classic Enviro 200 122, SN16OGP, was pictured.
Richard Godfrey

Several of the buses dedicated to Chester city routes carry the former Chester Corporation colours. Illustrating them while operating the city centre circular is Enviro 400 142, X111ACL. At Chester the rail station is some distance from the walled city centre. *Richard Godfrey*

121	H	YX65RFN	ADL E20D 8.9m	ADL Enviro 200	N29F	2015	
122	H	SN16OGP	ADL E20D 8.9m	ADL Enviro 200	N29F	2016	
	H	UK66ACL	Irizar i6 12.8m	Irizar	C57FT	2016	
1001	M	XL66ACL	BCI Enterprise BRZ2 12.5m	BCI	NC61/37F	2016	
	M	LX17DZB	BCI Excellence BRZ1 12.5m	BCI	N51/27F	2017	Ensign, Purfleet, 2023
	M	LX17DZC	BCI Excellence BRZ1 12.5m	BCI	N51/27F	2017	Ensign, Purfleet, 2022
	M	LX17GZL	BCI Excellence BRZ1 12.5m	BCI	N51/27F	2017	Ensign, Purfleet, 2023
123	H	YX17NJO	ADL E20D 8.9m	ADL Enviro 200	N29F	2017	
124	H	YY67USP	ADL E20D 8.9m	ADL Enviro 200	N29F	2017	
	M	LX67DDU	BCI Excellence BRZ1 12.5m	BCI	N51/27F	2017	Ensign, Purfleet, 2022
1	H	JC72ACL	ADL E40D	ADL Enviro 400 MMC	NC5135F	2022	
	H	UK23ACL	Irizar i6s 12.8m	Irizar	C55FT	2023	
2	H	AC73ACL	ADL E40D	ADL Enviro 400 MMC	NC5135F	2024	

Special event vehicles: (original owners shown)

980	JCK892	Leyland Tiger Cub PSUC1/2T	Burlingham	C23F	1956	Ribble
1274	RRN423	Leyland Atlantean PDR1/1	Weymann	BC39/20F	1962	Ribble
RM1289	HKF151	AEC Routemaster 2R2RH	Park Royal	B36/28R	1962	London Transport
RM1620	620DYE	AEC Routemaster 2R2RH	Park Royal	B36/28R	1963	London Transport
RCL2243	CUV243C	AEC Routemaster R2RH/1	Park Royal	B36/29RD	1965	London Transport
249	HRN249G	Bristol RELL6G	Eastern Coach Works	B41D	1969	Ribble
1000	KCK381H	Leyland Leopard PSU4A/4R	Plaxton Panorama	C36F	1970	Ribble
7250	TUB250R	Foden NC	NCME	B43/31F	1977	WYPTE
6300	ROC300R	Foden NC	NCME	B43/33F	1977	WMPTE
1000	OHF858S	Leyland National 11351A/1R	Leyland	DP45F	1978	Merseybus
1032	A132HLV	Leyland Atlantean AN68D/1R	Alexander AL	B43/32F	1983	MPTE

Depots: Sefton Lane Industrial Estate, Maghull (M) and Hooton Road, Ellesmere Port (H).

ATLANTIC TRAVEL

Atlantic Travel (GB) Limited, Northolt Drive, Mikar Business Park, Bolton, BL3 6RE

BJ11DSV	Volvo B9TL	Wrightbus Gemini 2	N39/27F	2011	Tower Transit, 2021
BJ11DVH	Volvo B9TL	Wrightbus Gemini 2	N39/27F	2011	Tower Transit, 2021
BN61MXD	Volvo B9TL	Wrightbus Gemini 2	N39/27F	2011	Tower Transit, 2021
BN61MXH	Volvo B9TL	Wrightbus Gemini 2	N39/27F	2011	Tower Transit, 2021
YT61GOX	Scania N230 UD	Optare Omnidekka	N51/35F	2011	Nottingham CT, 2023
YT61GPZ	Scania N230 UD	Optare Omnidekka	N51/35F	2011	Nottingham CT, 2023
KE12OEY	Volvo B9TL	Wrightbus Gemini 2	N39/27F	2011	Golden Tours, 2021
PO12MXD	Mercedes-Benz Vario 0816	Unvi	C24F	2012	
BF62UYN	Volvo B9TL	MCV eVoSeti	N45/27F	2012	Golden Tours, 2021
BF62UYP	Volvo B9TL	MCV eVoSeti	N45/27F	2012	Golden Tours, 2021
BT13ZCZ	Volvo B9TL	MCV eVoSeti	N45/27F	2013	Golden Tours, 2021
BT13LCT	Van Hool TX16 Alicron	Van Hool	C53FT	2013	Leon's, Stafford, 2021
SM63XAF	Van Hool TX16 Alicron	Van Hool	C57FT	2014	Ogden, St Helens, 2018
BF63HEJ	Volvo B9TL	MCV eVoSeti	N45/27F	2014	Golden Tours, 2022
SN16BRV	Mercedes-Benz Atego 1023L	Unvi	C33F	2015	David Dove, Sunderland
YX71OHA	ADL E20D 10.8m	ADL Enviro 200 MMC	N41F	2021	
YX71OHB	ADL E20D 10.8m	ADL Enviro 200 MMC	N41F	2021	
YX71OHC	ADL E20D 10.8m	ADL Enviro 200 MMC	N41F	2021	
YX71OHD	ADL E20D 10.8m	ADL Enviro 200 MMC	N41F	2021	
YX71OHE	ADL E20D 10.8m	ADL Enviro 200 MMC	N41F	2021	
YX71OHF	ADL E20D 10.8m	ADL Enviro 200 MMC	N41F	2021	
SK22BVZ	ADL E40D	ADL Enviro 200 MMC	NC51/34F	2022	
SK22BWA	ADL E40D	ADL Enviro 200 MMC	NC51/34F	2022	
SK22BWB	ADL E40D	ADL Enviro 200 MMC	NC51/34F	2022	
SK22BWC	ADL E40D	ADL Enviro 200 MMC	NC51/34F	2022	
SK22BWD	ADL E40D	ADL Enviro 200 MMC	NC51/34F	2022	
BV22WRJ	Mercedes-Benz Tourismo M2	Mercedes-Benz	C53FT	2022	
BV22WRK	Mercedes-Benz Tourismo M2	Mercedes-Benz	C53FT	2022	
BV22WRL	Mercedes-Benz Tourismo M2	Mercedes-Benz	C53FT	2022	
BF23CMK	Mercedes-Benz Tourismo M2	Mercedes-Benz	C53FT	2023	
BF23CMO	Mercedes-Benz Tourismo M2	Mercedes-Benz	C53FT	2023	
BF23CMU	Mercedes-Benz Tourismo M2	Mercedes-Benz	C53FT	2023	
AT14NTC	Mercedes-Benz Tourismo M2	Mercedes-Benz	C53FT	2023	
YT73BVB	Scania K360 CB4	Higer Touring	C51FT	2023	
YT73BVC	Scania K360 CB4	Higer Touring	C51FT	2023	

Based in Bolton; Atlantic Travel provides luxury coach travel throughout the UK as well as private hire in the Bolton area. Enviro 400 MMC SK22BWD is shown.
John Birtwistle

BEESTON'S

Beeston's (Hadleigh) Ltd; The Coach Depot, Ipswich Road, Hadleigh, Ipswich, IP7 6BG

BUS91A	Scania N94 UB	East Lancs OmniTown	N33F	2004	Nottingham, 2019
NSV371	Scania N94 UD	East Lancs Omnidekka	N47/33F	2004	Ralph Bullock, 2010
NSV372	Scania N94 UD	East Lancs Omnidekka	N47/33F	2004	Ralph Bullock, 2010
YN54NXL	Scania OmniCity CN94 UB	Scania	N42F	2004	Hatton's, St Helens, 2021
524FN	Scania N94 UD	East Lancs Omnidekka	N45/33F	2005	
526FN	Scania N94 UD	East Lancs Omnidekka	N47/33F	2005	Forsyth, Glasgow, 2021
YN55NDY	Scania N94 UD	East Lancs Omnidekka	N47/33F	2005	Forsyth, Glasgow, 2021
BUS91C	Scania N94 UD	East Lancs Omnidekka	PO47/33F	2005	Thames Travel, 2008
BUS91R	Scania N94 UD	East Lancs Omnidekka	PO47/33F	2005	Reading Buses, 2010
BUS91D	Scania N94 UD	East Lancs Omnidekka	PO47/33F	2005	Reading Buses, 2010
BUS91E	Scania N94 UD	East Lancs Omnidekka	PO47/33F	2006	Ralph Bullock, 2010
DRM195S	Volvo B7RLE	Wrightbus Eclipse 2	N45F	2010	Henry Cooper, 2023
226LRB	Volvo B8R	Plaxton Panther	C59F	2021	
229LRB	Volvo B8R	Plaxton Panther	C59F	2021	
FHJ565	Volvo B8R	Plaxton Leopard	S59F	2022	
523FN	Volvo B8R	Plaxton Leopard	S72F	2023	
219GRA	Volvo B8RLE	MCV eVoRa	N38F	2023	
221GRA	Volvo B8RLE	MCV eVoRa	N38F	2023	
MUN56N	Volvo B8L	MCV eVoSeti	NC60/38F	2024	
MUN59N	Volvo B8L	MCV eVoSeti	NC60/38F	2024	
-	Volvo B8L	MCV eVoSiti	NC60/38F	2025	
-	Volvo B8L	MCV eVoSiti	NC60/38F	2025	
-	Volvo B8RLE	MCV eVoRa	N38F	2025	

Special event vehicle:

BCF802	Austin K4 CXB	Plaxton	C29F	1948

Web: www.beestons.co.uk

Representing Beeston's operation is Scania YN55NDY, pictured as it heads home from Ipswich. *Steve Rice*

BLACKPOOL TRANSPORT

Blackpool Transport Services Ltd, Rigby Road, Blackpool, FY1 5DD

217-220		ADL E20D 9.6m		ADL Enviro 200 MMC		N34F	2019	
217	YX19OOU	**218**	YX19OOV	**219**	YX19OOW		**220**	YX19OOY

221-238		ADL E20D 9.6m		ADL Enviro 200 MMC		N34F	2018	
221	YX18KWA	**226**	YX18KWF	**231**	YX18KWL		**235**	YX18KWP
222	YX18KWB	**227**	YX18KWG	**232**	YX18KWM		**236**	YX18KWR
223	YX18KWC	**228**	YX18KWH	**233**	YX18KWN		**237**	YX18KWS
224	YX18KWD	**229**	YX18KWJ	**234**	YX18KWO		**238**	YX18KWT
225	YX18KWE	**230**	YX18KWK					

411-435		ADL E40D		ADL Enviro 400 City		N45/27F	2016-17	
411	SN17MFJ	**418**	SN17MFY	**424**	SN17MGV		**430**	SN17MHF
412	SN17MFK	**419**	SN17MFZ	**425**	SN17MGX		**431**	SN17MHJ
413	SN17MFO	**420**	SN17MGE	**426**	SN17MGY		**432**	SN17MHK
414	SN17MFP	**421**	SN17MGJ	**427**	SN17MGZ		**433**	SN17MHL
415	SN17MFU	**422**	SN17MGO	**428**	SN17MHA		**434**	SN17MHM
416	SN17MFV	**423**	SN17MGU	**429**	SN17MHE		**435**	SN17MHO
417	SN17MFX							

436-455		ADL E40D		ADL Enviro 400 City		N45/27F	2016-17	
436	SN67WZA	**441**	SN67WZF	**446**	SN67WZL		**451**	SN67WZS
437	SN67WZB	**442**	SN67WZG	**447**	SN67WZM		**452**	SN67WZT
438	SN67WZC	**443**	SN67WZH	**448**	SN67WZO		**453**	SN67WZU
439	SN67WZD	**444**	SN67WZJ	**449**	SN67WZP		**454**	SN67WZV
440	SN67WZE	**445**	SN67WZK	**450**	SN67WZR		**455**	SN67WZW

Blackpool Transport selected the Enviro 400 City model for a major fleet renewal in 2016. Our frontispiece shows 415 as it passes the Windmill on Langdale Road, while below is 423, SN17MGU, pictured on Cherry Tree Road in Mereside. *Richard Godfrey*

On 26 March 2022, it was announced that funding worth £198 million has been awarded to twelve local transport authorities under the then government's standard process of the ZEBRA programme. This included £19,600,000 for Blackpool Council for the move towards electric buses. Twenty-six Enviro 200 MMCs joined the fleet and following tenders are to be found on services outside the borough, such as Preston to Fleetwood. Illustrating the model while heading towards Cleveleys is 227, YX18KWG.
Mark Lyons

456-459		ADL E40D		ADL Enviro 400 City	N45/27F	2020	
456	SK20AUN	**457**	SK20AUO	**458**	SK20AUP	**459**	SK20AUT

555-559		Mercedes-Benz Citaro		Mercedes-Benz	N39F	2015	
555	BJ15UVX	**557**	BG15BTY	**558**	BJ15AVX	**559**	BJ15BEO
556	BJ15BEU						

561-586		ADL E20D 11.5m		ADL Enviro 200 MMC	N43F	2019-20	
561	YX19OPA	**568**	YX19OPH	**575**	YX20OFD	**581**	YX20OFL
562	YX19OPB	**569**	YX19OPJ	**576**	YX20OFE	**582**	YX20OFM
563	YX19OPC	**570**	YX19OPK	**577**	YX20OFG	**583**	YX20OFN
564	YX19OPD	**571**	YX19OPL	**578**	YX20OFH	**584**	YX20OFO
565	YX19OPE	**572**	YX20OFA	**579**	YX20OFJ	**585**	YX20OFP
566	YX19OPF	**573**	YX20OFB	**580**	YX20OFK	**586**	YX20OFR
567	YX19OPG	**574**	YX20OFC				

Special event vehicles:

364	B364UBV	Leyland Atlantean AN68C/2R	East Lancs	BC45/29F	1984	
857	D257FYM	Leyland Olympian ONLXB/1RH	Eastern Coach Works	O42/26D	1987	Ensignbus, 2007

Ancillary vehicles:

T292	YJ07EJL	Optare Solo M950	Optare	tv	2007
T554	BJ15UVW	Mercedes-Benz Citaro	Mercedes-Benz	N39F	2015
T977	BF60UVL	Volvo B7RLE	Plaxton Centro	tv	2010
T978	BF60UVM	Volvo B7RLE	Plaxton Centro	tv	2010

One of the oldest electric tramways in the world, the Blackpool Tramway runs from Blackpool to Fleetwood on the Fylde in Lancashire, England. The line dates back to 1885 within the borough. It then extended northwards to link up with the Blackpool and Fleetwood Tramroad in 1900. Since its modernisation in 2012, it has seen modern light-rail trams operating along the eleven miles of coastline to Fleetwood. 008 is seen heading south past the Metropole. *John Young*

Trams:

001-018 Bombardier Flexity 2 32.2m Bombardier N74T 2011-17

001	**004**	**007**	**009**	**011**	**013**	**015**	**017**
002	**005**	**008**	**010**	**012**	**014**	**016**	**018**
003	**006**						

Preserved and historic fleet:

636		Test car	EMB M4d	Brush	S48C	1937
671 w	C	Parts	English Electric M4s	English Electric	S53C	1960
704	C	Stored	English Electric M4d	English Electric	D54/40C	1934
706	C	Operational	English Electric M4d	English Electric	OD52/40C	1934
707	B	Stored	English Electric M4d	English Electric	D52/40C	1934
709	B	Stored	English Electric M4d	English Electric	D52/40C	1934
711	B	Stored	English Electric M4d	English Electric	D52/40C	1934
713	B	Stored	English Electric M4d	English Electric	D54/40C	1934
715	C	Operational	English Electric M4d	English Electric	D54/40C	1935
717	C	Operational	English Electric M4d	English Electric	D54/40C	1934
718	B	Stored	English Electric M4d	English Electric	D54/40C	1934
719	B	Stored	English Electric M4d	English Electric	D44/34C	1935
720	B	Stored	English Electric M4d	English Electric	D44/40C	1935
723	C	Operational	English Electric M4d	English Electric	D52/40C	1935
724	B	Stored	English Electric M4d	English Electric	D54/40C	1935
732	C	Stored	English Electric M4d	Blackpool	?	1962
733	C	Operational	English Electric M4d	Blackpool	35-seat	1962
734	C	Operational	Dick Kerr B4s	Blackpool	60-seat	1962
736	C	Operational	Dick Kerr M4d	Blackpool	S71R	1965
737	C	Operational	EMB M4d	Brush	S48C	2001
T2	C	Operational	Maley & Taunton M4d	MCW	S61C	1960
754		Works	Blackpool Transport	East Lancs	n/a	1992

BRYLAINE

Brylaine Travel Ltd, 291 London Road, Boston, PE21 7DD

	LX51FJF	Dennis Trident 10.5m	Alexander ALX400	N45/28F	2001	Stagecoach, 2014
	LX51FJO	Dennis Trident 10.5m	Alexander ALX400	N45/28F	2001	Stagecoach, 2014
	LX51FKB	Dennis Trident 10.5m	Alexander ALX400	N45/28F	2001	Stagecoach, 2014
		TransBus Trident 10.5m	TransBus ALX400	N45/29F	2003	Stagecoach, 2015
	LX03BTZ	LX03BWW	LX03BVV			LX03BWZ
	LX03BUA	LX03BVT				
	SN53EUW	TransBus Trident 10.5m	TransBus ALX400	N45/29F	2003	Belle Vue, Manchester, '21
	KX04RVJ	TransBus Trident 10.5m	TransBus ALX400	N45/29F	2004	Stagecoach, 2021
		TransBus Trident 10.5m	TransBus ALX400	N45/29F	2004	Stagecoach, 2017
	LX04FXM	LX04FYA	LX04FYM			LX04FYT
w	LX04FXZ	LX04FYF	LX04FYG			
w	YJ54UBY	Optare Solo M920	Optare	N31F	2004	Stuarts, Carluke, 2016
w	YJ05WCF	Optare Solo M850 SL	Optare	N25F	2005	Harrogate CT, 2019
		Optare Solo M950	Optare	N37F	2005	
w	YJ05JXD	w YJ05JXF	YJ05JXH			YJ05JXL
w	YJ05JXE	YJ05JXG	w YJ05JXK			
	YJ55BKO	Optare Tempo X1200	Optare	NC41F	2005	Stagecoach, 2019
	YJ06XLM	Volvo B7TL	Wrightbus Genini	N45/29F	2006	First, 2023
	AE06GZR	TransBus Trident 10.5m	TransBus ALX400	N47/28F	2006	Stagecoach, 2020
	AE06TWU	Optare Solo M850	Optare	N27F	2006	Stagecoach, 2021
	YJ06YSP	Optare Tempo X1200	Optare	N42F	2006	Harrogate CT, 2019
	YJ56ATU	Optare Tempo X1200	Optare	N42F	2006	Harrogate CT, 2019
	MX07BVA	Volvo B9TL	Wrightbus Genini	N45/29F	2007	Vision, Bolton, 2023
	MX07BVD	Volvo B9TL	Wrightbus Genini	N45/29F	2007	Vision, Bolton, 2023
	MX07BVG	Volvo B9TL	Wrightbus Genini	N45/29F	2007	Vision, Bolton, 2023
	MX07BVL	Volvo B9TL	Wrightbus Genini	N45/29F	2007	Vision, Bolton, 2023

Brylaine operates several town services in Boston as well as school and other contract services for Lincolnshire County Council. An acquired fleet of Optare Tempo buses has been accumulated including YJ06YSP, seen in Skegness at the end of route B7. *Steve Rice*

Recent double-deck arrivals add more of the Wrightbus-bodied Volvo B9TLs new to Lothian Buses in 2008. With the coast behind, SN08BXK heads back to Boston. *Steve Rice*

YJ57EHX	Optare Tempo X1200	Optare	N42F	2007	Harrogate CT, 2019
YJ57EGY	Optare Tempo X1200	Optare	N42F	2007	Konectbus, Dereham, 2019
YK57FHM	Optare Tempo X1200	Optare	N43F	2008	Stagecoach, 2019
	Optare Solo M880 SL	Optare	N27F	2008	
MX08DHF	YJ08PHV	YJ08PHX			YJ08PHY
	Volvo B9TL	Wrightbus Eclips Gemini	N48/33F	2008	Lothian Buses, 2021
SN08BWO	SN08BWU	SN08BXF			SN08BYH
SN08BWP	SN08BXE	SN08BXK			
	Volvo B9TL	Wrightbus Eclips Gemini	N48/33F	2008	Stott, Oldham, 2023
SN08BWM	SN08BWW	SN08BWZ			SN08BXB
SN08BWV	SN08BWX	SN08BXA			
YN58FXH	Optare Tempo X1200	Optare	N43F	2008	Stagecoach, 2019
YJ09MHY	Optare Tempo X1200	Optare	N42F	2009	Konectbus, Dereham, 2019
YJ09MHZ	Optare Tempo X1200	Optare	N42F	2009	Konectbus, Dereham, 2019
R13TYB	Optare Tempo X1200	Optare	N42F	2009	Hulleys of Baslow, 2022
YJ59NNZ	Optare Tempo X1200	Optare	N43F	2010	Stagecoach, 2019
YJ10MDE	Optare Tempo X1200	Optare	N41F	2010	Yellow Buses, 2020
YJ10MDU	Optare Tempo X1200	Optare	N41F	2010	Yellow Buses, 2020
YJ60KGE	Optare Versa V1100	Optare	N34F	2010	RATP. London, 2021
WK11APV	Optare Solo M995	Optare	N35F	2011	Faresaver, 2019
WK11APX	Optare Solo M995	Optare	N35F	2011	Faresaver, 2019
YD63UZV	Optare Solo M890	Optare	N34F	2013	igo, Birmingham, 2019
YD63UZW	Optare Solo M890	Optare	N34F	2013	igo, Birmingham, 2019
YD63UZX	Optare Solo M890	Optare	N34F	2013	igo, Birmingham, 2019

Depots: London Road, Boston; Old Boston Lane, Coningsby and Hassall Road, Skegness.

BUS VANNIN

Isle of Man Public Transport, Banks Circus, Lake Road, Douglas, Isle of Man, IM1 5PT

101-108		Mercedes-Benz Citaro K		Mercedes-Benz		NC32F	2016/19	
101	MMN101L	**103**	MMN103L	**105**	NMN105K		**107**	NMN107K
102	MMN102L	**104**	MMN104L	**106**	NMN106K		**108**	NMN108K
109	-	Mercedes-Benz Citaro K Hybrid		Mercedes-Benz		NC32F	on order	
110	-	Mercedes-Benz Citaro K Hybrid		Mercedes-Benz		NC32F	on order	
141-145		Mercedes-Benz Sprinter 45		Mercedes-Benz		N17F	2013-16	
141	MAN41H	**143**	MAN43H	**144**	MMN144G		**145**	MMN145G
142	MAN42H							
171-182		Volvo B9TL		Wrightbus Eclipse Gemini		NC41/30F	2013-14	
171	LMN171K	**174**	LMN174K	**177**	LMN177N		**180**	LMN180N
172	LMN172K	**175**	LMN175K	**178**	LMN178N		**181**	LMN181N
173	LMN173K	**176**	LMN176K	**179**	LMN179N		**182**	LMN182N
183	MMN183U	Volvo B5TL		Wrightbus Gemini 3		NC43/29F	2017	
184	MMN184U	Volvo B5TL		Wrightbus Gemini 3		NC43/29F	2017	
204-222		Mercedes-Benz Citaro L		Mercedes-Benz		NC41F	2011-12	
204	KMN204L	**214**	KMN214U	**218**	KMN218U		**222**w	KMN222U
210	KMN210L	**215**	KMN215U	**219**	KMN219U			
225	LMN225D	Mercedes-Benz Citaro L		Mercedes-Benz		N42F	2012	Evobus demonstrator, 2013
226	LMN226H	Mercedes-Benz Citaro L		Mercedes-Benz		N42F	2012	Evobus demonstrator, 2013
227-230		Mercedes-Benz Citaro L		Mercedes-Benz		NC41F	2013	
227	LMN227H	**228**	LMN228H	**229**	LMN229H		**230**	LMN230H
251-264		Mercedes-Benz Citaro N		Mercedes-Benz		NC40F	2019-20	
251	NMN251M	**255**	NMN255M	**259**	NMN259X		**262**	NMN262X
252	NMN252M	**256**	NMN256M	**260**	NMN260X		**263**	NMN263X
253	NMN253M	**257**	NMN257M	**261**	NMN261X		**264**	NMN264X
254	NMN254M	**258**	NMN258M					
265-270		Mercedes-Benz Citaro H 12m		Mercedes-Benz		NC40F	2020	
265	PMN265D	**267**	PMN267D	**269**	PMN269D		**270**	PMN270D
266	PMN266D	**268**	PMN268D					

Bus Vannin has invested in a fleet of Mercedes-Benz Sprinters for its rural routes. Some have Mellor conversions while others are factory-built like 141, MAN41H, shown. Currently, none are the low-floor variant. *John Young*

2020 saw the arrival of six of the Citaro H model from Mercedes-Benz. The H (hybrid) variant features a 14 kW electric motor that generates energy when coasting and braking. This can reduce the fuel consumption by up to 8.5 percent. 267, PMN267D is seen on route 12. *Richard Cranmer*

271	-	Mercedes-Benz Citaro H 12m	Mercedes-Benz	NC--F	on order
272	-	Mercedes-Benz Citaro H 12m	Mercedes-Benz	NC--F	on order
273	-	Mercedes-Benz Citaro H 12m	Mercedes-Benz	NC--F	on order

301-310 Wrightbus StreetDeck (6cyl) | Wrightbus | NC45/28F | 2020

301	PMN301E	**304**	PMN304E	**307**	PMN307E	**309**	PMN309E
302	PMN302E	**305**	PMN305E	**308**	PMN308E	**310**	T10MAN
303	PMN303E	**306**	PMN306E				

801-804 Mercedes-Benz Sprinter 514 cdi | Mercedes-Benz Transfer 45 | B16F | 2017

801	NMN801A	**802**	NMN802A	**803**	R651MAN	**804**	NMN804A

805-812 Mercedes-Benz Sprinter 514 CDI | Mercedes-Benz Transfer 35 | B16F | 2020

805	NMN805V	**807**	NMN807V	**809**	NMN809V	**811**	NMN811V
806	NMN806V	**808**	NMN808V	**810**	NMN810V	**812**	NMN812V

821	PMN821G	Mercedes-Benz Sprinter 414 cdi	Mellor	B16F	2021
822	PMN822G	Mercedes-Benz Sprinter 414 cdi	Mellor	B16F	2021
823	PMN823G	Mercedes-Benz Sprinter 414 cdi	Mellor	B16F	2021

824-837 Mercedes-Benz Sprinter | Mellor | B16F | 2023

824	RMN824E	**828**	RMN828E	**832**	RMN832E	**835**	RMN835E
825	RMN825E	**829**	RMN829G	**833**	RMN833E	**836**	RMN836E
826	RMN826E	**830**	RMN830E	**834**	RMN834E	**837**	RMN827E
827	RMN827E	**831**	RMN831E				

850w	LMN103J	Mercedes-Benz Sprinter 514 cdi	Mercedes-Benz Mobility 45	B16F	2015
852	MMN882B	Mercedes-Benz Sprinter 514 cdi	Mercedes-Benz Mobility 45	B16F	2015
853	MMN883B	Mercedes-Benz Sprinter 514 cdi	Mercedes-Benz Mobility 45	B16F	2015

854-861 Mercedes-Benz Sprinter 514 cdi | Mercedes-Benz Mobility 35 | B16F | 2016

854	MMN854L	**856**	MMN856L	**858**	MMN858L	**860**	MMN860L
855	MMN855L	**857**	MMN857L	**859**	MMN859L	**861**	MMN861L

Bus Vannin is the government-owned bus service on the Isle of Man. The name was adopted in June 2009 to replace Isle of Man Transport. A private hire Heritage Fleet, which includes AEC and Leyland double decker buses ranging from 1948 to 1967, is also maintained. Pictured leaving Laxey, 205, KMN205L, is one of the early Mercedes-Benz Citaro buses that have now been replaced with later, hybrid models. *John Young*

862	MMN862T	Mercedes-Benz Sprinter 45	Mercedes-Benz	N16F	2017
863	MMN863T	Mercedes-Benz Sprinter 45	Mercedes-Benz	N16F	2017
864	MMN864T	Mercedes-Benz Sprinter 45	Mercedes-Benz	N16F	2017
865	MMN865T	Mercedes-Benz Sprinter 45	Mercedes-Benz	N16F	2017

866-875 Mercedes-Benz Sprinter 45 — Mercedes-Benz — N16F — 2016

866	MMN866T	**869**	NMN869B	**872**	NMN872B	**874**	NMN874B
867	MMN867T	**870**	NMN870B	**873**	NMN873B	**875**	NMN875B
868	NMN868B	**871**	NMN871B				

876-881 Mercedes-Benz Sprinter 45 — Mercedes-Benz — N16F — 2018

876	NMN876H	**878**	NMN878H	**880**	NMN880H	**881**	NMN881H
877	NMN877H	**879**	NMN879H				

882-889 Mercedes-Benz Sprinter 514 cdi — Mellor — M16F — 2021

882	PMN882G	**884**	PMN884G	**886**	PMN886G	**888**	PMN888G
883	PMN883G	**885**	PMN885G	**887**	PMN887G	**889**	PMN889G

890-896 Mercedes-Benz Sprinter 515 cdi — Mellor — N16F — 2024

890	RMN890J	**892**	RMN892J	**894**	RMN894J	**896**	RMN8906
891	RMN891J	**893**	RMN893J	**895**	RMN895J		

Special event vehicles:

2	KMN504	Leyland Titan PD2/1	Leyland	B30/26R	1948	Isle of Man RS
13 u	MN5454	Thornycroft BC	Hall Lewis	B28D	1928	Isle of Man RS
15	410LMN	AEC Regent V	Willowbrook	B36/28F	1968	Douglas Corporation
32 u	XMN346	Leyland Titan PD3/3	MCW Orion	B41/32R	1958	Isle of Man RS
54	3680MN	Leyland Tiger Cub	Willowbrook	B43F	1961	Isle of Man RS
58 u	HMN689	AEC Regent III	Northern Counties	B30/26R	1947	Douglas Corporation
64	MN1082	AEC Regent III	Northern Counties	B30/26R	1949	Douglas Corporation
67	67UMN	Leyland Titan PD3A/6	MCW	B41/32R	1964	Isle of Man RS
99 u	DMN16R	Leyland Olympian	Alexander RH	B47/31F	1990	Dublin Bus
117 u	MN5105	Leyland Lion PLSC1	Massey	B28R	1927	Isle of Man RS

CARDIFF BUS

Cardiff City Transport Services Ltd, Sloper Road, Leckwith, Cardiff, CF1 8AF

101-120		Mercedes-Benz Citaro O530		Mercedes-Benz		N40F	2013	
101	CE63NYU	**106**	CE63NYZ	**111**	CE63NZS	**116**	CE63NYO	
102	CE63NYV	**107**	CE63NZA	**112**	CE63NZT	**117**	CE63NYP	
103	CE63NYW	**108**	CE63NZB	**113**	CE63NYL	**118**	CE63NYR	
104	CE63NYX	**109**	CE63NZC	**114**	CE63NYM	**119**	CE63NYS	
105	CE63NYY	**110**	CE63NZD	**115**	CE63NYN	**120**	CE63NYT	

121-130		Mercedes-Benz Citaro O530		Mercedes-Benz		N41F	2015
121	CN65ABF	**124**	CN65ABU	**127**	CN65ABZ	**129**	CN65ACJ
122	CN65ABK	**125**	CN65ABV	**128**	CN65ACF	**130**	CN65ACO
123	CN65ABO	**126**	CN65ABX				

131-140		Mercedes-Benz Citaro O295		Mercedes-Benz		N41F	2017
131	CN17FZS	**134**	CN17FZV	**137**	CN17FZY	**139**	CN17GNX
132	CN17FZT	**135**	CN17FZW	**138**	CN17FZZ	**140**	CN17GNY
133	CN17FZU	**136**	CN17FZX				

141-152		Mercedes-Benz Citaro O530 L		Mercedes-Benz		N41F*	2011-12	Bus Vannin, 2021 *141/2 are N42F
141	CN11KFZ	**144**	CX11FZS	**147**	CX12FLD	**150**	CX12FLE	
142	CX11FZT	**145**	CX11FZR	**148**	CU12MDN	**151**	CX12FNG	
143	CN11KFY	**146**	CX12FTT	**149**	CX12FLF	**152**	CX12FNH	

153	BF68ZHB	Mercedes-Benz Citaro O295 H	Mercedes-Benz	N41F	2018	Evobus demonstrator, 2013

251-270		ADL E20D		ADL Enviro 200		N39F*	2013-14	*261-70 are N38F
251	CE63NZF	**256**	CE63NZM	**261**	CN64FWJ	**266**	CN64FWP	
252	CE63NZG	**257**	CE63NZN	**262**	CN64FWK	**267**	CN64FWR	
253	CE63NZH	**258**	CE63NZO	**263**	CN64FWL	**268**	CN64FWS	
254	CE63NZJ	**259**	CE63NZP	**264**	CN64FWM	**269**	CN64FWT	
255	CE63NZK	**260**	CE63NZR	**265**	CN64FWO	**270**	CN64FWU	

Linking the city centre with Rhiwbina, Whitchurch and Pantmawr, Caerdydd's Mercedes-Benz Citaro 113, CE63NYL, was pictured as it passed through Whitchurch. In 2021 further examples of the type joined the fleet from the Isle of Man. *John Young*

Green Farm Road in the Ely district of Cardiff provides the location for this view of Enviro 400 MMC 301, CN65AAE. It is one of ten that joined the fleet in 2015. *Richard Godfrey*

301-310		ADL E40D		ADL Enviro 400 MMC	NC51/34F	2015	
301	CN65AAE	**304**	CN65AAK	**307**	CN65AAV	**309**	CN65AAY
302	CN65AAF	**305**	CN65AAO	**308**	CN65AAX	**310**	CN65AAZ
303	CN65AAJ	**306**	CN65AAU				

311-317		ADL E40D		ADL Enviro 400 MMC	N51/34F	2022	On loan
311	YX22OJB	**313**	SK22BVF	**315**	YX72OLK	**317**	YX72OLM
312	YX22OJC	**314**	YX72OLJ	**316**	YX72OLL		

321	SN65OHZ	ADL E40D		ADL Enviro 400 MMC	N51/29F	2015	Bournemouth. 2022

341-346		Scania OmniCity N230 UD		Scania	N41/16F	2022	RATP, 2022
341	YR59FZB	**343**	YT59PBV	**345**	YT59PBZ	**346**	YT59PCO
342	YR59FZD	**344**	YT59PBY				

351-358		Scania N270 UD		Optare Omnidekka	N51/33F	2010	Nottingham CT, 2022
351	YT10UWJ	**353**	YT10UWL	**355**	YT10UWN	**357**	YT10UWP
352	YT10UWK	**354**	YT10UWM	**356**	YT10UWO	**358**	YT10UWR

399	V524ESC	Dennis Trident		Plaxton President	O45/26F	1999	Reading Buses, 2022

401-436		Yutong E12		Yutong	N37F	2021	
401	CE71YCD	**410**	CE71YDF	**419**	CE71YDA	**428**	CE71YXN
402	CE71YCF	**411**	CE71YDG	**420**	CE71YDB	**429**	CE71YXO
403	CE71YCG	**412**	CE71YDH	**421**	CE71YXF	**430**	CE71YXP
404	CE71YCH	**413**	CE71YDJ	**422**	CE71YXG	**431**	CE71YXR
405	CE71YCJ	**414**	CE71YXD	**423**	CE71YXH	**432**	CE71YXT
406	CE71YCK	**415**	CE71YCN	**424**	CE71YXJ	**433**	CE71YXU
407	CE71YCL	**416**	CE71YCO	**425**	CE71YXK	**434**	CE71YCB
408	CE71YCM	**417**	CE71YCP	**426**	CE71YXL	**435**	CE71YDC
409	CE71YDD	**418**	CE71YCR	**427**	CE71YXM	**436**	CE71YXV

The Yutong E12 is the choice of electric bus for Cardiff with over fifty now in service. Illustrating the model is 434, CE71YCB. Seen in Westgate Street it was working route 49 which connects the city with Llanrumney. *Steve Rice*

437-455		Yutong E12		Yutong		N37F	2024	
437	CK24AVU	**442**	CK24AUT	**447**	CK24AVX	**452**	CK24AUW	
438	CK24AVZ	**443**	CK24AUX	**448**	CK24AWF	**453**	CK24AVC	
439	CK24AWG	**444**	CK24AVG	**449**	CK24AWM	**454**	CK24AVJ	
440	CK24AWN	**445**	CK24AVN	**450**	CK24AUJ	**455**	CK24AVO	
441	CK24AUM	**446**	CK24AVT	**451**	CK24AUP			

541-550		ADL E20D		ADL Enviro 200		N33F	2017
541	CN17EYL	**544**	CN17EYO	**547**	CN17EYS	**549**	CN17EYV
542	CN17EYM	**545**	CN17EYP	**548**	CN17EYU	**550**	CN17EYW
543	CN17EYN	**546**	CN17EYR				

551	CN17BGK	ADL E20D	ADL Enviro 200 MMC	N33F	2017	
552	CN17BGO	ADL E20D	ADL Enviro 200 MMC	N33F	2017	
701	CN73AZX	Scania K280 CB4	Higer Fencer F1	NC39F	2023	
702	CN73AZZ	Scania K280 CB4	Higer Fencer F1	NC39F	2023	
720w	YN56FBK	Scania OmniCity N270 UB	Scania	N41F	2006	Reading Buses, 2021
731w	CN57BJU	Scania OmniCity N270 UB	Scania	N41F	2007	

737-744		Scania OmniCity N270 UB		Scania		N41F	2009
737	CN09EFJ	**739**	CN09EFL	**741**	CN59CKV	**743**	CN59CKY
738	CN09EFK	**740**	CN59CKU	**742**	CN59CKX	**744**	CN59CLF

761 t	CN58FFZ	Scania N230 UB	Wrightbus Solar	N41F	2008	
762 t	CN58FFY	Scania N230 UB	Wrightbus Solar	N41F	2008	
769	WX06JXT	Scania L94 UB	Wrightbus Solar	N40F	2006	Go-South Coast, 2021
771	WX57TLY	Scania K230 UB	Wrightbus Solar	N40F	2008	Go-South Coast, 2021
772	WX57TLU	Scania K230 UB	Wrightbus Solar	N40F	2008	Go-South Coast, 2021
773 t	WX57TLV	Scania K230 UB	Wrightbus Solar	N40F	2008	Go-South Coast, 2021
781	YN17ONJ	Scania K250 UB	Irizar i3	N41F	2017	Reading Buses, 2022
782	YN17ONK	Scania K250 UB	Irizar i3	N41F	2017	Reading Buses, 2022
783	YN17ONL	Scania K250 UB	Irizar i3	N41F	2017	Reading Buses, 2022

Ancilliary vehicle:

161	W161EAX	Dennis Dart SLF 8.8m	Plaxton Mini Pointer	N29F	2000

COMPASS TRAVEL

Compass Travel (Sussex) Ltd, Pilgrim House. 51-63 St. Dunstan's Road
Worthing, BN13 1AA

1108	GX62CNN	ADL E20D 10.8m	ADL Enviro 200	N39F	2012	
1109	GX62COA	ADL E20D 10.8m	ADL Enviro 200	N39F	2012	

1110-1116 ADL E20D 10.8m ADL Enviro 200 N39F 2015-16

1110	SK15HBC	**1112**	SK15HBE	**1115**	SN66WKD	**1116**	SN66WKE
1111	SK15HBD	**1113**	YY15NHM				

1117	MX62AKY	ADL E20D 10.8m	ADL Enviro 200	N39F	2012	Sheffield CT, 2018
1118	MX62AKZ	ADL E20D 10.8m	ADL Enviro 200	N39F	2012	Sheffield CT, 2018
1120	YN13GBY	ADL E20D 10.8m	ADL Enviro 200	N39F	2013	
1121	YN13GDY	ADL E20D 10.8m	ADL Enviro 200	N39F	2013	
1122	YY15NHN	ADL E20D 10.8m	ADL Enviro 200	N39F	2015	Silverline, Solihull, 2020
1123	YY17GPF	ADL E20D 10.8m	ADL Enviro 200	N33F	2017	Manchester Airport, 2020
1124	YY17GPJ	ADL E20D 10.8m	ADL Enviro 200	N33F	2017	Manchester Airport, 2020
1125	YY17GPK	ADL E20D 10.8m	ADL Enviro 200	N33F	2017	Manchester Airport, 2020
1126	YY17GPO	ADL E20D 10.8m	ADL Enviro 200	N33F	2017	Manchester Airport, 2020
1127	YY17GPU	ADL E20D 10.8m	ADL Enviro 200	N39F	2017	Mistral rental, 2021
1128	YX18KUE	ADL E20D 10.8m	ADL Enviro 200	N39F	2018	First, 2023
1129	SN16OSV	ADL E20D 10.8m	ADL Enviro 200	N39F	2016	Manchester Airport, 2023
1204 w	YX09FKT	ADL Dart 4 10.2m	ADL Enviro 200	N33F	2009	Metroline, 2018
1205	YX09FNJ	ADL Dart 4 10.2m	ADL Enviro 200	N33F	2009	Metroline, 2018
1301	YX18KNY	ADL E20D 10.8m	ADL Enviro 200 MMC	N41F	2018	First, 2023
1302	YX23OUM	ADL E20D 10.8m	ADL Enviro 200 MMC	N41F	2023	
1303	YX23OUN	ADL E20D 10.8m	ADL Enviro 200 MMC	N41F	2023	
1304	YX23OUO	ADL E20D 10.8m	ADL Enviro 200 MMC	N41F	2023	
1305	YX23OUP	ADL E20D 10.8m	ADL Enviro 200 MMC	N41F	2023	
1306	YX24OWM	ADL E20D 10.8m	ADL Enviro 200 MMC	N40F	2024	
3105	SN61CYY	ADL Enviro 300 12m	ADL Enviro 300	N36F	2011	Trustybus, Harlow, 2018
3204	BA58GHA	Volvo B7RLE	Wrightbus Eclipse Urban	N45F	2009	GHA, Ruabon, 2017
4101 w	GX57AFV	ADL Dart 4 8.9m	ADL Enviro 200	N29F	2007	

4105-4120 ADL E20D 8.9m ADL Enviro 200 N29F 2012-16

4105	GX62CKP	**4109**	GX62CSF	**4114**	GX13FSP	**4118**	YY15NHL
4106	GX62CMY	**4110**	GX13FSS	**4115**	GX13FSU	**4119**	SN16OGS
4107	GX62CJO	**4112**	GX13FSN	**4117**	YY15NHK	**4120**	YX16OCV
4108	GX62CJU	**4113**	GX13FSO				

4121	YX67UYD	ADL E20D 9.3m	ADL Enviro 200	N33F	2017	
4122	YX67UYE	ADL E20D 9.3m	ADL Enviro 200	N33F	2017	
4123	YX67UYF	ADL E20D 9.3m	ADL Enviro 200	N33F	2017	
4124	YX12FRC	ADL E20D 8.9m	ADL Enviro 200	N29F	2012	Wheelers, N Baddesley, '20
4125	YY64TZX	ADL E20D 8.9m	ADL Enviro 200	N29F	2014	Wheelers, N Baddesley, '20
4127	YX63GXP	ADL E20D 8.9m	ADL Enviro 200	N29F	2013	Roberts, Coalville, 2023
4128	YX63GXR	ADL E20D 8.9m	ADL Enviro 200	N29F	2013	Roberts, Coalville, 2023
4129	YX18KUK	ADL E20D 8.9m	ADL Enviro 200	N29F	2018	Ratho, Newbridge, 2023
4130	YX18KUN	ADL E20D 8.9m	ADL Enviro 200	N29F	2018	Ratho, Newbridge, 2023

4201-4204 ADL E20D 9.3m ADL Enviro 200 N33F 2016

4201	YY66PFZ	**4202**	YY66PGE	**4203**	YY66PGF	**4204**	YY66PGK

4205	SN65OEW	ADL E20D 9.3m	ADL Enviro 200	N33F	2015	Prentice, Haddington, 2023
4206	SN65OEX	ADL E20D 9.3m	ADL Enviro 200	N33F	2015	Prentice, Haddington, 2023
4301	YX68UJU	ADL E20D 9.7m	ADL Enviro 200 MMC	N34F	2018	
4302	YX68UJV	ADL E20D 9.7m	ADL Enviro 200 MMC	N34F	2018	
4303	YX68UJW	ADL E20D 9.7m	ADL Enviro 200 MMC	N34F	2018	
4305	YX21RTO	ADL E20D 9.7m	ADL Enviro 200 MMC	N34F	2021	
4306	YX21RTU	ADL E20D 9.7m	ADL Enviro 200 MMC	N34F	2021	
4307	YX21RTV	ADL E20D 9.7m	ADL Enviro 200 MMC	N34F	2021	

Compass Travel operates services in West Sussex, East Sussex and Surrey. Representing the fleet is classic Enviro 200 4109, GX62CSF, pictured while on Worthing town service 900 to Asda. *Mark Doggett*

4308-4311		ADL E20D 9.7m		ADL Enviro 200 MMC	N34F	2024	
4308	YX24OXE	**4309**	YX24OXF	**4310** YX24OXG		**4311**	YX24OXH
4401-4405		ADL E20D		ADL Enviro 200 MMC	N30F	2023	
4401	YX73PJJ	**4403**	YX73PJU	**4404** YX73PJV		**4405**	YX73PJY
4402	YX73PJO						

6111	BX11PTO	ADL Trident 2 10.5m	ADL Enviro 400	N41/31F	2011	ADL development vehicle
6112	SN13CHJ	ADL E40D	ADL Enviro 400	N41/31F	2013	Tower Transit, 2021
6170	YT59DYS	Scania OmniCity N230 UD	Scania	N41/26F	2009	Go-Ahead London, 2022
6171	YT59DYU	Scania OmniCity N230 UD	Scania	N41/26F	2009	Go-Ahead London, 2022
6172	YT59DYV	Scania OmniCity N230 UD	Scania	N41/26F	2009	Go-Ahead London, 2022
6173	YT59DYW	Scania OmniCity N230 UD	Scania	N41/26F	2009	Go-Ahead London, 2022
6174	PN09ENH	Scania N230 UD	Optare Olympus	N45/27F	2009	Go-Ahead London, 2023
6175	PN09ENK	Scania N230 UD	Optare Olympus	N45/27F	2009	Go-Ahead London, 2023
8005	Y24COM	Scania K360 EB4	Irizar i6	C53FT	2015	Solus, Tamworth, 2019
8006	Y26COM	Scania K360 EB4	Irizar i6	C53FT	2015	Solus, Tamworth, 2019
8007	Y25COM	Scania K360 EB4	Irizar i6	C53FT	2015	?, 2019
8101	VA61BFN	Ford Transit	Ford	M17	2011	Micro Buzz, 2015

CONNEXIONS BUSES

Harrogate Coach Travel Ltd, 6 St Thomas's Way, Green Hammerton, York, YO26 8BE

S900RGE	Scania N94 UD	East Lancs Omnidekka	N51/39F	2003	Go-Ahead London, 2018
YN04UJL	Scania N94 UD	East Lancs Omnidekka	N51/39F	2004	Nottingham, 2018
YN04UJY	Scania N94 UD	East Lancs Omnidekka	N51/39F	2004	Nottingham, 2018
YRW194	Scania N94 UD	East Lancs Omnidekka	N51/39F	2004	Stagecoach, 2020
YN05GXA	Scania L94 UB	Wrightbus Solar	N42F	2005	Eddie Brown, 2022
YN05GXB	Scania L94 UB	Wrightbus Solar	N42F	2005	Eddie Brown, 2014
YN05GXC	Scania L94 UB	Wrightbus Solar	N42F	2005	Eddie Brown, 2022
YN05WKF	Scania L94 UB	Wrightbus Solar	N42F	2005	Stagecoach, 2017
YN05WKJ	Scania L94 UB	Wrightbus Solar	N42F	2005	Stagecoach, 2017
MX05CKJ	Volvo B7RLE	Wrightbus Eclipse	N44F	2005	First, 2023
URH806	Scania N94 UD	East Lancs Omnidekka	N51/39F	2005	RATP, London, 2018
5385WX	Scania N94 UD	East Lancs Omnidekka	N51/39F	2005	RATP, London, 2018
XNT421	Scania N94 UD	East Lancs Omnidekka	N47/33F	2005	First, 2022
IUI6411	Scania N94 UD	East Lancs Omnidekka	N47/33F	2005	First, 2022
SN05HWX	Scania N94 UD	East Lancs Omnidekka	N47/33F	2005	First, 2022
YN05GXB	Scania L94 UB	Wrightbus Solar	N44F	2005	Eddie Brown, 2022
789FAY	Scania L94 UB	Wrightbus Solar	N44F	2005	Trent-Barton, 2021
FJ55BZP	Scania L94 UB	Wrightbus Solar	N44F	2005	Trent-Barton, 2021
J800CXB	Scania L94 UB	Wrightbus Solar	N44F	2005	Trent-Barton, 2021
K200CXB	Scania L94 UB	Wrightbus Solar	N44F	2005	Trent-Barton, 2021
DM56BUS	Scania OmniCity CN94 UB	Scania	N42F	2006	DRM, Bromyard, 2014
S400SLT	Scania OmniCity CN94 UB	Scania	N42F	2006	South Lancs, Atherton, '18
7396LJ	Scania OmniCity CN94 UB	Scania	N42F	2006	First, 2023
YN06WMT	Scania OmniCity CN94 UB	Scania	N42F	2006	First, 2023
ESU912	Scania OmniCity CN94 UB	Scania	N36F	2006	Ipswich Buses, 2019
YN56NVF	Scania OmniCity CN94 UB	Scania	N36F	2006	Ipswich Buses, 2019
YN56NVG	Scania OmniCity CN94 UB	Scania	N36F	2006	Ipswich Buses, 2019
K300RSA	Scania OmniCity CN94 UB	Scania	N36F	2006	Go North East, 2021
YN56FBY	Scania OmniCity N94 UD	Scania	N41/23F	2006	happy Al's, 2023
Y20CXB	Scania OmniCity N94 UD	Scania	N45/31F	2006	RATP, London, 2022
5209UA	Scania OmniCity N94 UD	Scania	N41/25F	2008	RATP, London, 2022
WX6025	Scania OmniCity N94 UD	Scania	N41/25F	2008	RATP, London, 2022

Illustrating the colours of Connexions Buses is Scania OmniCity, K300RSA, originally NK56KHF. It was pictured in Leeds. *Steve Rice*

Another view of K300RSA, this time in June 2023 when it was working route 64. This service links Aberford with Leeds on a thirty-minute frequency. *John Young*

CN06GFG	Scania OmniCity CN94 UA	Scania	AN53D	2006	Cardiff Bus, 2022
YN07EYM	Scania N270 UD	East Lancs Omnidekka	N51/37F	2007	Nottingham, 2018
6539FN	Scania OmniCity N94 UD	Scania	N45/28F	2007	Ace Travel, Airdrie, 2019
9936UB	Scania OmniCity N230 UD	Scania	N45/31F	2007	Lothian Buses, 2022
SN57DAU	Scania OmniCity N230 UD	Scania	N45/31F	2007	Lothian Buses, 2022
UUG384	Scania OmniCity N230 UB	Scania	N41F	2007	Go North East, 2022
4078NU	Scania OmniCity N270 UB	Scania	N41F	2007	Cardiff Bus, 2023
8548VF	Scania OmniCity N270 UB	Scania	N41F	2007	Cardiff Bus, 2023
JSU721	Scania OmniCity N270 UB	Scania	N41F	2007	Cardiff Bus, 2023
YN08DFK	Scania OmniCity N230 UB	Scania	N33F	2008	Nash, Smethwick, 2023
YN08DFL	Scania OmniCity N230 UB	Scania	N33F	2008	Nash, Smethwick, 2023
5147UA	Scania OmniCity CN230 UD	Scania	N45/28F	2008	RATP, 2019
5515LJ	Scania OmniCity CN230 UD	Scania	N45/28F	2008	RATP, 2019
M500JJR	Scania OmniCity CN230 UD	Scania	N45/28F	2008	RATP, 2019
L600CKB	Scania OmniCity CN230 UD	Scania	N45/28F	2008	RATP, 2019
LX59CRF	Scania OmniCity N230 UB	Scania	N41/22D	2009	ComfortDelGro, 2023
638UYC	Scania OmniCity CN230 UD	Scania	N45/28F	2009	Stagecoach, 2019
P700CXB	Scania OmniCity CN230 UD	Scania	N45/28F	2010	ComfortDelGro, 2022
NK61DBZ	Optare Solo M880 SR	Optare	N27F	2011	Go North East, 2023
NK61FMD	Optare Solo M880 SR	Optare	N27F	2011	Go North East, 2023
BK13XYF	Mercedes-Benz Citaro O530N	Mercedes-Benz	N42F	2013	Yourbus, Heanor, 2019.
L50LOW	Optare Solo M9250 SL	Optare	N30F	2015	
BV23NUB	Volvo B8RLE	MCV eVoRa	N46F	2023	

Special event vehicles:

AUB170J	AEC Swift 5P2R	Roe	B48D	1971	Leeds City Transport
SUG588M	Leyland Atlantean AN68/2R	Roe	B45/33D	1973	West Yorkshire PTE
XER134T	AEC Reliance	Plaxton Supreme IV	C57F	1979	Miller Brothers, Foxton
CVE12V	Volvo B58-61	Plaxton Supreme IV	C50F	1980	Kenzies Coaches
FWA475V	Leyland National NL106L11/1R	Leyland National 2	N44F	1980	South Yorkshire PTE
B144RWY	Leyland Olympian ONLXB/1R	Roe	BC47/27F	1984	West Yorkshire PTE
D574LFX	Leyland Royal Tiger	Van Hool Alizée	C53F	1986	Travellers, Carnforth
M393VWX	Volvo B10B	Alexander	BC49F	1995	Harrogate & District

DRM

D R Morris, The Coach Garage, Bromyard, HR7 4NT

SN55OUF	Mercedes-Benz Atego 1223L	Ferqui Solera	C30F	2005	Malbank, Nantwich, 2023
YN06MXR	Volvo B7R	Plaxton Profile	C57F	2006	Cresswell, Evesham, 2023
FJ56PFG	Scania K340 EB4	Caetano Levanté	C49FT	2006	First, 2022
YN07LDY	Scania OmniLink K270 UB6	Scania	N55F	2007	Nottingham CT, 2014
YN57FYV	Scania OmniLink K270 UB6	Scania	N55F	2008	Tyrer, Bolton, 2023
YN57FYW	Scania OmniLink K270 UB6	Scania	N55F	2008	Tyrer, Bolton, 2023
YN57FYX	Scania OmniLink K270 UB6	Scania	N55F	2008	Tyrer, Bolton, 2023
YT09FLZ	Scania OmniExpress K340 UB6	Scania	N55FT	2009	Lucketts, 2022
DK09DZE	Volvo B7RLE	Wrightbus Eclipse Urban	N45F	2009	Compass Bus, 2020
DM09DRM	Scania OmniCity CN230 UB	Scania	N41F	2009	Scania demonstrator, 2010
DM10DRM	Scania OmniLink K230 UB4	Scania	N46F	2010	Scania demonstrator, 2011
KV60WDF	Volkswagen Crafter	Volkswagen	M8	2010	
DM12DRM	Scania OmniLink K230 UB6	Scania	N54F	2012	
DM63DRM	Scania OmniLink K230 UB6	Scania	N54F	2014	
DM66DRM	Volvo B8RLE	MCV eVolution	N46F	2016	
BV73MTZ	Volvo B8RLE	MCV eVoRa	N38F	2023	
-	Volvo B8RLE	MCV eVoRa	N38F	2024	

D R Morris is based in Bromyard, a town in Herefordshire, in the valley of the River Frome. DRM's main service connects Hereford with Ledbury. Recent fleet changes have seen the sale of the Enviro 200 MMC and an order for a further Volvo B8RLE. The earlier MCV eVoRa delivered in 2023, BV73MTZ, is seen in Ledbury while heading south on route 476. *Bill Potter*

DELAINE

Delaine Buses Ltd, 8 Spalding Road, Bourne, PE10 9LE

135	Y8OCT	Volvo B7TL	East Lancs Vyking	N45/31F	2001	
136	AD03OCT	Volvo B7TL	East Lancs Vyking	N45/31F	2003	
139	AD04OCT	Volvo B7TL	East Lancs Vyking	N45/31F	2004	
140	AD05OCT	Volvo B7TL	East Lancs Vyking	N45/31F	2005	
141	AD56DBL	Volvo B9TL	East Lancs Olympus	N47/31F	2006	
142	AD07DBL	Volvo B9TL	East Lancs Olympus	N47/31F	2007	
143	AD08DBL	Volvo B9TL	East Lancs Olympus	N47/31F	2008	
144	AD58DBL	Volvo B9TL	East Lancs Olympus	N47/31F	2008	
145	AD59DBL	Volvo B9TL	East Lancs Olympus	N47/31F	2009	
150	AD61DBL	Volvo B9TL	Wrightbus Gemini 2	N45/30F	2011	
152	AD12DBL	Volvo B9TL	Wrightbus Gemini 2	N45/30F	2012	
153	AD62DBL	Volvo B9TL	Wrightbus Gemini 2	N45/30F	2012	
154	AD63DBL	Volvo B9TL	Wrightbus Gemini 2	N45/30F	2013	
155	KX57BWD	Volvo B7RLE	Wrightbus Eclipse Urban	N45F	2008	Jim Stones, Leigh, 2013
156	AD14DBL	Volvo B9TL	Wrightbus Gemini 2	N45/30F	2014	
157	AD64DBL	Volvo B9TL	Wrightbus Gemini 2	N45/30F	2014	
158	AD15DBL	Volvo B9TL	Wrightbus Gemini 2	N45/30F	2015	
159	AD65DBL	Volvo B5TL	Wrightbus Gemini 3	N45/30F	2015	
160 u	AD51DLD	Volvo B7TL	Alexander ALX400	N49/31F	2001	Dublin Bus, 2015
161 u	AD51DLE	Volvo B7TL	Alexander ALX400	N49/31F	2001	Dublin Bus, 2015
162	AD66DBL	Volvo B5TL	Wrightbus Gemini 3	N45/30F	2016	
163	AD17DBL	Volvo B5TL	Wrightbus Gemini 3	N45/30F	2016	
164	AD68DBL	Volvo B8RLE	Wrightbus Eclipse Urban 3	N45F	2018	
166	AD56DLD	Volvo B7TL	ADL ALX400	N49/27F	2006	Dublin Bus, 2019

September in Witham and Enviro 400 171, LJ09CCN operates route 201. It is one of three acquired from Abellio in 2023. *Richard Godfrey*

The origins of Delaine Buses of Bourne Lincolnshire can be traced back to 1890 when the family introduced horse-drawn vehicles to cater for local people wishing to travel to markets throughout the surrounding area. In 2015 the family founded the Delaine Heritage Trust and established the Delaine Bus Museum which houses the extensive Delaine Archive, with the centrepiece being the Delaine Heritage Fleet which consists of former Delaine vehicles dating back to the 1950s. April in Werrington and Enviro 200 MMC 168, AD21DBL, wends its way back to Bourne from Peterborough. *Richard Godfrey*

167	AD70DBL	ADL E20D 11.8m	ADL Enviro 200 MMC	N43F	2020	
168	AD21DBL	ADL E20D 11.8m	ADL Enviro 200 MMC	N43F	2021	
169	AD71DBL	ADL E20D 11.8m	ADL Enviro 200 MMC	N43F	2021	
170	AD22DBL	ADL E20D 11.8m	ADL Enviro 200 MMC	N43F	2022	
171	LJ09CCN	ADL Trident	ADL Enviro 400	N41/31F	2009	Abellio, London, 2022
172	LJ09CCO	ADL Trident	ADL Enviro 400	N41/31F	2009	Abellio, London, 2022
173	LJ09CCF	ADL Trident	ADL Enviro 400	N41/31F	2009	Abellio, London, 2022
174	AD72DBL	ADL E20D 11.8m	ADL Enviro 200 MMC	N43F	2022	
175	AD23DBL	ADL E20D 11.8m	ADL Enviro 200 MMC	N43F	2023	
176	AD73DBL	ADL E40D	ADL Enviro 400 City	N45/32F	2023	
177	AD74DBL	ADL E40D	ADL Enviro 400 City	N45/32F	2024	

Delaine Heritage Trust:

45	KTL780	Leyland Titan PD2/20	Willowbrook	B35/28R	1956
47	MTL750	Leyland Tiger Cub PSUC1/2	Yeates Europa	BC43F	1958
50	RCT3	Leyland Titan PD3/1	Yeates	B39/34R	1960
72	ACT540L	Leyland Atlantean AN68/2R	Northern Counties	B47/35F	1973
100	E100AFW	Leyland Tiger TRCTL11/2RZ	Duple Dominant	B59F	1987
116	M1OCT	Volvo Olympian	East Lancs	B51/35F	1995
130	X7OCT	Volvo B7TL	East Lancs Vyking	N45/31F	2000

Named vehicles: 141 Hugh Delaine-Smith MBE; 142 Thomas Arthur Smith; 143 Emma Jane Smith; 144 Derek Vickers Tilley; 145 Beryl Philippa Tilley. Web: www.delainebuses.com

EASTERN TRANSPORT HOLDINGS

Stephensons - NIBS

Stephensons of Essex Ltd, Riverside Ind Est., South Street, Rochford, SS4 1BS
NIBS Buses Ltd, The Coach Station, Bruce Grove, Wickford, SS11 8BZ

161	S	1842PP	Volvo B9R	Caetano Levanté	C48FT	2012	Galloway, 2024
200	S	X400MTT	Volvo B10M-62	Plaxton Paragon	C57F	2000	Motts, Aylesbury
323	S	EU07FVN	Optare Solo M780 SE	Optare	N24F	2007	
325	S	YJ58PHO	Optare Solo M880 SL	Optare	N28F	2008	UNO, Hatfield, 2021
326	S	EU58AXX	Optare Solo M880 SL	Optare	N28F	2008	
327	S	MX06BPZ	Optare Solo M850 SL	Optare	N28F	2006	
328	S	YJ58PHW	Optare Solo M850 SL	Optare	N28F	2008	
401	N	YX16OBP	ADL E20D 8.9m	ADL Enviro 200 MMC	N29F	2016	Abellio, London, 2021
402	N	YX16OBR	ADL E20D 8.9m	ADL Enviro 200 MMC	N29F	2016	Abellio, London, 2021
413	S	SK07HLN	ADL Dart 4 8.9m	ADL Enviro 200	N26F	2007	
414	S	SK07HLV	ADL Dart 4 8.9m	ADL Enviro 200	N26F	2007	
418	N	MX59AVN	ADL Dart 4 8.9m	ADL Enviro 200	N29F	2009	Ensignbus, 2019
419	N	CN11FBE	ADL Dart 4 8.9m	ADL Enviro 200	N29F	2011	Ensignbus, 2019
421	S	EU09NYO	ADL Dart 4 8.9m	ADL Enviro 200	N29F	2009	
422	S	EU60CAV	ADL Dart 4 8.9m	ADL Enviro 200	N29F	2010	
424	S	EU15AZT	ADL Dart 4 8.9m	ADL Enviro 200	N29F	2015	
425	S	MX62APK	ADL Dart 4 8.9m	ADL Enviro 200	N29F	2012	Go Goodwins, Eccles, 2015
426	S	MX62APO	ADL Dart 4 8.9m	ADL Enviro 200	N29F	2012	Go Goodwins, Eccles, 2015
427	S	YY15NJO	ADL E20D 8.9m	ADL Enviro 200	N29F	2015	Holmeswood Coaches,'17
428	S	YX17NYW	ADL E20D 8.9m	ADL Enviro 200	N29F	2016	Tamar, Plymouth, 2023
429	S	YX17NYZ	ADL E20D 8.9m	ADL Enviro 200	N29F	2016	Tamar, Plymouth, 2023

431-434			ADL Dart 4 10.4m			ADL Enviro 200			N34F	2010	
431	S	EU10NVP	**432**	S	EU10NVR	**433**	S	EU10NVS	**434**	S	EU10NVT

435	S	YY67USC	ADL E20D 9.7m	ADL Enviro 200	N33F	2017	Yourbus, Heanor, 2020
436	S	YY67USD	ADL E20D 9.7m	ADL Enviro 200	N33F	2017	Yourbus, Heanor, 2020
438	N	YY15FZC	ADL E20D 9.7m	ADL Enviro 200	N33F	2015	Omniserv, Heathrow, 2021
439	N	YY15FZD	ADL E20D 9.7m	ADL Enviro 200	N33F	2015	Omniserv, Heathrow, 2021
440	S	SN16ORS	ADL E20D 9.4m	ADL Enviro 200	N33F	2016	Silcox, Pembroke Dock, '16
441	S	SN16ORU	ADL E20D 9.4m	ADL Enviro 200	N33F	2016	Silcox, Pembroke Dock, '16

442-452			ADL Dart 4 10.2m			ADL Enviro 200			N36F	2010	Abellio London, 2019
442	S	YX10FEH	**445**	N	YX10FFA	**449**	S	YX10FFK	**451**	N	YX10FFM
443	N	YX10FEU	**447**	N	YX10FFE	**450**	N	YX10FFL	**452**	N	YX10FFN
444	N	YX10FEV	**448**	S	YX10FFG						

461	S	EU60CBF	ADL Dart 4 10.8m	ADL Enviro 200	N37F	2010	
462	S	YX11CTO	ADL Dart 4 10.8m	ADL Enviro 200	N39F	2011	
463	S	YX11CTU	ADL Dart 4 10.8m	ADL Enviro 200	N39F	2011	
464	S	EU62FDF	ADL E20D 10.8m	ADL Enviro 200	N39F	2012	
465	S	EU62FBO	ADL E20D 10.8m	ADL Enviro 200	N39F	2012	
466	S	DK57OPZ	ADL Dart 4 10.8m	ADL Enviro 200	N37F	2008	HTL Huyton Travel, 2012
467	S	SN66WKF	ADL Dart 4 10.8m	ADL Enviro 200	N39F	2016	
468	S	SN66WKG	ADL Dart 4 10.8m	ADL Enviro 200	N39F	2016	
469	S	SN66WLL	ADL E20D 10.8m	ADL Enviro 200	N39F	2016	Yourbus, Heanor, 2020
470	S	SN66WLO	ADL E20D 10.8m	ADL Enviro 200	N39F	2016	Yourbus, Heanor, 2020

471-481			ADL E20D 10.8m			ADL Enviro 200			NC38F	2015-16	
471	S	EU65EOG	**474**	S	EU65EOK	**477**	S	EU66AVB	**480**	S	EU66AVF
472	S	EU65EOH	**475**	S	EU65EOL	**478**	S	EU66AVC	**481**	S	EU66AVG
473	S	EU65EOJ	**476**	S	EU65EOM	**479**	S	EU66AVD			

491-496			ADL E20D 10.8m			ADL Enviro 200			NC40F	2013	Nottingham CT, 2024
491	S	YX63GXV	**493**	S	YX63KFG	**495**	S	YX63KFK	**496**	S	YX63LHU
492	S	YX63GXW	**494**	S	YX63KFJ						

Stephensons of Essex can trace its origins back to the mid 1970's, when operations started with a single Bedford coach. It now operates a fleet of over one hundred buses and coaches throughout south and mid-Essex and west Suffolk and along with NIBS and Galloways it is part of Eastern Transport Holdings. Illustrating the Stephensons livery is classic Enviro 200 461, EU60CBF. *Mark Doggett*

501	S	EU58BRX	Scania N230 UD	Optare Olympus	N51/29F	2008	
502	S	EU09AUK	Scania N230 UD	Optare Olympus	N51/29F	2009	
503	S	EU59BHX	Scania N230 UD	Optare Olympus	N51/29F	2009	
504	S	YN07LHU	Scania N230 UD	East Lancs Olympus	NC45/25F	2007	RATP, London, 2011
505	S	YN07LHX	Scania N230 UD	East Lancs Olympus	NC45/25F	2007	RATP, London, 2011
506	S	YN07LHD	Scania OmniCity CN270 UB	Scania	N41/29F	2007	Reading Buses, 2011
507	S	YT59NZM	Scania N230 UD	Optare Olympus	N51/28F	2009	Rotala, 2016
509	S	YN07LHP	Scania N230 UD	East Lancs Olympus	NC45/27F	2007	Centrebus, 2012
510	S	YN08OAM	Scania N230 UD	East Lancs Olympus	N51/28F	2008	Centrebus, 2013
511	S	YN08OAO	Scania N230 UD	East Lancs Olympus	N51/28F	2008	Centrebus, 2013
512	S	YN08OAP	Scania N230 UD	East Lancs Olympus	N51/28F	2008	Centrebus, 2013
513	N	YN08OCR	Scania N270 UD	Optare Olympus	N51/30F	2008	
514	N	EU58BLJ	Scania N270 UD	Optare Olympus	N51/30F	2008	
515	S	EU59BFK	Scania N270 UD	Optare Olympus	N51/30F	2009	
516	N	PN09EKT	Scania N230 UD	Optare Olympus	N45/29F	2009	Go-Ahead London, 2019

521-528			Scania OmniCity CN230 UB			Scania		N48/27F	2008		
521	N	LX08ECD	**523**	N	LX08ECF	**525**	N	LX08ECN	**527**	N	LX08ECV
522	N	LX08ECE	**524**	N	LX08ECJ	**526**	N	LX08ECT	**528**	N	LX08ECW

531	S	YT09ZCF	Scania OmniCity N230 UD	Scania	NC51/25F	2009	RATP, 2023
532	S	YR59FYP	Scania OmniCity N230 UD	Scania	NC51/25F	2009	RATP, 2023
533	S	YR59FYU	Scania OmniCity N230 UD	Scania	NC51/25F	2009	RATP, 2023
534	S	YT59DXZ	Scania OmniCity N230 UD	Scania	NC51/25F	2009	RATP, 2023
535	S	YT59SFY	Scania OmniCity N230 UD	Scania	NC51/25F	2009	RATP, 2023

601-608			Scania N230 UD			ADL Enviro 400		N47/28F	2012-14	*607/8 are NC47/28F	
601	S	EU12HXW	**603**	S	EU13EBK	**605**	S	EX63UZV	**607**	S	EU64CVP
602	S	EU12HXY	**604**	S	EU13EBL	**606**	S	EX63UZW	**608**	S	EU64CVR

As well as an integral bus, the Enviro 400 body was available on Scania N-series chassis. While most used the N230UD chassis, two were built for Express Motors on the N280 variant. Both of these are now with Stephensons, represented by the first of the pair, 609, CY12EMS. *Mark Doggett*

609	S	CY12EMS	Scania N280 UD	ADL Enviro 400	N47/28F	2012	Express Motors, 2018
610	S	CX14EMS	Scania N280 UD	ADL Enviro 400	N47/28F	2014	Express Motors, 2018
611	S	SN15ETD	Scania N230 UD	ADL Enviro 400	NC47/28F	2014	Lloyds Cs, 2024
612	S	SN15ETE	Scania N230 UD	ADL Enviro 400	NC47/28F	2014	Lloyds Cs, 2024
613	S	SN15ETF	Scania N230 UD	ADL Enviro 400	NC47/28F	2014	Lloyds Cs, 2024
621	S	EU23BZL	Scania N230 UD	ADL Enviro 400 MMC	NC47/28F	2023	

626-630 Scania N94 UD — East Lancs Omnidekka — N51/29F — 2004-05

626	N	YN04YJR	**628**	N	BIL4710	**629**	N	BIL9406	**630**	N	EU05ECV
627	N	BIL7894									

631-647 Scania N94 UD — East Lancs Omnidekka — N45/33F — 2005 — RATP, London, 2014

631	S	YN55NHA	**636**	S	YN55NHV	**640**	S	YN55NJV	**644**	S	YN55NKH
632	N	YN55NHB	**637**	S	YN55NJE	**641**	S	YN55NKA	**645**	S	YN55NKJ
634	N	YN55NHF	**638**	S	YN55NJF	**642**	S	YN55NKC	**646**	S	YN55NKK
635	S	YN55NHP	**639**	S	YN55NJK	**643**	S	YN55NKE	**647**	S	YN55NKL

648	S	BV55UCT	Scania N94 UD	East Lancs Omnidekka	N45/33F	2005	Go-Ahead London, 2016
649	S	BV55UCW	Scania N94 UD	East Lancs Omnidekka	N45/33F	2005	Go-Ahead London, 2016

801-805 ADL E20D — ADL Enviro 400 MMC — NC(86)F — 2024

801	S	EU24LWT	**803**	S	-	**804**	S	-	**805**	S	-
802	S	EU24LWV									

901-905 Scania N94 UD 12m — East Lancs Omnidekka — N51/39F — 2003 — Nottingham CT, 2015

901	S	YN53CFP	**903**	S	YN53CFV	**904**	S	YN53CFX	**905**	S	YN53CFY
902	S	YN53CFU									

906	S	YN54AFF	Scania N94 UD 12m	East Lancs Omnidekka	N51/39F	2004	Reading Buses, 2011
907	S	YN54AFJ	Scania N94 UD 12m	East Lancs Omnidekka	N51/39F	2004	Reading Buses, 2011

NIBS started out in 1984 as the Nelsons Independent Bus Services brand operating between Romford and Southend Airport. Illustrating the NIBS livery is Scania OmniCity double-deck 528, LX08ECW, which was new to Docklands Buses operation and was pictured in Basildon. *Richard Godfrey*

Special event vehicles:

1424	S	424DCD	Leyland PD3/4	Northern Counties	CO39/30F	1964	Southdown
3129	S	XHK234X	Bristol VR	ECW	H74F	1981	Eastern National

Ancillary vehicles:

9033	tv	LK03NLG	TransBus Dart SLF	Caetano Nimbus	N29D	2003	Metroline, 2015
7054	tv	A17SOE	Scania OmniCity N230 UB	Scania	N42F	2004	Nottingham CT, 2019

Associated operation:
GALLOWAY EUROPEAN COACHLINES, Denters Hill, Mendlesham, Suffolk, IP15 5RR

84	M	AX14GXS	Ford Tourneo MPV	Ford	M8	2014
85	M	MX67XWY	Ford Tourneo MPV	Ford Custom	M8	2017
102	G	BF68LCE	Scania K410EB6	Caetano Levanté III	C55FT	2019
104	G	BF68LCJ	Scania K410EB6	Caetano Levanté III	C55FT	2019
105	G	BF68LCK	Scania K410EB6	Caetano Levanté III	C55FT	2019
107	G	BF68LCM	Scania K410EB6	Caetano Levanté III	C55FT	2019
108	G	BF68LCN	Scania K410EB6	Caetano Levanté III	C55FT	2019
143	G	1482PP	Mercedes-Benz Tourismo	Mercedes Tourismo	C49FT	2015
144	G	4092PP	Van Hool TX16 Astron	Van Hool	C53FT	2016
145	G	4178PP	Van Hool TX16 Astron	Van Hool	C53FT	2016
151	G	5048PP	Setra S416 GT-HD	Setra	C53F	2010
152	G	6399PP	Mercedes-Benz Tourismo	Mercedes-Benz	C53F	2010
153	G	2086PP	Volvo 9700	Volvo	C53FT	2012
154	G	5611PP	Volvo 9700	Volvo	C53FT	2013
155	G	1440PP	Volvo B9R	Plaxton Panther 2	C53FT	2013
156	G	1754PP	Volvo B9R	Plaxton Panther 2	C53FT	2013

Depots: Stephensons of Essex Ltd (S) Riverside Industrial Estate, South Street, Rochford, SS4 1BS, Quayside industrial Estate, Maldon, CM9 5FA, Waltham Road Industrial Estate, Boreham, CM3 3AW, Springwood Industrial Estate, Braintree, CM7 7YN, Lufkins Farm, Frating,CO7 7HN, Duddery Hill, Haverhill, CB19 8DR. NIBS Buses Ltd (N), Bruce Grove, Wickford Bruce Grove, Wickford, SS11 8BZ, CGreys Coaches, Common Road, Witchford, CB6 2HY and Denters Hill Farm, Mendlesham, Stowmarket, IP14 5RR.

FALCON

Falcon Buses, 20a, Wintersells Road, Byfleet, KT14 7LF

NIL8354	Volvo B12B	Berkhof Axial 50	C49FT	2006	Kavanagh, Urlingford
SK07DFP	Volvo B7RLE	Wrightbus Eclipse	N37F	2007	Lothian Biuses, 2024
KX58GVE	ADL Dart 4 8.9m	ADL Enviro 200	N29F	2009	APCOA, Uxbridge
E7ATD	Mercedes-Benz Vario 0816	Sitcar Beluga	C25F	2009	Dundee Airport, 2021
HIL5657	Ford Transit	Ford	M16	2012	
YT13HKZ	Scania OmniLink K230 UBFord	Scania	N45F	2013	Rotala, 2023
HN64DAO	Ford Transit	Ford	M16	2014	
KX14FHJ	Mercedes-Benz Vario 0816	Plaxton Cheetah 2	C29F	2014	Taunton mini coaches
KX14FHK	Mercedes-Benz Vario 0816	Plaxton Cheetah 2	C29F	2014	Taunton mini coaches
SW65GSW	ADL E20D 10.8m	ADL Enviro 200 MMC	N41F	2015	Selwyn, Runcorn, 2023
WW65GSW	ADL E20D 10.8m	ADL Enviro 200 MMC	N41F	2015	Selwyn, Runcorn, 2023
ET16ZVM	Ford Transit	Ford	M16	2016	
HN16XOB	Ford Transit	Ford	M16	2016	
YX17NZA	ADL E20D 8.9m	ADL Enviro 200 MMC	N30F	2017	Townlynx, Wrexham, 2023
YX67VGJ	ADL E20D 9.7m	ADL Enviro 200	N33F	2017	White Bus, Windsor, 2021
YX67VGK	ADL E20D 9.7m	ADL Enviro 200	N33F	2017	White Bus, Windsor, 2021
TUI1438	Irizar i6	Irizar	C53FT	2016	Golden Boy, 2023
TUI1440	Irizar i6	Irizar	C53FT	2016	Golden Boy, 2023
YN18ZPB	Irizar i4	Irizar	S70F	2018	
KX18NMM	Mercedes-Benz Sprinter 514 cdi	Trekka	C20F	2018	
YX18KNN	ADL E20D 10.8m	ADL Enviro 200 MMC	N41F	2018	Arriva, 2023
YX18KUT	ADL E20D 10.8m	ADL Enviro 200 MMC	N41F	2018	Qpark, Heathrow
YX68UJP	ADL E20D 8.9m	ADL Enviro 200 MMC	N30F	2018	
YX68UJR	ADL E20D 8.9m	ADL Enviro 200 MMC	N30F	2018	
YX68ULP	ADL E20D 8.9m	ADL Enviro 200 MMC	N30F	2018	
YX68ULR	ADL E20D 8.9m	ADL Enviro 200 MMC	N30F	2018	
YX68ULS	ADL E20D 8.9m	ADL Enviro 200 MMC	N30F	2018	
YX68ULT	ADL E20D 8.9m	ADL Enviro 200 MMC	N30F	2018	
YX68ULU	ADL E20D 8.9m	ADL Enviro 200 MMC	N30F	2018	
TUI4762	Volvo B8R	Sunsundegui SB3	S72F	2019	
TUI4763	Irizar i4	Irizar	S70F	2019	
YT19DWY	Scania K360 IB4	Higer Touring	C51FT	2019	
YT19DWZ	Scania K360 IB4	Higer Touring	C51FT	2019	
YN69XVC	Scania K360 IB4	Irizar i6s	C53FT	2019	
YY69TMZ	ADL E20D 8.9m	ADL Enviro 200 MMC	N41F	2019	White Horse holiday park
HK69FYR	Ford Transit	Ford	M16	2019	

Pictured in Chertsey Lane, Egham, is Falcon's Enviro 200 MMC SW65GSW. *Richard Godfrey*

The Enviro 200 MMC is the principal model used by Falcon, making it one of the most modern fleets in Surrey. Falcon Buses is a trading name of Falcon Coaches Ltd, and the company can trace its history back some forty years. Pictured in Ripley during May 2024 is YX73OTY, a 10.8 metre example. *Richard Godfrey*

YX19ONK	ADL E20D 10.8m	ADL Enviro 200 MMC	N41F	2019	Somerset PS, 2022
YX19ONL	ADL E20D 10.8m	ADL Enviro 200 MMC	N41F	2019	Somerset PS, 2022
YX19ONM	ADL E20D 10.8m	ADL Enviro 200 MMC	N41F	2019	Somerset PS, 2022
YX19ONN	ADL E20D 10.8m	ADL Enviro 200 MMC	N41F	2019	Somerset PS, 2022
YX19ONO	ADL E20D 10.8m	ADL Enviro 200 MMC	N41F	2019	Somerset PS, 2022
YX19ONP	ADL E20D 10.8m	ADL Enviro 200 MMC	N41F	2019	Somerset PS, 2022
YX20OCY	ADL E20D 8.9m	ADL Enviro 200 MMC	N30F	2020	
YX20OCZ	ADL E20D 8.9m	ADL Enviro 200 MMC	N30F	2020	
YX70OKU	ADL E20D 8.9m	ADL Enviro 200 MMC	N30F	2020	
YX70OKV	ADL E20D 8.9m	ADL Enviro 200 MMC	N30F	2020	
YX70OKW	ADL E20D 8.9m	ADL Enviro 200 MMC	N30F	2020	
YX70OKZ	ADL E20D 8.9m	ADL Enviro 200 MMC	N30F	2020	
SK21FHX	ADL E20D 8.9m	ADL Enviro 200 MMC	N30F	2021	Air Sym, Heathrow, 2023
YX21RPO	ADL E20D 8.9m	ADL Enviro 200 MMC	N30F	2021	Caelloi, Pwllheli, 2023
YX71OGZ	ADL E20D 10.8m	ADL Enviro 200 MMC	N41F	2021	
YX71OJH	ADL E20D 8.9m	ADL Enviro 200 MMC	N30F	2021	
YX71OJN	ADL E20D 8.9m	ADL Enviro 200 MMC	N30F	2021	
HK22HKW	Ford Transit	Ford	M16	2022	
HK22RVF	Ford Transit	Ford	M16	2022	
HV22HJN	Ford Transit	Ford	M16	2022	
YX22OHZ	ADL E20D 8.9m	ADL Enviro 200 MMC	N30F	2022	Cobra, Fleet, 2023
YX72OJY	ADL E20D 8.9m	ADL Enviro 200 MMC	N30F	2022	
YX72OJZ	ADL E20D 8.9m	ADL Enviro 200 MMC	N30F	2022	
YX23ORV	ADL E20D 8.9m	ADL Enviro 200 MMC	N30F	2023	
YX23OSZ	ADL E20D 8.9m	ADL Enviro 200 MMC	N30F	2023	
YX23OYH	ADL E20D 8.9m	ADL Enviro 200 MMC	N30F	2023	
YG73PGY	ADL E20D 10.8m	ADL Enviro 200 MMC	N41F	2023	
YX73OTY	ADL E20D 10.8m	ADL Enviro 200 MMC	N41F	2023	
YX73OYP	ADL E20D 8.9m	ADL Enviro 200 MMC	N30F	2023	
YX73OYR	ADL E20D 8.9m	ADL Enviro 200 MMC	N30F	2023	
SK24XPC	ADL E20D 8.9m	ADL Enviro 200 MMC	N30F	2024	
SK24XPD	ADL E20D 8.9m	ADL Enviro 200 MMC	N30F	2024	
SK24XPF	ADL E20D 8.9m	ADL Enviro 200 MMC	N30F	2024	
SK24XPG	ADL E20D 8.9m	ADL Enviro 200 MMC	N30F	2024	
SK24XPH	ADL E20D 8.9m	ADL Enviro 200 MMC	N30F	2024	

FARESAVER

Faresaver Buses, The Coach Yard, Vincents Road, Chippenham, SN14 6QA

KBK750	ADL E20D 10.8m	ADL Enviro 200	N33F	2008	ADL testbed
PSV444	Volvo B9TL	Wrightbus Eclipse Gemini	N39/27F	2009	Metroline, 2022
RRU345	Volvo B9TL	Wrightbus Eclipse Gemini	N39/27F	2009	Metroline, 2022
LVR164	Volvo B9TL	Wrightbus Eclipse Gemini	N39/27F	2009	Metroline, 2022
NUH527	Volvo B9TL	Wrightbus Eclipse Gemini	N39/27F	2009	Metroline, 2022
YJ59GGK	Optare Solo M980	Optare	N29F	2009	Go Coach, Swanley, 2023
AM05BUS	ADL Dart 4 10.2m	ADL Enviro 200	N32F	2010	Go-Ahead London, 2019
BV10WVP	Volvo B9TL	Wrightbus Gemini 2	N39/27F	2011	Metroline, 2023
YJ10MGX	Optare Solo M950	Optare	N33F	2010	Henderson, Hamilton, 2014
NJ11EXJ	Optare Solo M1020	Optare	N35F	2011	Phoenix, Blyth, 2017
BU51TOY	ADL Dart 4 10.8m	ADL Enviro 200	N39F	2011	Ensignbus, 2019
SN11FFT	ADL Dart 4 10.8m	ADL Enviro 200	N39F	2011	Ensignbus, 2019
FA54VER	Volvo B9TL	Wrightbus Gemini 2	N43/27F	2011	Tower Transit, 2019
BJ11DVN	Volvo B9TL	Wrightbus Gemini 2	N43/27F	2011	Tower Transit, 2019
BJ11DVO	Volvo B9TL	Wrightbus Gemini 2	N43/27F	2011	Tower Transit, 2019
BJ11DVT	Volvo B9TL	Wrightbus Gemini 2	N43/27F	2011	Tower Transit, 2019
BJ11EAC	Volvo B9TL	Wrightbus Gemini 2	N43/27F	2011	Tower Transit, 2019
BJ11EBM	Volvo B9TL	Wrightbus Gemini 2	N43/27F	2011	Tower Transit, 2019
BX12CVK	Volvo B9TL	Wrightbus Gemini 2	N43/27F	2012	Tower Transit, 2016
BX12CVM	Volvo B9TL	Wrightbus Gemini 2	N43/27F	2012	Tower Transit, 2016
YX12TAT	ADL E20D 10.8m	ADL Enviro 200	N39F	2012	Tates, Barnsley, 2016
YJ62FDK	Optare Solo M960	Optare	N34F	2012	Tanet Valley, 2023
YX62ECT	ADL E20D 10.8m	ADL Enviro 200	N37F	2012	Marshall, Sutton, 2019
YX62EDO	ADL E20D 10.8m	ADL Enviro 200	N37F	2012	Weavaway, Newbury, 2016
YX62EDP	ADL E20D 10.8m	ADL Enviro 200	N37F	2012	Weavaway, Newbury, 2016
YX62FET	ADL E20D 8.9m	ADL Enviro 200	N29F	2013	Tate, Barnsley, 2016
YJ13HKX	Optare Solo M925	Optare	N30F	2013	Garelochhead, 2023
MX13KUB	ADL E20D 10.8m	ADL Enviro 200	N39F	2013	Wilfreda Beehive, 2020
YX63ZVP	ADL E20D 10.8m	ADL Enviro 200	N37F	2014	Weavaway, Newbury, 2021
YX63ZVS	ADL E20D 10.8m	ADL Enviro 200	N37F	2014	Weavaway, Newbury, 2021
YY64YKJ	ADL E20D 8.9m	ADL Enviro 200	N29F	2014	TLC, Keighley, 2024
YJ64DBV	Optare Solo M9600 SR	Optare	N27F	2014	Blind Veterans, Brighton,'22
YJ64DVZ	Optare Solo M8900 SR	Optare	N32F	2014	Wheelers, Andover,'22

Devizes, a market town in Wiltshire, is the location for this view of Enviro 200 YX63ZVS. It had just arrived on route 272 which links the town with Bath via Melksham. *John Young*

Passing the West End Inn at Melksham, Volvo B9TL BJ11DVO is one of eight acquired from Tower Transit in 2019. All have subsequently been converted from dual-door layout. Route X34 runs from Frome to Chippenham passing through Trowbridge and Melksham. *John Young*

YY15CMX	ADL E20D 8.9m	ADL Enviro 200	N29F	2015	Weardale, 2023
YY15CNA	ADL E20D 10.8m	ADL Enviro 200	N35F	2015	GHA, Ruabon, 2016
YY15CNC	ADL E20D 10.8m	ADL Enviro 200	N35F	2015	GHA, Ruabon, 2017
YY15CNE	ADL E20D 10.8m	ADL Enviro 200	N35F	2015	GHA, Ruabon, 2018
YJ15AYE	Optare Solo M970 SE	Optare	N30F	2015	GHA, Ruabon, 2019
YJ15AYF	Optare Solo M970 SE	Optare	N30F	2015	Blue Bus, Shotts, 2020
YJ15AYG	Optare Solo M970 SE	Optare	N30F	2015	Blue Bus, Shotts, 2020
YJ15AYH	Optare Solo M970 SE	Optare	N30F	2015	GHA, Ruabon, 2016
BF15KFJ	Volvo B9TL	Wrightbus Gemini 3	N47/28F	2013	Yellow Buses, 2023
BF15KFL	Volvo B9TL	Wrightbus Gemini 3	N47/28F	2013	Yellow Buses, 2023
SN65OFO	ADL E20D 10.8m	ADL Enviro 200	N39F	2015	
SN65OFP	ADL E20D 10.8m	ADL Enviro 200	N39F	2015	
YJ16DXR	Optare Solo M9250 SE	Optare	N30F	2015	Dales & District, 2024
YJ66ANU	Optare Solo M890 SR	Optare	N30F	2017	igo, Birmingham, 2019
YJ66ANV	Optare Solo M890 SR	Optare	N30F	2017	igo, Birmingham, 2019
YJ66ANX	Optare Solo M890 SR	Optare	N30F	2017	igo, Birmingham, 2019
YJ66AOA	Optare Solo M890 SR	Optare	N30F	2017	igo, Birmingham, 2019
YJ66AOS	Optare Solo M9250 SR	Optare	N29F	2016	Stuarts, Carluke, 2023
YJ66AOT	Optare Solo M9250 SR	Optare	N29F	2016	Stuarts, Carluke, 2023
YX17NJN	ADL E20D 10.8m	ADL Enviro 200	N39F	2017	Yourbus, Heanor, 2020
YX17NRO	ADL E20D 10.8m	ADL Enviro 200	N39F	2017	CT Plus 2023
YX17NSJ	ADL E20D 10.8m	ADL Enviro 200	N39F	2017	Yourbus, Heanor, 2020
YX17NTN	ADL E20D 10.8m	ADL Enviro 200	N39F	2017	Coach Serv, Thetford, 2023
YY17GPX	ADL E20D 10.8m	ADL Enviro 200	N37F	2017	Lloyds, Machynlleth, 2024
YX18KUD	ADL E20D 10.8m	ADL Enviro 200	N39F	2018	Lloyds, Machynlleth, 2024
SK22BVV	ADL E20D 10.8m	ADL Enviro 200 MMC	NC41F	2022	
SK22BVW	ADL E20D 10.8m	ADL Enviro 200 MMC	NC41F	2022	

	Volvo B8RLE	MCV eVoRa	N38F	2023-24
BV73MJE	BV73MJK	BC24EHL	BC24EHN	
BV73MJF	BC24EHJ	BC24EHM	BC24EKZ	
BV73MJJ	BC24EHK			

GLOBE

Globe - Rosa

Globe Holidays Ltd, 60 Eldon Street, Barnsley, S70 2JL

1021	PG02YWA	Volvo B10M	Jonckheere Mistral	C53F	2002	Yorkshire Rose
3	CA52JJZ	Scania OmniCity CN94UB	Scania	N42F	2002	Newport Transport
1	YS03ZLN	Scania OmniCity CN94UB	Scania	N42F	2003	Bakers, Biddulph
2	YN05GXD	Scania L94 UB	Wrightbus Solar Eclipse	N43F	2005	
1551	SN55HSU	ADL Dart	ADL Pointer	N38F	2005	
-	FN06FLD	Volvo B12B	Caetano Levanté	S70F	2006	Rotala
-	YN06PFF	Volvo B12M	Plaxton Panther	S70F	2006	Tellings GM
-	YN07OPG	Volvo B12M	Plaxton Panther	C53FT	2007	Moffat & Williamson
2	YN05GXD	Scania L94 UB	Wrightbus Solar Eclipse	N43F	2005	
	M50RSW	Mercedes-Benz Atego 1223L	Ferqui Solera	C39F	2005	Watersons, Barnsley, 2024
5	NK07KPT	Mercedes-Benz Citaro O530	Mercedes-Benz	N40F	2007	
-	KX07HDF	Volvo B12B	Plaxton Panther	C57F	2007	Grammar School, Leeds
1072	KX07HDU	ADL Dart 4	ADL Enviro 200	N27F	2007	Kent Top Travel
1073	KX07HEU	ADL Dart 4	ADL Enviro 200	N27F	2007	Kent Top Travel
1074	KX07HEV	ADL Dart 4	ADL Enviro 200	N27F	2007	Kent Top Travel
1075	KX07HFA	ADL Dart 4	ADL Enviro 200	N27F	2007	Kent Top Travel
1076	KX07HFC	ADL Dart 4	ADL Enviro 200	N27F	2007	Kent Top Travel
	YJ57BTX	VDL SB4000	Van Hool T9 Alizée	C53FT	2007	
-	KX08HLR	Volvo B12B	Plaxton Panther	C57F	2008	Grammar School, Leeds
1581	KX58GSZ	ADL Dart 4 8.9m	ADL Enviro 200	N29F	2009	Falcon Buses, Woking
1582	MV58FMY	ADL Dart 4 8.9m	ADL Enviro 200	N29F	2008	Bus Eireann
4	MIL8163	Scania OmniCity CN230 UB	Scania	N38F	2009	Halton Buses
1101	KX10DVF	ADL E300	ADL Enviro 300	N45F	2010	Waterson, Pontefract
1102	KX10DVG	ADL E300	ADL Enviro 300	N45F	2010	Waterson, Pontefract
1103	KX10DVM	ADL Dart 4 8.9m	ADL Enviro 200	N29F	2010	Falcon Buses, Woking
1104	KX10DVJ	ADL E300	ADL Enviro 300	N45F	2010	Courtney, Reading
1105	KX10DVH	ADL E300	ADL Enviro 300	N45F	2010	Courtney, Reading
1601	KX60DVP	ADL E20D 10.8m	ADL Enviro 200	N29F	2010	Turner, Chulmleigh
1602	KX60DVO	ADL E20D 8.9m	ADL Enviro 200	N29F	2010	Falcon Buses, Woking
-	FT11EBT	Volvo B9R	Plaxton Panther	C53FT	2011	Eddie Brown
-	GT11EBT	Volvo B9R	Plaxton Panther	C53FT	2011	Eddie Brown
-	YN12CSO	Volvo B9R	Plaxton Panther	C53FT	2012	Logan, Dunloy
-	YJ62FMZ	Optare Versa V1110	Optare	N37F	2012	Waterson, Pontefract
1641	BX64AEV	King Long XMQ6130C	King Long	S73F	2014	Tate, Low Barugh
1651	YX65RHA	ADL E20D 8.9m	ADL Enviro 200	N29F	2015	Hanson, Birmingham
1652	YX65RHA	ADL E20D 8.9m	ADL Enviro 200	N29F	2015	Hanson, Birmingham
1191	GL19BES	Van Hool EX16M	Van Hool	C57FT	2019	
1192	YJ19BBX	Van Hool EX16M	Van Hool	C57FT	2019	
-	YX19MKE	Volvo B8R	Plaxton Panther	C53FT	2019	Cooper, Killamarsh
-	YX19MLY	Volvo B11R	Plaxton Panther	C53FT	2019	Lakeside, Ellesmere
-	YX19MLZ	Volvo B11R	Plaxton Panther	C53FT	2019	Lakeside, Ellesmere
1181	YX18KUY	ADL E20D 10.8m	ADL Enviro 200 MMC	N41F	2018	Jones, Braintree
1701	YX70OKR	ADL E20D 10.8m	ADL Enviro 200 MMC	N41F	2021	
1702	YX70OKT	ADL E20D 10.8m	ADL Enviro 200 MMC	N41F	2021	
1211	SK21FKF	ADL E20D 10.8m	ADL Enviro 200 MMC	N41F	2021	MP Travel, Warrington
1212	SK21FKE	ADL E20D 10.8m	ADL Enviro 200 MMC	N41F	2021	MP Travel, Warrington
1213	YX21RSV	ADL E20D 10.8m	ADL Enviro 200 MMC	N41F	2021	Johnson, Henley-in-Arden
1214	YX21RTZ	ADL E20D 10.8m	ADL Enviro 200 MMC	N41F	2021	Johnson, Henley-in-Arden
1215	YX21RYH	ADL E20D 10.8m	ADL Enviro 200 MMC	N41F	2021	Roberts, Leicester
1711	YX71OHU	ADL E20D 8.9m	ADL Enviro 200 MMC	N30F	2021	
1712	YX71OHU	ADL E20D 8.9m	ADL Enviro 200 MMC	N30F	2021	
1221	YX22OGJ	ADL E20D 8.9m	ADL Enviro 200 MMC	N30F	2022	
1222	YX22OGP	ADL E20D 8.9m	ADL Enviro 200 MMC	N30F	2022	
1721	YX72OJE	ADL E20D 10.8m	ADL Enviro 200 MMC	N41F	2022	
1722	YX72OJF	ADL E20D 10.8m	ADL Enviro 200 MMC	N41F	2022	
1241	SK24CUJ	ADL E20D 10.8m	ADL Enviro 200 MMC	N41F	2024	
1242	SK24CUH	ADL E20D 10.8m	ADL Enviro 200 MMC	N41F	2024	

GO-COACH

Go-Coach - Hulleys - Silver Service

Go Coach Hire, 10 Vestry Ind Est, Vestry Rd, Sevenoaks, TN14 5EL
Henry Hulley & Sons Ltd, Derwent Garage, Derwent Drive, Baslow, Bakewell, DE45 1RP

1	H	YX23OYB	ADL E20D 10.8m	ADL Enviro 200 MMC	N40F	2023	
2	H	YX70OHS	ADL E20D 9.7m	ADL Enviro 200 MMC	N34F	2020	White Bus, Windsor, 2023
3	H	LK09EKU	ADL Trident 2	ADL Enviro 400	N41/31F	2009	Metroline, 2021
5	H	LK09EKP	ADL E40D	ADL Enviro 400	N41/30F	2009	Metroline, 2023
6	H	YJ09OTH	Optare Solo M950	Optare	N33F	2009	Southern, Bury, 2020
7	H	YX09HZJ	ADL Dart 4 10.8m	ADL Enviro 200	N37F	2009	Tates, Barnsley, 2016
8	H	YX12DHN	ADL Dart 4 8.9m	ADL Enviro 200	N39F	2012	Newport Buses, 2022
9	H	MX09AOF	Optare Solo M880 SL	Optare	N28F	2009	
10	H	YJ09MHN	Optare Solo M880	Optare	N28F	2009	RATP, London, 2020
13	H	WK11APY	Optare Solo M995	Optare	N35F	2011	Bluebus, Shotts, 2021
12	H	BV23NVH	Volvo B8RLE	MCV eVoRa	N46F	2023	
15	H	MK63XAU	ADL Dart 4 10.8m	ADL Enviro 200	N39F	2013	Coach Services, 2018
16	H	LJ09CCK	ADL Trident 2	ADL Enviro 400	N41/31F	2009	Abellio, London, 2022
17	H	MX11CZM	ADL Dart 4 10.8m	ADL Enviro 200	N38F	2011	
21	H	Y100HOB	Volvo B8RLE	MCV eVoRa	N46F	2024	
22	H	LR52KXJ	Dennis Trident	Plaxton President	N41/27F	2002	JH, Chester-le-Street, 2023
601	G	LX19CXN	Renault Master ZE	Renault	M6	2019	

701-704			Ford Transit Tourneo			Flexicab Crown			M7		2020
701	G	WF20ENX	**702**	G	WF20EOA	**703**	G	WF20EOO	**704**	G	WF20KJK

2801	G	YJ59GFG	Optare Solo M780 SE	Optare	N23F	2009	*operated for Kent CC*
3619	H	YK05CAO	Optare Solo M780 SL	Optare	N34F	2005	CT Coaches, Bath, 2023
3801	G	YJ59PKN	Optare Solo M810 SL	Optare	N24F	2010	igo, Birmingham, 2019
3802	G	YJ59PKV	Optare Solo M810 SL	Optare	N24F	2010	igo, Birmingham, 2019
3901	G	YJ11EKA	Optare Solo M780 SE	Optare	N25F	2011	Network Warrington, 2015
3902	H	YJ11EKB	Optare Solo M780 SE	Optare	N25F	2011	Network Warrington, 2015
3903	G	YJ11EKD	Optare Solo M780 SE	Optare	N25F	2011	Network Warrington, 2015
4501	G	YJ09MMK	Optare Solo M890	Optare	N25F	2009	Arriva S Counties, 2017
4502	H	YJ09MMO	Optare Solo M890	Optare	N25F	2009	Arriva S Counties, 2017
4504	H	YJ11EJA	Optare Solo M880	Optare	N28F	2011	RATP, London, 2020
4503	G	YJ09MMU	Optare Solo M890	Optare	N25F	2009	Arriva S Counties, 2017
5013	G	YJ62FUD	Optare Solo M970	Optare	N25D	2012	RATP, 2018
5014	G	YJ62FUG	Optare Solo M970	Optare	N25D	2012	RATP, 2018
5015	G	YJ62FVN	Optare Solo M970	Optare	N25D	2012	RATP, 2018
5025	H	YJ57ZWP	Optare Solo M950 SL	Optare	N32F	2007	Go-Coach, 2021
5318	H	YJ11EJD	Optare Solo M880	Optare	N33F	2011	RATP, London, 2021
5501	G	YJ14BFY	Optare MetroCity V990 MC	Optare	N28D	2014	RATP, 2022
5601	G	YJ59GFO	Optare Versa V1100	Optare	N40F	2009	*operated for Kent CC*
5602	G	YJ59GFK	Optare Versa V1100	Optare	N40F	2009	*operated for Kent CC*
5714	H	YX11AEN	ADL E20D	ADL Enviro 200	N33F	2011	Vision, Bolton, 2023
6003	G	LX58CHO	Optare Versa V1040	Optare	N27D	2009	Stagecoach, 2017
6004	G	LX58CHV	Optare Versa V1040	Optare	N27D	2009	Stagecoach, 2017
6008	G	YJ58VBX	Optare Versa V1040	Optare	N27D	2009	RATP, 2019
6201	H	YJ18DKX	Optare MetroCity V1080 MC	Optare	N37F	2018	
6202	G	YD63UZL	Optare MetroCity V1080 MC	Optare	N29D	2013	RATP, 2019
6311	H	SW64SAR	ADL E20D 10.8m	ADL Enviro 200	N38F	2014	Leasks, Lerwick, 2020
6323	H	YX11CSY	ADL Dart 4 8.9m	ADL Enviro 200	N28F	2011	Whitelaws, 2015
6326	H	LJ09KPK	ADL Dart 4 10.8m	ADL Enviro 200	N28F	2009	Stanton, Stoke, 2024
6327	H	LJ09KRD	ADL Dart 4 10.8m	ADL Enviro 200	N28F	2009	Panther Travel, 2024
7801	G	YJ11EHN	Optare Tempo X1200	Optare	N34D	2011	RATP, 2019
7802	G	YJ11EHR	Optare Tempo X1200	Optare	N34D	2011	RATP, 2019
7803	G	YJ11EHX	Optare Tempo X1200	Optare	N34D	2011	RATP, 2019

8343-8347			ADL E20D			ADL Enviro 200 MMC			N27D	2016	*On loan from Abellio*
8343	G	YX66WFD	**8345**	G	YX66WFF	**8346**	G	YX66WFG	**8347**	G	YX66WFH
8344	G	YX66WFE									

The origins of Hulleys can be traced back to 1914 when Henry Hulley purchased a Ford Model T taxi. In December 2023, Hulleys of Baslow acquired Go-Coach, a Sevenoaks operator, though Go-Coach has retained branding for the southern element. The Derbyshire village of Holymoorside, to the west of Chesterfield, is the location for this view of Enviro 400 LK09EKU. A bus in the Go Coach colours is in the vehicle index. *John Young*

9001-9010 ADL Trident 2 10.2m | ADL Enviro 400 | N41/26D | 2007 | RATP London, 2020

9001	G	SK07DZA	**9004**	G	SK07DZD	**9006**	G	SK07DZF	**9009**	G	SK07DZJ
9002	G	SK07DZB	**9005**	G	SK07DZE	**9007**	G	SK07DZG	**9010**	G	SK07DZL
9003	G	SK07DZC									

9011	G	LK57AXT	ADL Trident 2 10.2m	ADL Enviro 400	N41/26D	2007	Metroline, 2020
9012	G	LK57AYB	ADL Trident 2 10.2m	ADL Enviro 400	N41/26D	2007	Metroline, 2020

9506-9518 ADL Trident 2 10.2m | ADL Enviro 400 | N41/26D | 2009 | *On loan from Abellio*

9506	G	SN59AVT	**9514**	H	SN59AWC	**9515**	G	SN59AWF	**9518**	G	SN59AWJ
9513	G	SN59AWA									

Special event vehicles:

364	312YUK	Bedford QL	Sammut	B40F	1943	Malta Bus
RML2472	JJD472D	AEC Routemaster	Park Royal	B42/32R	1965	London Transport
RML2699	SMK699F	AEC Routemaster	Park Royal	B42/32R	1965	London Transport
623	WXG316	AEC Swift	Park Roayal	B40F	1970	Malta Bus
5003	S519KFL	Dennis Dart SLF 9.3m	Marshall Capital C39	N27F	1998	Metroline, 2009
8601	S869HCG	Volvo Olympian OLY-50	Alexander RH	N47/31F	1998	DublinBus, 2010

GRANT PALMER

Grant Palmer Ltd, 2C Commerce Way, Flitwick, Bedford, MK45 5BP

105	YJ05WDC	Optare Solo M850 SL	Optare	N27F	2005	Befordshire CC, 2011
209	YX09FMJ	ADL Dart 4	ADL Enviro 200	N26F	2009	Ensignbus, 2017
210	CA05GHA	Dennis Dart SLF	Plaxton Mini Pointer	N29F	2005	GHA, Ruabon, 2016
211	YX11HPU	ADL Dart 4	ADL Enviro 200	N29F	2011	Ensignbus, 2015
212	YX12DHG	ADL E20D 8.9m	ADL Enviro 200	N29F	2012	
213	YX12DHJ	ADL E20D 8.9m	ADL Enviro 200	N29F	2012	
214	YX09HZF	ADL Dart 4	ADL Enviro 200	N29F	2012	Yellow Buses, 2017
215	SK15HFP	ADL E20D 8.9m	ADL Enviro 200	N29F	2015	
216	YX16OHT	ADL E20D 10.8m	ADL Enviro 200	N39F	2016	
217	YX16OHU	ADL E20D 10.8m	ADL Enviro 200	N39F	2016	
218	SN66WPJ	ADL E20D 8.9m	ADL Enviro 200	N29F	2017	
219	YY66OFE	ADL E20D 8.9m	ADL Enviro 200	N29F	2017	
220	YX18KND	ADL E20D 9.7m	ADL Enviro 200	N33F	2016	
221	YX18KNE	ADL E20D 9.7m	ADL Enviro 200	N33F	2016	
222	YX60FUH	ADL Dart 4	ADL Enviro 200	N29F	2011	Go-Ahead London, 2019
223	YX60FUD	ADL Dart 4	ADL Enviro 200	N29F	2011	Go-Ahead London, 2019
224	MK63WZY	ADL E20D 8.9m	ADL Enviro 200	N29F	2013	Connexions, York, 2019
225	YX69NXK	ADL E20D 8.9m	ADL Enviro 200 MMC	N30F	2019	
226	MK12DZJ	ADL E20D 8.9m	ADL Enviro 200	N29F	2012	Halton Buses, 2020
227	KX59CYW	ADL Dart 4	ADL Enviro 200	N29F	2009	iGo, Aston, 2020
228	KX08HME	ADL Dart 4	ADL Enviro 200	N29F	2008	Dawson Rentals, 2020
229	YX70OKG	ADL E20D 8.9m	ADL Enviro 200 MMC	N30F	2020	
230	YX70OKH	ADL E20D 8.9m	ADL Enviro 200 MMC	N30F	2020	
231	YX71OJF	ADL E20D 8.9m	ADL Enviro 200 MMC	N30F	2022	
232	YX71OJG	ADL E20D 8.9m	ADL Enviro 200 MMC	N30F	2022	
233tv	LJ56ONN	ADL E20D 10.8m	ADL Enviro 200	N30D	2006	Ensignbus, 2022
233	YX72OKS	ADL E20D 10.8m	ADL Enviro 200 MMC	N41F	2022	
234	YX72OKT	ADL E20D 10.8m	ADL Enviro 200 MMC	N41F	2022	
706	BU54WAY	Volvo B7TL	Writghbus Gemin Eclipse	N41/27F	2006	Go-Ahead London, 2017
707	BU51WAY	Volvo B7TL	Writghbus Gemin Eclipse	N41/27F	2006	Go-Ahead London, 2017
708	BU58WAY	Volvo B9TL	Optare Olympus	N51/30F	2008	Ensignbus, 2020
709	BU57WAY	Volvo B9TL	Writghbus Gemin Eclipse	N44/29F	2007	Lothian Buses, 2021
710	BU52WAY	Volvo B9TL	Writghbus Gemin Eclipse	N44/29F	2008	Lothian Buses, 2021
711	BU53WAY	Volvo B9TL	Writghbus Gemin Eclipse	N44/29F	2008	Lothian Buses, 2021
712	BU56WAY	Volvo B9TL	Writghbus Gemin Eclipse	N48/32F	2008	Lothian Buses, 2021
713	GP55BUS	Volvo B9TL	Writghbus Gemin Eclipse	N44/29F	2008	Lothian Buses, 2021
714	BU59WAY	Scania N230 UD	Optare Omnidekka	N51/35F	2011	Nottingham CT, 2023
715	GP56BUS	Scania N230 UD	Optare Omnidekka	N51/35F	2011	Nottingham CT, 2023

Special event vehicle:

	CUV299C	AEC Routemaster	Park Royal	B42/32R	1965	London Transport

Seen passing through Flitwick is Grant Palmers' latest Enviro 200 MMC 234, YX72OKT. Route 42 links Dunstable with Bedford via Flitwick and Ampthill.
Mark Doggett

HORNSBY TRAVEL

Hornsby Travel Services Ltd, 51 Ashby High Street, Scunthorpe, DN16 2NB

w	YN54AJX	Scania N94 UD	East Lancs Omnidekka	N45/29D	2004	Go-Ahead London, 2019
	7455RH	Volvo B12B	Plaxton Panther	C49FT	2004	
	LF55CZB	Volvo B7TL	Wrightbus Eclipse Gemini	N45/27F	2006	Abellio, London, 2021
	BX55XNO	Volvo B7TL	Wrightbus Eclipse Gemini	N45/24D	2006	Isle, Scunthorpe, 2023
	7419RH	Volvo B12B	Plaxton Panther	S70F	2007	Whittle, Kidderminster, '19
	2553RH	Volvo B12B	Plaxton Panther	C49FT	2007	East Yorkshire, 2016
	MX09CHK	Man 12.240	Plaxton Centro	N38F	2009	Holmes James, Speke, '12
	MX09CHL	Man 12.240	Plaxton Centro	N38F	2009	Holmes James, Speke, '12
	2732RH	Volvo B9R	Plaxton Panther	C53FT	2009	Andersons, London 2012
	MX59AWA	ADL Dart 8.9m	ADL Enviro 200	N29F	2009	Swans, Chadderton, 2017
w	YX09HYV	ADL Dart 4 10.8m	ADL Enviro 200	N37F	2009	Myles, Crieff, 2011
	YT09ZCE	Scania OmniCity N230 UD	Scania	N45/32F	2009	Stephensons, Rochford, '23
	YT59SFF	Scania OmniCity N230 UD	Scania	N45/32F	2009	RATP, 2023
	YX59CAA	Man 12.240	Plaxton Centro	N38F	2009	Tees Valley, 2013
	YR10BDV	Scania N230 UD	Optare Omnidekka	N45/32F	2009	RATP, 2023
	NH10BUS	ADL E20D 8.9m	ADL Enviro 200	N29F	2010	Abellio, 2019
	NH11BUS	ADL E20D 8.9m	ADL Enviro 200	N29F	2011	Tates, Barnsley, 2017
	YN11FBG	Ford Transit	Stamford	M6	2011	
	3730RH	Volvo B9R	Caetano Levanté	C48FT	2011	Galloway, 2019
	6053RH	Volvo B9R	Caetano Levanté	C48FT	2011	Galloway, 2019
	NH04BUS	ADL E20D 9.6m	ADL Enviro 200	N33F	2012	
	NH12BUS	ADL E20D 8.9m	ADL Enviro 200	N29F	2013	Stephenson, Easingwold
	NH07BUS	ADL E20D 10.8m	ADL Enviro 200	N39F	2013	Nottingham CT, 2024
	NH09BUS	ADL E20D 10.8m	ADL Enviro 200	N39F	2013	Nottingham CT, 2024
	1642RH	Volvo B9R	Plaxton Panther	C53FT	2013	Logans, Dunloy, 2018
	8955RH	Volvo B11R	Plaxton Panther	C53FT	2014	
	NH13BUS	ADL E20D 10.8m	ADL Enviro 200	N39F	2016	
	NH14BUS	ADL E20D 10.8m	ADL Enviro 200	N39F	2016	
	NH15BUS	ADL E20D 10.8m	ADL Enviro 200	N39F	2016	
	NH16BUS	ADL E20D 10.8m	ADL Enviro 200	N39F	2016	
	NH17BUS	Mercedes-Benz 516 cdi	Mellor Strata	N22F	2017	

Special event vehicles:

	EDR793	Bedford OB	Duple Vista	C29F	1949	van de Merve, 2017
	YJ06LFW	VDL SB120	Wrightbus Cadet	N39F	2006	

Hornsby Travel Services has been running for more than forty-four years, based in Scunthorpe. Seen in NHS livery for a hospital park and ride service is NH16BUS. *Richard Godfrey*

HOUSTON'S

Houston's Coaches, Broomhouses 1 Industrial Estate, Lockerbie DG11 2RZ

	MV07EFT	Volvo B12B	VDL Jonckheere SHV	C53F	2007	
	HIL2464	Volvo B12M	VDL Jonckheere SHV	C53FT	2008	
	SF08VTK	Volvo B12M	VDL Jonckheere SHV	C53FT	2008	Parks of Hamilton, 2020
	WX58BVV	Mercedes-Benz Sprinter 515 cdi	Unvi	B9F	2008	
	SK10AFP	Optare Solo M880 SL	Optare	N27F	2010	Vale, Aylesbury,
	SK10AJP	Optare Solo M880 SL	Optare	N27F	2010	Vale, Aylesbury,
	YJ60KHE	Optare Solo M880 SL	Optare	N27F	2010	
	CN11EFX	Mercedes-Benz Sprinter 515 cdi	Treka	B16F	2011	
	YJ12GSV	Optare Solo M880 SL	Optare	N29F	2012	*op for SWestTrans*
	YJ12GSZ	Optare Solo M880 SL	Optare	N28F	2012	*op for SWestTrans*
	YJ12GTF	Optare Solo M880 SL	Optare	N29F	2012	*op for SWestTrans*
	KY63VTC	Optare Solo M890	Optare	N32F	2012	Accessible Transport, 2020
	P24HOU	Volvo B9R	Plaxton Elite	C48FT	2014	Parks of Hamilton, 2024
	P25HOU	Volvo B9R	Plaxton Elite	C48FT	2014	Parks of Hamilton, 2024
	KX14FJE	Optare Solo M890	Optare	N32F	2014	Accessible Transport, 2020
	AT64KZT	Mercedes-Benz Tourismo	Mercedes-Benz	C49FT	2015	Aston Manpr, Birmingham
W	SN15LRY	ADL E20D 10.8m	ADL Enviro 200	N39F	2015	
	YJ15APF	Optare Solo M890 SR	Optare	N31F	2015	*op for SWestTrans*
	YJ15APU	Optare Solo M890 SR	Optare	N30F	2015	*op for SWestTrans*
	SN15CCE	Ford Transit	Ford	M17	2015	

Houston's YJ12GSZ and KX14FJE illustrate the different body shapes of the initial and later 'SR-style' of the Optare Solo. They were pictured at Sandyhills terminus in August 2023. GSZ also shows the colours of *Swestrans,* **a Regional Transport Partnerships headed by the Dumfries and Galloway Council. Houston's Mini Coaches which was established in 1975 having expanded with depots both in Lockerbie and Castle Douglas. It is now managed by the second generation of the family.** *Murdoch Currie*

The latest arrivals with Houstons are four Volvo B8RLE buses with MCV eVoRa bodies, a model launched in 2018. Manufacturing Commercial Vehicles (MCV) is an Egyptian manufacturer for buses located in Salheya. It entered the British market after it purchased Marshall Bus in 2002. SJ73HSV is seen in Edinburgh. *John Birtwistle*

N22HOU	Mercedes-Benz Sprinter 516 cdi	EVM Avantgarde	C19F	2015	Reays, Wigton, 2023
DC16OBY	Mercedes-Benz Sprinter 516 cdi	Mellor Strata	N22F	2016	Mellor demonstrator
DT17UHP	Ford Transit	Ford	M16	2017	
N33HOU	Mercedes-Benz Atego 1021L	UNVI Voyager GT	N33F	2017	Star, Cowdenbeath, 2023
PY66OSE	Mercedes-Benz Atego 1021L	UNVI Voyager GT	N33F	2017	Reays, Wigton, 2023
YY67HBG	ADL E20D 10.8m	ADL Enviro 200	N40F	2018	Bay Travel, Keighley
YJ18DHC	Optare Solo M9250 SR	Optare	N31F	2018	
YJ18DHD	Optare Solo M9250 SR	Optare	N31F	2018	
YX19MKN	Volvo B8R	Plaxton Elite	C57F	2019	Owens, Oswestry, 2023
SJ69EYM	Fiat Ducato	Mellor Strider	N18F	2020	
YJ22AYL	Optare Solo M9250 SL	Optare	N24F	2022	
RX72TNV	Mercedes-Benz Sprinter 516 cdi	EVM Cityline	N18F	2022	
GX23CZE	Mercedes-Benz Sprinter 516 cdi	Altas Novus	N16F	2023	
GX23CZF	Mercedes-Benz Sprinter 516 cdi	Altas Novus	N16F	2023	
YL23FUG	Mercedes-Benz Sprinter 516 cdi	Altas Novus	N16F	2023	
YL23FSA	Mercedes-Benz Sprinter 516 cdi	EVM Cityline	N16F	2023	
GX73AYB	Mercedes-Benz Sprinter 516 cdi	EVM Cityline	N16F	2023	
GX73AYD	Mercedes-Benz Sprinter 516 cdi	EVM Cityline	N16F	2023	
SJ73HSV	Volvo B8RLE 10.8m	MCV eVoRa	N38F	2023	
SJ73HSX	Volvo B8RLE 10.8m	MCV eVoRa	N38F	2023	
SJ73HSY	Volvo B8RLE 10.8m	MCV eVoRa	N38F	2023	
SJ73HVO	Volvo B8RLE 11.3m	MCV eVoRa	N46F	2023	

IPSWICH BUSES

Ipswich Buses Ltd, 7 Constantine Road, Ipswich, IP1 2DL

1	SGZ1001	Volvo B7R	VDL Jonckheere Modulo	C57F	2002	Smith, Tring. 2019
2	SGZ1002	Volvo B11R	Caetano Levanté	C55FT	2015	
3	SGZ1003	Volvo B11R	Caetano Levanté	C55FT	2015	
5	SN65OHZ	ADL E20D	ADL Enviro 400 MMC	N47/32F	2015	Yellow Buses, 2024
6	SN65OJA	ADL E20D	ADL Enviro 400 MMC	N47/32F	2015	Yellow Buses, 2024
7	SN65OJB	ADL E20D	ADL Enviro 400 MMC	N47/32F	2015	Yellow Buses, 2024
25	YT11LTF	Scania N230 UD	Optare Omnidekka	N41/35F	2011	Nottingham CT, 2023
26	YT61GOJ	Scania N230 UD	Optare Omnidekka	N41/35F	2011	Nottingham CT, 2023
29	YR59FYT	Scania OmniCity N230 UD	Scania	N45/27F	2009	RATP, 2023

30-45 Scania OmniCity CN230 UD | Scania | N45/27F | 2011 | Metroline, 2017

30	YR61RPV	**34**	YR61RSV	**38**	YR61RUU	**42**	YR61RUJ
31	YR61RPY	**35**	YR61RTV	**39**	YR61RUV	**43**	YR61RUL
32	YR61RRU	**36**	YR61RUC	**40**	YR61RUW	**44**	YR61RRZ
33	YR61RRV	**37**	YR61RUH	**41**	YR61RVF	**45**	YR61RVE

46	SGZ3346	Scania OmniCity CN230 UD	Scania	N45/27F	2008	RATP, 2020
47	SGZ3347	Scania OmniCity CN230 UD	Scania	N45/27F	2008	RATP, 2020
48	SGZ3348	Scania OmniCity CN230 UD	Scania	N45/27F	2008	RATP, 2020
49	SGZ3349	Scania OmniCity CN230 UD	Scania	N45/27F	2008	RATP, 2020
50	SGZ3350	Scania OmniCity CN230 UD	Scania	N45/27F	2008	RATP, 2020
51	SGZ3351	Scania OmniCity CN230 UD	Scania	N45/27F	2008	RATP, 2020
55	PN52XBO	DAF DB250	East Lancs Lowlander	N43/29F	2002	
57w	PN52XBU	DAF DB250	East Lancs Lowlander	N43/29F	2002	
58w	PJ53OLA	DAF DB250	East Lancs Lowlander	N43/29F	2003	
60	PJ54YZT	Scania N94 UD	East Lancs Omnidekka	N47/33F	2005	
61	PJ54YZU	Scania N94 UD	East Lancs Omnidekka	N47/33F	2005	
62	PJ54YZV	Scania N94 UD	East Lancs Omnidekka	N47/33F	2005	
63	YN06TFZ	Scania N94 UD	East Lancs Omnidekka	N47/33F	2006	Arriva The Shires, 2021
64	SGZ6664	Scania N94 UD	East Lancs Omnidekka	N47/33F	2006	Vision, Bolton, 2021
71	LX58LMO	ADL E20D 8.9m	ADL Enviro 200	N29F	2009	Bus Eireann, 2020
72	LX58LMM	ADL E20D 8.9m	ADL Enviro 200	N29F	2009	Bus Eireann, 2020
73	YX18KNW	ADL E20D 10.8m	ADL Enviro 200 MMC	N41F	2018	Caelloi, Pwllheli, 2024
74	DU60LOJ	ADL E20D 10.8m	ADL Enviro 200	N37F	2010	Tanat Valley, Oswestry, '20
75	GD10MVM	ADL E20D 8.9m	ADL Enviro 200	N29F	2009	Beeston, Hadleigh, 2020
76	LX58LML	ADL E20D 10.8m	ADL Enviro 200	N38F	2009	Bus Eireann, 2020

Commemorating 120 years of buses in Ipswich, Scania OmniCity 29, YR59FYT, heads for the local hospital.
Mark Doggett

Ipswich operates three of the shorter (klein) model of the Mercedes-Benz Citaro. 154, BF65HVU, illustrates this 10-metre version as it works route 3. *Mark Doggett*

78-82 — ADL E20D 10.8m — ADL Enviro 200 — N39F — 2013-14

78	YX14RWL	**80**	YX63ZVV	**81**	YX63LGE	**82**	YX63LGF
79	YX63ZVW						

83	KX58GUW	ADL E20D 8.9m	ADL Enviro 200	N29F	2008	Completely, Norwich, 2020
84	YX63GXS	ADL E20D 10.8m	ADL Enviro 200	N40F	2013	Nottingham CT, 2024
85	KX59GNY	ADL E20D 10.8m	ADL Enviro 200	N37F	2009	Premier, Nottingham, 2016
86	YX63GXY	ADL E20D 10.8m	ADL Enviro 200	N40F	2013	Nottingham CT, 2024

87-99 — Optare Tempo X1200 SR — Optare — N41F — 2012 — TrentBuses, 2020

87	YJ12GWA	**91**	YJ12GWF	**94**	YJ12GWL	**97**	YJ12GWO
88	YJ12GWC	**92**	YJ12GWG	**95**	YJ12GWM	**98**	YJ12GWP
89	YJ12GWD	**93**	YJ12GWK	**96**	YJ12GWN	**99**	YJ12GWU
90	YJ12GWE						

101-108 — ADL E20D — ADL Enviro 200 — N39F — 2016

101	SN16OGG	**103**	SN16OGJ	**105**	YX66WCJ	**107**	YX66WCL
102	SN16OGH	**104**	SN16OGK	**106**	YX66WCK	**108**	YX66WCM

153	BF65HVT	Mercedes-Benz Citaro K O295	Mercedes-Benz	N40F	2015	
154	BF65HVU	Mercedes-Benz Citaro K O295	Mercedes-Benz	N40F	2015	
155	BF65HVV	Mercedes-Benz Citaro K O295	Mercedes-Benz	N40F	2015	
161	SN57DCX	Volvo B7RLE	Wrightbus Eclipse Urban	N38F	2007	Lothian Buses, 2022

JMB TRAVEL

JMB Travel Ltd, 101 Main Street, Newmains, Wishaw, ML2 9BG

R366DJN	Volvo Olympian OLY-56	East Lancashire Pyoneer	B51/36F	1997	Golden Eagle, 2023
UNZ9789	Volvo B10M-62	Jonckheere Mistral	S70F	1999	Stagecoach
SN51AYL	Dennis Trident	Plaxton President	N45/26F	2001	McNairn, Coatbridge, 2023
YD02PXM	Bova Futura	Bova	S70F	2002	McNairn, Coatbridge, 2023
RG03BVU	Bova Futura	Bova	S70F	2003	McNairn, Coatbridge, 2023
B88BUS	Volvo B10M-62	Jonckheere Mistral	C53F	2004	Stagecoach
NK04LBE	ADL Dart 4	ADL Pointer	N38F	2004	Stagecoach
NK04NPJ	ADL Dart 4	ADL Pointer	N38F	2004	Stagecoach
SF04VTE	ADL Dart 4	ADL Pointer	N38F	2004	Stagecoach
PX05ELH	ADL Dart 4	ADL Pointer	N38F	2005	Stagecoach
PX05ELO	ADL Dart 4	ADL Pointer	N38F	2005	Stagecoach
PX05ELU	ADL Dart 4	ADL Pointer	N38F	2005	Stagecoach
PX05ELV	ADL Dart 4	ADL Pointer	N38F	2005	Stagecoach
PX05ELW	ADL Dart 4	ADL Pointer	N38F	2005	Stagecoach
PX05EMJ	ADL Dart 4	ADL Pointer	N38F	2005	Stagecoach
PX05EMK	ADL Dart 4	ADL Pointer	N38F	2005	Stagecoach
SV55BZL	ADL Dart 4	ADL Pointer	N38F	2005	Stagecoach
SV55BZM	ADL Dart 4	ADL Pointer	N38F	2005	Stagecoach
SV55CCN	ADL Dart 4	ADL Pointer	N38F	2005	Stagecoach
SP55CXJ	Optare Solo M850	Optare	N27F	2005	Stagecoach
SP06FVC	Volvo B7R	Plaxton Profile	S70F	2006	Stagecoach
SP06FVE	Volvo B7R	Plaxton Profile	C49F	2006	Stagecoach
SV56BVR	Volvo B7R	Plaxton Profile	C49F	2006	Stagecoach
SV56BVZ	Volvo B7R	Plaxton Profile	C49F	2006	Stagecoach
SV56BWA	Volvo B7R	Plaxton Profile	C49F	2006	Stagecoach
SF56FKX	ADL Dart 4	ADL Pointer	N38F	2006	Stagecoach
SF56FKY	ADL Dart 4	ADL Pointer	N38F	2006	Stagecoach
YK06DTZ	BMC Condor	BMC	N57F	2006	Dunn, Airdrie, 2023
VNZ1742	Volvo B7TL	Wrightbus Eclipse Gemini	N48/33F	2006	Lothian Buses
VNZ2901	Volvo B7TL	Wrightbus Eclipse Gemini	N48/33F	2006	Lothian Buses
MXZ3334	Volvo B7TL	Wrightbus Eclipse Gemini	N48/33F	2006	Lothian Buses
MXZ3335	Volvo B7TL	Wrightbus Eclipse Gemini	N48/33F	2006	Lothian Buses
MXZ3336	Volvo B7TL	Wrightbus Eclipse Gemini	N48/33F	2006	Lothian Buses
MXZ3337	Volvo B7TL	Wrightbus Eclipse Gemini	N48/33F	2006	Lothian Buses
MXZ3338	Volvo B7TL	Wrightbus Eclipse Gemini	N48/33F	2006	Lothian Buses
MXZ3339	Volvo B7TL	Wrightbus Eclipse Gemini	N48/33F	2006	Lothian Buses
SP07HHT	Volvo B7R	Plaxton Profile	C49F	2007	Stagecoach, 2023
RX57MDZ	Optare Solo M710 SE	Optare	N23F	2007	Ballantyre, Bellshill
YN07DSU	Irisbus Eurorider 397E.12.43A	Beulas Cygnus	C53F	2007	
VNZ7605	ADL Dart 4	ADL Enviro 200	N37F	2008	Abellio, London
VNZ7647	ADL Dart 4	ADL Enviro 200	N37F	2008	Abellio, London
EM09BUS	Optare Solo M710 SE	Optare	N22F	2009	Ballantyre, Bellshill
DRZ1305	Neoplan Tourliner N2216 SHD	Neoplan	C49FT	2010	McNairn, Coatbridge, 2023
YJ11EJN	Optare Solo M710 SE	Optare	N22F	2011	Ballantyre, Bellshill
YJ13HNN	Optare Solo M710 SE	Optare	N22F	2013	Ballantyre, Bellshill
VHZ3765	Mercedes-Benz Sprinter 45	Mercedes-Benz	N17F	2014	Avis, Bracknell, 2023
UNZ9141	Mercedes-Benz Sprinter 45	Mercedes-Benz	N17F	2014	Avis, Bracknell, 2023
UNZ9109	Mercedes-Benz Sprinter 45	Mercedes-Benz	N17F	2014	Avis, Bracknell, 2023
BJ15UVP	Mercedes-Benz Sprinter 45	Mercedes-Benz	N17F	2015	
BJ15UVV	Mercedes-Benz Sprinter 45	Mercedes-Benz	N17F	2015	
CG15BUS	Mercedes-Benz Sprinter 45	Mercedes-Benz	N17F	2015	
YJ15ANX	Optare Solo M710 SE	Optare	N17F	2015	*Operated for SPT*
YJ15AOB	Optare Solo M710 SE	Optare	N17F	2015	*Operated for SPT*
YY15NHU	ADL E20D 10.8m	ADL Enviro 200	N37F	2015	Stephenson's, Tholthorpe
SN16OSA	ADL E20D 10.8m	ADL Enviro 200	N37F	2016	
SN16OSB	ADL E20D 10.8m	ADL Enviro 200	N37F	2016	
OE16WHZ	Neoplan Tourliner N2216 SHD	Neoplan	C49FT	2016	
OE16WJD	Neoplan Tourliner N2216 SHD	Neoplan	C49FT	2016	
BT66UAP	Mercedes-Benz Sprinter 45	Mercedes-Benz	N17F	2016	
BT66UAR	Mercedes-Benz Sprinter 45	Mercedes-Benz	N17F	2016	
BT66UAS	Mercedes-Benz Sprinter 45	Mercedes-Benz	N17F	2016	
YJ17CPV	Optare Solo M7900 SE	Optare	N22F	2017	McGill, 2023

Illustrating the colours of JMB Travel is recently withdrawn classic Enviro 200 YX66WHB. It is seen loading passengers in Lanark while heading towards Hamilton. *John Young*

BW67EVP	Scania K450 EB6	Caetano Levanté 2	C65FT	2018	Bruce, Airdrie, 2023
BW67EVR	Scania K450 EB6	Caetano Levanté 2	C65FT	2018	Bruce, Airdrie, 2023
RX18LNM	Mercedes-Benz Sprinter 516 cdi	EVM Cityline	N15F	2018	Arriva, 2023
RK68GWL	Mercedes-Benz Sprinter 516 cdi	EVM Cityline	N15F	2018	Arriva, 2023
SJ22GZR	Volvo B8RLE	MCV eVoRa	N37F	2022	
SJ22GZS	Volvo B8RLE	MCV eVoRa	N37F	2022	
SJ22GZT	Volvo B8RLE	MCV eVoRa	N37F	2022	
SJ22GZU	Volvo B8RLE	MCV eVoRa	N37F	2022	
SJ22GZV	Volvo B8RLE	MCV eVoRa	N37F	2022	
SJ22GZW	Volvo B8RLE	MCV eVoRa	N37F	2022	
SJ22GZX	Volvo B8RLE	MCV eVoRa	N37F	2022	
SJ22GZY	Volvo B8RLE	MCV eVoRa	N37F	2022	
SJ22GZZ	Volvo B8RLE	MCV eVoRa	N37F	2022	
SJ72HVT	Volvo B8R	Sunsundegui SC3	S70F	2023	
SJ72HVU	Volvo B8R	Sunsundegui SC3	S70F	2023	
SJ72HVV	Volvo B8R	Sunsundegui SC3	S70F	2023	
SJ72HVW	Volvo B8R	Sunsundegui SC3	S70F	2023	
SJ24HWA	Volvo B8RLE	MCV eVoRa	N38F	2024	
SJ24HWB	Volvo B8RLE	MCV eVoRa	N38F	2024	

LANDFLIGHT

Landflight - Silverline

Silverline Landflight, Argent House, Vulcan Road, Solihull B91 2JY

YN64CAV	Mercedes-Benz Sprinter 516 cdi	Irmãos Mota	C16F	2014	
RE15WAJ	Mercedes-Benz Sprinter 513 cdi	Mercedes-Benz	M16	2015	
RO15GJP	Mercedes-Benz Sprinter 513 cdi	Mercedes-Benz	M16	2015	
RA65LZB	Mercedes-Benz Sprinter 513 cdi	Mercedes-Benz	M16	2015	
BF65HTT	Mercedes-Benz Tourismo	Mercedes-Benz	C49FT	2015	
BF65HTU	Mercedes-Benz Tourismo	Mercedes-Benz	C49FT	2015	
YX16OCZ	ADL E20D 10.8m	ADL Enviro 200	N39F	2015	
YR17ATU	Mercedes-Benz Sprinter 513 cdi	Mercedes-Benz	M16	2017	
BF67WFM	Mercedes-Benz Tourismo	Mercedes-Benz	C49FT	2017	
YX18KWU	ADL E20D 10.8m	ADL Enviro 200 MMC	N41F	2018	
YW68PFA	ADL E20D 10.8m	ADL Enviro 200 MMC	N41F	2019	
YW68PFD	ADL E20D 10.8m	ADL Enviro 200 MMC	N41F	2019	
YW68PFE	ADL E20D 10.8m	ADL Enviro 200 MMC	N41F	2019	
YW68PFF	ADL E20D 10.8m	ADL Enviro 200 MMC	N41F	2019	
YW68PFG	ADL E20D 10.8m	ADL Enviro 200 MMC	N41F	2019	
YW68PFJ	ADL E20D 10.8m	ADL Enviro 200 MMC	N41F	2019	
YW68PFK	ADL E20D 10.8m	ADL Enviro 200 MMC	N41F	2019	
YD19HGE	Yutong TC9	Yutong	C37F	2019	
YD19HGF	Yutong TC9	Yutong	C37F	2019	
BV69LTZ	Mercedes-Benz Tourismo	Mercedes-Benz	C53F	2019	
YX69KZD	Volvo B8R	Plaxton Panther	C61F	2019	Taf Valley Coaches
YX69NUC	ADL E20D 8.9m	ADL Enviro 200 MMC	N30F	2019	
YX69NUE	ADL E20D 8.9m	ADL Enviro 200 MMC	N30F	2019	
YX69NUF	ADL E20D 8.9m	ADL Enviro 200 MMC	N30F	2019	
YX22OHD	ADL E20D 10.8m	ADL Enviro 200 MMC	N41F	2022	
YX22OHE	ADL E20D 10.8m	ADL Enviro 200 MMC	N41F	2022	
YD23FLX	Yutong TCe12	Yutong	C50FT	2023	
YD23FNJ	Yutong GT12	Yutong	C53FT	2023	
YD23FNK	Yutong GT12	Yutong	C53FT	2023	
YD23FNL	Yutong GT12	Yutong	C53FT	2023	

Station Road in Solihull, Landflight's Enviro 200 MMC YW68PFA is heading for Acocks Green. *John Young*

LLOYDS

Lloyds Coaches Ltd, Old Crosville Garage, Heol y Dol, Machynlleth, Powys, SY20 8BH

NHG541	Optare Solo M850	Optare	N27F	2004	Somerbus, Paulton, 2019
LC06WYN	Volvo B12B	Plaxton Paragon	C53FT	2006	
YN06MXP	Mercedes-Benz Vario 0814	Plaxton Beaver 2	B16F	2006	CT Plus, Hackney, 2020
LC08WYN	Volvo B12B	Plaxton Panther	C53FT	2008	KTs, Kendal, 2019
YJ09OTP	Optare Versa V1110	Optare	N39F	2009	GHA, Ruabon, 2016
SB09PEG	Optare Solo M850	Optare	N27F	2009	Somerbus, Paulton, 2019
YJ60KFU	Optare Solo M890	Optare	N28F	2010	Connexions, 2018
CY11GNK	Ford Transit	Ford	M8	2011	Mach, Machynlleth, 2013
DM11OWD	Mercedes-Benz Sprinter 516 cdi	EVM Elegance	C16F	2011	
LL07WYN	Mercedes-Benz Sprinter 313 cdi	Mercedes-Benz	M8	2011	
LL09WYN	Mercedes-Benz Sprinter 313 cdi	Mercedes-Benz	M8	2011	
YN11FUA	Mercedes-Benz Vario 0816	Plaxton Cheetah	C33F	2011	Greenfields Travel, 2018
YJ62FYN	Optare Versa V1110	Optare	N37F	2012	Hulleys, Baslow, 2021
KP14ZDK	Mercedes-Benz Sprinter 312 cdi	Mercedes-Benz	M8	2014	
LC14WYN	VDL Futura FHD2-129.365	VDL	C53FT	2014	
YJ14BCO	Optare Solo M900	Optare	N33F	2014	Vision, Bolton, 2021
YJ14BCU	Optare Solo M900	Optare	N33F	2014	Vision, Bolton, 2021
YJ14BCV	Optare Solo M890	Optare	N30F	2014	
YJ14BCX	Optare Solo M890	Optare	N30F	2014	
YJ14BCY	Optare Versa V1110	Optare	N39F	2014	
YJ14BCZ	Optare Versa V1170	Optare	N42F	2014	
YJ14BEU	Optare Solo M900	Optare	N33F	2014	Vision, Bolton, 2021
WA14NWW	Mercedes-Benz Vario 0816	Plaxton Cheetah	C33F	2014	Lucketts, 2024
SK15HBG	ADL E20D 8.9m	ADL Enviro 200	N41F	2015	NX Airports, 2023
YY15JNJ	Ford Transit	Ford	M8	2015	
YJ65EUM	Optare MetroCity V1080 MC	Optare	N38F	2015	
YJ65EUN	Optare MetroCity V1080 MC	Optare	N38F	2015	
L25WYN	Irizar i6	Irizar	C57FT	2016	Vision, Widnes, 2019
BU16UYL	Volvo B11R	Jonckheere JHV	C53FT	2016	
BU16UYM	Volvo B11R	Jonckheere JHV	C53FT	2016	
YN16WTX	Scania K360 IB4	Irizar i6	C53FT	2016	Falcon, Shepperton, 2021
YN16WTY	Scania K360 IB4	Irizar i6	C53FT	2016	Falcon, Shepperton, 2021
YN16WTZ	Scania K360 IB4	Irizar i6	C53FT	2016	Falcon, Shepperton, 2021
LC66WYN	Optare Solo M9250SR	Optare	N30F	2016	

Dyserth is a village in Denbighshire and it is here that Optare Solo YJ60KFU is seen during a turn on route 19 towards Cornist Brushwood Avenue in Flint. *John Young*

WA66DVN	Peugeot Boxer	GM Coachworks	M16	2016	
YS66YFA	Ford Transit	Ford	M8	2016	
YS66YFB	Ford Transit	Ford	M8	2016	
YS66YFC	Ford Transit	Ford	M8	2016	
YS66YFD	Ford Transit	Ford	M8	2016	
LC61WYN	ADL E40D	ADL Enviro 400 MMC	N45/22F	2016	
LC62WYN	ADL E40D	ADL Enviro 400 MMC	N45/22F	2016	
DX17EOS	Optare MetroCity V1080 MC	Optare	N38F	2017	
YJ17FYY	Optare MetroCity V1080 MC	Optare	N38F	2017	
YJ17FYZ	Optare MetroCity V1080 MC	Optare	N38F	2017	
YJ67FZL	Optare Solo M9250 SR	Optare	N30F	2017	
YJ67FZM	Optare Solo M9250 SR	Optare	N30F	2017	
YJ67FZN	Optare Solo M9250 SR	Optare	N30F	2017	
YJ67FZO	Optare Solo M9250 SR	Optare	N30F	2017	
YJ67FZP	Optare MetroCity V1080 MC	Optare	N38F	2017	
BU18YSM	Mercedes-Benz Tourismo M2	Mercedes-Benz	C48FT	2018	Shearings, Wigan, 2021
BU18YSS	Mercedes-Benz Tourismo M2	Mercedes-Benz	C48FT	2018	Shearings, Wigan, 2020
LC18ZSL	Ford Transit	Ford	M8	2018	
EA18NZZ	Ford Transit	Ford	M8	2018	
YT18PHX	Ford Transit	Ford	M8	2018	
YT18PHZ	Ford Transit	Ford	M8	2018	
YX18KUH	ADL E20D	ADL Enviro 200	N39F	2018	First, 2023
YX18KUY	ADL E20D	ADL Enviro 200 MMC	N39F	2018	Transdev, 2023
YX18KYE	ADL E20D	ADL Enviro 200 MMC	N39F	2018	Transdev, 2023
YX68UJO	ADL E20D	ADL Enviro 200 MMC	N41F	2018	Acklams, Beverley, 2023
LC07WYN	Iveco Daily 70C18	Noone Touras 700	C29F	2019	
DY61AXB	ADL E20D 10.8m	ADL Enviro 200 MMC	N41F	2019	
DY61AXC	ADL E20D 10.8m	ADL Enviro 200 MMC	N41F	2019	
CT19XCZ	Ford Transit	Ford	M8	2019	
MP20BUS	Volvo B8RLE	MCV eVoRa	N46F	2020	
BV21OOW	Volvo B8RLE	MCV eVoRa	N46F	2021	Volvo demonstrator, 2022
WP21XFB	Mercedes-Benz Sprinter 516 cdi	Illesbus i-City	N19F	2021	Illesbus demonstrator, 2023
RO21TZF	Mercedes-Benz Sprinter 516 cdi	EVM Cityline	N16F	2021	*Op for Transport for Wales*
RO21TZG	Mercedes-Benz Sprinter 516 cdi	EVM Cityline	N16F	2021	*Op for Transport for Wales*
RO21VKU	Mercedes-Benz Sprinter 516 cdi	EVM Cityline	N16F	2021	*Op for Transport for Wales*
BV22HBG	Volvo B8R	Sunsundegui SB3	S72F	2022	
LC73WYN	Iveco Daily 65C18	Illesbus i-City	N19F	2023	
BV73MLN	Volvo B8RLE	MCV eVoRa	N38F	2023	
BV73MLO	Volvo B8RLE	MCV eVoRa	N38F	2023	
BV24LME	Volvo B8RLE	MCV eVoRa	N38F	2023	
BV24LMF	Volvo B8RLE	MCV eVoRa	N38F	2023	
BV24LMJ	Volvo B8RLE	MCV eVoRa	N38F	2023	
BV24LMK	Volvo B8RLE	MCV eVoRa	N38F	2023	
BV24LML	Volvo B8RLE	MCV eVoRa	N38F	2023	
BV24LMM	Volvo B8RLE	MCV eVoRa	N38F	2023	
BV24LMO	Volvo B8RLE	MCV eVoRa	N38F	2023	
BV24LMU	Volvo B8RLE	MCV eVoRa	N38F	2023	
BV24LMX	Volvo B8RLE	MCV eVoRa	N38F	2023	

Depots: Treowain Enteprise Park, Forge Road, Machynlleth, SY208EG, Arran Road, Dolgellau, LL40 1LA, Old Station Yard, Heol Y Doll, Machynlleth, SY20 8BL and Lodge Farm, Tre Ddol, Machynlleth SY20 8QD.

LYNX

Coastal Red Ltd, Saddlebow Industrial Estate, Acer Road, King's Lynn, PE34 3HN

2	YJ55BJE	Optare Tempo X1200	Optare	N41F	2005	Pygalls, Peterlee, 2014
3	YJ55BKG	Optare Tempo X1200	Optare	N41F	2005	Arriva NW&W
7	YJ56WVA	Optare Tempo X1200	Optare	N42F	2007	Connectbus, 2018
11-19		Optare Tempo X1200	Optare	N42F	2005-07	Trent-Barton, 2017
11	YJ07VSK	**13** YJ07VSM	**15** FD54JYA		**17** FD54JYC	
12	YJ07VSL	**14** YJ07VSN	**16** FD54JYB		**19** FD54JYF	
21-27		Optare Tempo X1200	Optare	N43F	2010	Transdev, 2017
21	YJ60KAA	**23** YJ60KAK	**25** YJ60KAU		**27** YJ60KBF	
22	YJ60KAE	**24** YJ60KAO	**26** YJ60KAX			
28	T28KLN	Optare Tempo X1200	Optare	N41F	2009	Yellow Buses, 2019
29	T29KLN	Optare Tempo X1200	Optare	N41F	2009	Yellow Buses, 2019
30	MX05ELH	Optare Tempo X1200	Optare	N41F	2005	Konectbus, 2019
31-34		ADL E20D	ADL Enviro 200 MMC	N43F	2024	
31	YY24EKZ	**32** YY24ELC	**33** YY24ELH		**34** YY24ELJ	
52	LJ53BFU	DAF DB250	Wrightbus Eclipse Gemini	N43/29F	2003	Reading Buses, 2017
53	LJ53BGU	DAF DB250	Wrightbus Eclipse Gemini	N43/29F	2003	Reading Buses, 2018
56	LJ04LDL	VDL DB250	Wrightbus Eclipse Gemini	N43/29F	2004	Reading Buses, 2019
57	LJ04LEU	VDL DB250	Wrightbus Eclipse Gemini	N41/29F	2004	Reading Buses, 2019
61	SK21FNG	ADL E40D	ADL Enviro 400 MMC	N44/32F	2021	ADL demonstrator, 2022
62	SK21FNH	ADL E40D	ADL Enviro 400 MMC	N44/32F	2021	ADL demonstrator, 2022
63	YX22OLN	ADL E40D	ADL Enviro 400 MMC	NC44/32F	2022	
64	YX22OLO	ADL E40D	ADL Enviro 400 MMC	NC44/32F	2022	
65	YX22OLP	ADL E40D	ADL Enviro 400 MMC	N47/32F	2022	
66	YX23OSE	ADL E40D	ADL Enviro 400 MMC	N47/32F	2023	
67	YX73PNJ	ADL E40D	ADL Enviro 400 MMC	N47/32F	2023	
81	DU61DVY	ADL E40D	ADL Enviro 400	N47/32F	2011	Reading Buses, 2022
82	UWW2X	ADL E40D	ADL Enviro 400	N47/32F	2012	Reading Buses, 2022

Representing the Lynx operation is Optare Tempo 22, YJ60KAE. Lynx commenced operations in 2015 and since then it has expended into new areas such as Wells-next-the-Sea, Fakenham, Downham Market, Wisbech and Marham. *Mark Doggett*

MARSHALLS

Marshalls of Sutton-on-Trent Ltd, 11 Main Street, Sutton-on-Trent, Newark, NG23 6PF

VL70	JKV441	Volvo B12B	Plaxton Panther	C49FT	2005	
OP86	YJ60KBO	Optare Versa V1110	Optare	N40F	2010	
OP89	YJ11EKY	Optare Versa V1110	Optare	N40F	2011	
VDL97	PM14JAM	VDL Futura FHD2 127.365	VDL	C53FT	2014	
DD98	S4YRR	Volvo B7TL	Alexander ALX400	N49/33F	2000	Dublin Bus, 2014
DD99	T3YRR	Volvo B7TL	Alexander ALX400	N49/33F	2000	Dublin Bus, 2014
OP100	MX09AOS	Optare Solo M950	Optare	N33F	2009	Coach Services, 2014
OP102	YJ65ERY	Optare MetroCity V1152 MC	Optare	N41F	2015	
MB104	PM16JAM	Mercedes-Benz Tourismo 0350	Mercedes-Benz	C53FT	2016	
OP105	YJ62FCD	Optare Versa V1100	Optare	N37F	2013	Webberbus, 2016

DD106-113		TransBus Trident	TransBus ALX400	N45/27F	2003	Stagecoach, 2016
DD106	LX53JZU	**DD108** LX53JZR	**DD110** LX03OTB		**DD112** LX03OSV	
DD107	LX53JZL	**DD109** LX53JZN	**DD111** LX03OSD		**DD113** LX03OSE	

MB114	PM17JAM	Mercedes-Benz Tourismo 0350	Mercedes-Benz	C53FT	2017	
IV115	YN67CFE	Iveco Daily 70C18	Noone Turas 600	C25F	2017	
VDL116	PM64JAM	VDL Futura FHD2 127.365	VDL	C53FT	2014	Coach Options, 2017
VDL119	PM19JAM	VDL Futura FHD2 106.365	VDL	N37FT	2019	

Marshalls of Sutton-on-Trent is a family business established over thirty years ago. Some years earlier Mister Marshall had taken his PSV test with Gash's of Newark and drove for them on a part time basis and later Lincolnshire Road Car. Today, some forty buses are used including OP89, YJ11EKY, an Optare Versa. *JohnYoung*

Nottingham rail station is the start of route 90 to Newark and Optare Versa OP86, YJ60KBO, is seen waiting its departure. *John Young*

OP120	YJ57XVO	Optare Versa V1110	Optare	N37F	2008	Marchants, Cheltenham, 21
VDL123	PM71JAM	VDL Futura FHD2 129.365	VDL	N53FT	2021	
MB124	SL17RSL	Mercedes-Benz Tourismo	Mercedes-Benz	C49FT	2017	Lawmans, Kettering, 2022
DD125	LX03BVG	TransBus Trident	TransBus ALX400	N45/31F	2003	Applegates, Berkeley, 2021
DD126	LX05LLP	ADL Trident	ADL ALX400	N45/31F	2005	Applegates, Berkeley, 2021
DD127	LX53JYH	TransBus Trident	TransBus ALX400	N45/27F	2005	Warwickshire Travel, 2021
OP128	YJ60LRX	Optare Solo M880	Optare	N23F	2011	Travel Wright, Newark, '14
OP129	YJ61JGZ	Optare Solo M880 SL	Optare	N24F	2012	Travel Wright, Newark, '14
FT130	YJ62AEC	Ford Transit	Ford	M16	2022	
IR131	PM22JAM	Irizar i6	Irizar	C53FT	2022	
MB132	PM23JAM	Mercedes-Benz Tourismo	Mercedes-Benz	C53FT	2023	
VDL133	PM24JAM	VDL Futura FHD2-129	VDL	C57F	2024	
VT134	SM24MAR	Yutong T122 HDH	Yutong	C53FT	2024	

Special event vehicles:

B101	C434HHL	Bedford YNT	Plaxton Paramount 3200	C53F	1985	Wainfleet, Nuneaton
1409	FW5696	Leyland Tiger TS7	Burlingham (1950)	B35F	1935	Lincolnshire RoadCar
DD7	LNN353	Daimler CVD6	Duple	L27/26RD	1950	Gash, Newark

Depots: Main Street, Sutton-on-Trent (Coaches) and Great North Road, Sutton-on-Trent (Buses).

MINSTERLEY MOTORS

Minsterley Motors Ltd, 2 The Farriers, Annscroft, Shrewsbury, SY5 8AN

FJ54ZCL	Volvo B7R	Jonckheere Module	C53F	2004	
N300MMS	Optare Solo M850 SL	Optare	N27F	2005	GHA, Ruabon, 2016
PL06TFV	Optare Solo M950 SL	Optare	N32F	2006	Country Bus, Exmouth
EE08OXF	Volvo B12B	Plaxton Panther	C48FT	2008	Holmeswood Coaches, '18
YN08CXA	Volvo B12M	Plaxton Panther	C49FT	2008	Roy McCarthy, 2017
YJ10DJX	VDL SB200	Wrightbus Cadet 2	N37F	2010	Manchester Airport, 2015
YN60FMF	Mercedes-Benz Vario 0816	Plaxton Cheetah	C33F	2010	Atlas, Harrow, 2019
YN12CRX	Volvo B9R	Plaxton Panther	C53FT	2012	
YN12CRZ	Volvo B9R	Plaxton Panther	C53FT	2012	
YJ12PMY	Optare Solo M960	Optare	N35F	2012	P&O Lloyd, 2023
YD63VEU	Optare Solo M960	Optare	N35F	2014	
YD63VFG	Optare Solo M900	Optare	N35F	2014	
YR63OKB	Mercedes-Benz Vario 0816	Irmaos Mota	C33F	2014	Bliss , Bermundsey, 2023
BU14EGD	Volvo B7RLE	MCV eVolution	N44F	2014	Simmonds, Diss, 2023
YJ14BBU	Optare Versa	Optare	N40F	2014	White Buses, Windsor, '20
YJ14BBV	Optare Versa	Optare	N40F	2014	White Buses, Windsor, '20
YX14EFM	Mercedes-Benz Vario 0816	Plaxton Cheetah	C25F	2014	
YT15AWC	Scania K360 EB4	Irizar i6	C53FT	2015	Bullock, Cheadle, 2017
CU15PJO	Ford Transit	Ford	M16	2015	
YJ65EVT	Optare MetroCity V1152 MC	Optare	N44F	2015	
YJ65EVU	Optare MetroCity V1152 MC	Optare	N44F	2015	
YJ65EVV	Optare MetroCity V1152 MC	Optare	N44F	2015	
YJ65EVW	Optare MetroCity V1152 MC	Optare	N44F	2015	
YJ65EVX	Optare MetroCity V1152 MC	Optare	N44F	2015	
BU16OZM	Volvo B11R	Jonckheere SHV	C53FT	2016	
YN16BNO	Mercedes-Benz Atego 921L	Noone Turas 900	C33F	2016	
GY66WYW	Ford Transit	Ford	M16	2016	
YY17GRZ	ADL E20D	ADL Enviro 200 MMC	N29F	2017	Xelabus, Eastleigh, 2023
YT19EBU	Scania Interlink K410 EB4	Scania	C53FT	2019	
YT19EBV	Scania Interlink K410 EB4	Scania	C53FT	2019	
SJ20KNL	Volvo B8RLE	MCV eVolution	N44F	2020	Lochs, Stornoway, 2023

Depots: The Farriers, Annscroft, SY5 8AN and Stiperstones, Snailbeach, SY5 0LZ

Minsterley Motors operates the main link between Shrewsbury, Pontesbury and Stiperstones to Bishops Castle along with several school duties. Seen passing through Lea Cross while heading away from Shrewsbury towards Minsterley and Stiperstones is MetroCity YJ65EVU. *Richard Godfrey*

MOFFAT & WILLIAMSON

Moffat & Williamson Ltd, The Old Railway Yard, St Fort, Newport-on-Tay, DD6 8RG

SJ04VNP	Ford Transit	Ford	M16	2004	
SN04EGF	Transbus Enviro 300	Transbus	N38F	2004	Stagecoach, 2023
YK05CDE	Optare Solo M920	Optare	N31F	2005	
YK05CDF	Optare Solo M920	Optare	N31F	2005	
SP05EOH	Optare Solo M850	Optare	N27F	2005	Stagecoach, 2023
SV05DKO	Optare Solo M850	Optare	N27F	2005	Stagecoach, 2023
SV55BZR	Optare Solo M850	Optare	N27F	2005	Stagecoach, 2023
SV55BZX	Optare Solo M850	Optare	N27F	2005	Stagecoach, 2023
SV55CCD	Optare Solo M850	Optare	N27F	2005	Stagecoach, 2020
SP55CXK	Optare Solo M850	Optare	N27F	2005	Stagecoach, 2023
SP55EEA	Optare Solo M850	Optare	N27F	2005	Stagecoach, 2023
SN55BKV	Volvo B7TL	Wrightbus Eclipse Gemini	N44/30F	2005	Lothian Buses, 2023
SN55BKY	Volvo B7TL	Wrightbus Eclipse Gemini	N44/30F	2005	Lothian Buses, 2023
SN55BKZ	Volvo B7TL	Wrightbus Eclipse Gemini	N44/30F	2005	Lothian Buses, 2023
SN55BOJ	Volvo B7TL	Wrightbus Eclipse Gemini	N44/30F	2005	Lothian Buses, 2023
SN55BPK	Volvo B7TL	Wrightbus Eclipse Gemini	N44/30F	2005	Lothian Buses, 2023
YN55KME	Volvo B12M	Plaxton Panther	C48FT	2005	Stagecoach, 2023
BX55XMH	Volvo B7TL	Wrightbus Eclipse Gemini	N45/31F	2005	Abelio, London, 2019
BX55XNP	Volvo B7TL	Wrightbus Eclipse Gemini	N45/31F	2005	Abellio, London, 2019
	Volvo B7TL	Wrightbus Eclipse Gemini	N43/27F	2006	Go-Ahead London. 2018
LX06DZJ	LX06DZK	LX06DZL			LX06DZM
KX56TXZ	Optare Solo M850	Optare	N27F	2006	Stagecoach, 2023
SP56CXF	Optare Solo M850	Optare	N27F	2006	Stagecoach, 2023
MX06ACV	Optare Solo M880SL	Optare	N27F	2006	Hulleys, Baslow, 2020
MX06ACZ	Optare Solo M850	Optare	N27F	2006	
MX06ADO	Optare Solo M850	Optare	N27F	2006	
YN06UGP	Optare Solo M850	Optare	N27F	2006	Stagecoach, 2020
PR06PET	Volvo B7R	Plaxton Profile	S70F	2006	Prospect, Lye
SP06FVA	Volvo B7R	Plaxton Profile	C49F	2006	Stagecoach, 2018
SP06FVB	Volvo B7R	Plaxton Profile	C49F	2006	Stagecoach, 2018
SP06FVD	Volvo B7R	Plaxton Profile	C49F	2006	Stagecoach, 2018
MX56ACF	Optare Solo M850	Optare	N28F	2006	Gibbs, Cupar, 2022
	Volvo B7TL	Wrightbus Eclipse Gemini	N45/30F	2006	Lothian Buses, 2019
SN56ABO	SN56ACF				
SN56ACU	SN56ADX	SN56AEW			SN56AEZ
SN56ACV	SN56AEU	SN56AEX			SN56AFA
SN56ADO	SN56AEV	SN56AEY			
SN56AXU	ADL E300	ADL Enviro 300	N38F	2007	Stagecoach, 2023
	Volvo B7R	Plaxton Profile	C49F*	2007	Stagecoach, 2017-18
					*several are now S70F
SF07LCJ	SP07HHO	SP07HHW			SJ57AAU
SF07LCK	SP07HHV	SJ57AAO			SJ57AAV
PX07HBF	Optare Solo M880	Optare	N27F	2007	Stagecoach, 2023
PX07HBH	Optare Solo M880	Optare	N27F	2007	Stagecoach, 2023
SV57BYW	ADL E300	ADL Enviro 300	N38F	2007	Stagecoach, 2023
MX57KXR	ADL E300	ADL Enviro 300	N38F	2007	Stagecoach, 2023
MX57OEL	ADL E300	ADL Enviro 300	N38F	2007	Stagecoach, 2023
OU08AYF	ADL Dart 4	ADL Enviro 200	N29F	2008	Heyfordian, Bicester, 2018
SF08GUU	Optare Solo M880	Optare	N27F	2008	Stagecoach, 2023
MW58HOW	Volvo B7R	Plaxton Profile	S70F	2008	
LX58CDY	Scania OmniCity N230 UD	Scania	P041/22D	2008	Stagecoach, 2023
YX58EEY	Volkswagen Transporter	Bluebird Tucana	N22F	2008	London Dial-a-Ride, 2019
BSK790	Volvo B12M	Plaxton Paragon	C53FT	2009	Parks of Hamilton, 2014

Moffat & Williamson has been operating coach and bus services in the area south of the River Tay for over seventy years. Markinch is a picturesque village in the heart of Fife and is also the location for this view of Optare Solo MX06ACZ. *John Young*

SF09ACV	Volvo B7R	Plaxton Profile	C49F	2009	Stagecoach, 2023
YX09ETA	Volkswagen Transporter	Bluebird Tucana	N22F	2009	
GN59CDV	Iveco Daily 45C15	Stanford	M16L	2009	
GN59FFM	Iveco Daily 45C15	Stanford	M16L	2009	
GN59FFR	Iveco Daily 45C15	Stanford	M16L	2009	
MW59JAV	Dennis Javelin 12m	Plaxton Profile	S70F	2009	
SP59BSX	Optare Versa V1110	Optare	N38F	2009	
SP59DCE	Optare Solo M950	Optare	N32F	2009	
OU10GYN	Volvo B9R	Plaxton Elite	C46FT	2010	Edwards, Llantwit Fardre
YN10ABX	Dennis Javelin	Plaxton Profile	C57F	2010	
YN10ABZ	Dennis Javelin	Plaxton Profile	C57F	2010	
YJ60GPZ	VDL SB180	VDL eVolution	N36F	2010	Stagecoach, 2023
SN60DJF	Volkswagen Crafter	-	C15F	2010	
FSU375	Volvo B9R	Plaxton Panther	C49FT	2010	
AE11FMF	Volvo B9R	Plaxton Panther	C49FT	2011	Stagecoach, 2023
SV11FFT	Volvo B9R	Plaxton Panther	C49FT	2011	Stagecoach, 2022
SV11FFX	Volvo B9R	Plaxton Panther	C49FT	2011	Stagecoach, 2022
KX61GDU	Volvo B9R	Plaxton Panther	C49FT	2011	Stagecoach, 2022
KX61GDV	Volvo B9R	Plaxton Panther	C49FT	2011	Stagecoach, 2022
KX61GDY	Volvo B9R	Plaxton Panther	C49FT	2011	Stagecoach, 2022
KX61GEJ	Volvo B9R	Plaxton Panther	C49FT	2011	Stagecoach, 2023
KX61GEK	Volvo B9R	Plaxton Panther	C49FT	2011	Stagecoach, 2023
KX61GEU	Volvo B9R	Plaxton Panther	C49FT	2011	Stagecoach, 2023
KX61GFA	Volvo B9R	Plaxton Panther	C49FT	2011	Stagecoach, 2023
SV61CTY	Volvo B9R	Plaxton Panther	C49FT	2011	Stagecoach, 2022
SV61CUA	Volvo B9R	Plaxton Panther	C49FT	2011	Stagecoach, 2022
SV61CUC	Volvo B9R	Plaxton Panther	C49FT	2011	Stagecoach, 2022
SV61CUG	Volvo B9R	Plaxton Panther	C49FT	2011	Stagecoach, 2022
SV61CUJ	Volvo B9R	Plaxton Panther	C49FT	2011	Stagecoach, 2022
CN61FBB	Van Hool TD927 Astromega	Van Hool	C63/24FT	2012	Stagecoach, 2022
CN61FBD	Van Hool TD927 Astromega	Van Hool	C63/24FT	2012	Stagecoach, 2022
DK61DJD	Mercedes-Benz Sprinter 513 cdi	Mellor	N16F	2012	Birmingham CC, 2021
DK12BXL	Mercedes-Benz Sprinter 513 cdi	Mellor	N16F	2012	Birmingham CC, 2021
SV12CJU	Optare Excel V1110	Optare	N30F	2012	Stagecoach, 2024

Joining the fleet in 2016 were six Enviro 200 MMCs, all being the shortest 8.9-metre model. One of the batch, SN66WHR, was photographed while leaving Dundee for Claverhouse on route 236. 236 is a local service fully subsidised by Dundee City Council. *John Young*

DK62OSZ	Mercedes-Benz Sprinter 513 cdi	Mellor	N16F	2012	Birmingham CC, 2023
DK64ETD	Mercedes-Benz Sprinter 513 cdi	Mellor	N15F	2014	Birmingham CC, 2023
MW14BUS	Volvo B9R	Plaxton Panther	C53FT	2014	
	Peugeot Boxer	Allied	M9	2014	
SF14UBE	SF14UBH	SF64VLH			SF64VLJ
SF14UBG					
MW15LUX	Volvo B11R	Plaxton Panther	C46FT	2015	
SJ16ZZV	Volvo B8RLE	MCV eVolution	N46F	2016	Mackie, Alloa, 2024
	ADL E20D 8.9M	ADL Enviro 200 MMC	N30F	2016	
SN66WHH	SN66WHK	SN66WHM			SN66WHR
SN66WHJ	SN66WHL				
KE66BVO	Mercedes-Benz Sprinter 513 cdi	Mellor Strider	N21F	2016	Redcar MBC, 2023
LO69AKV	Mercedes-Benz Sprinter 513 cdi	Mellor Strider	N21F	2020	McNairn's, Coatbridge, '24
MW17BUS	Volvo B11R	Plaxton Panther	C46FT	2017	
KW68VWC	Mercedes-Benz Sprinter 514 cdi	Stamford	N21F	2018	
MW18DEV	Volvo B11RT	Plaxton Panther	C61FT	2018	
	Mercedes-Benz Sprinter 516 cdi	Mellor Strata	N21F	2018-21	
LM18DZA	LM18DZC	LM18DZF			LN19TXP
LM18DZB	LM18DZD	LM18DZG			WN21UJO
LN20PWF	LM18DZE				
LV73ZHT	Mercedes-Benz Sprinter 516 cdi	Mellor Strata	N21F	2024	
LV73ZHU	Mercedes-Benz Sprinter 516 cdi	Mellor Strata	N21F	2024	
LV73ZPE	Mercedes-Benz Sprinter 516 cdi	Mellor Strata	N21F	2024	
LV73ZPH	Mercedes-Benz Sprinter 516 cdi	Mellor Strata	N21F	2024	
LY73EHT	Mercedes-Benz Sprinter 516 cdi	Mellor Strata	N21F	2024	
LY73EJG	Mercedes-Benz Sprinter 516 cdi	Mellor Strata	N21F	2024	

Depots: Boston Road, Glenrothes and Old Station Yard, St Fort, Wormit.

NEWPORT BUS

Newport Borough Transport Ltd, 160 Corporation Road, Newport, NP19 0WF

1	YN57FZT	Scania OmniCity N230 UB	Scania	N41F	2007	
2	YN57FZU	Scania OmniCity N230 UB	Scania	N41F	2007	
3	YN57FZV	Scania OmniCity N230 UB	Scania	N41F	2007	
6	YN57FZY	Scania OmniCity N230 UB	Scania	N41F	2007	
43w	YN54AOC	Scania OmniCity N94 UB	Scania	N42F	2004	
60w	YN53GGU	Scania OmniCity CN94 UB	Scania	N41F	2003	

110-117 Scania OmniCity CN94 UB — Scania — N41F — 2011

110	YT11LUL	**112**w	YT11LUP	**116**	YT11LUH	**117**w	YT11LUJ
111	YT11LUO	**115**w	YT11LUF				

233-243 Ford Transit — Ford — M16 — 2021

233	YS21JVE	**236**	YS21JVK	**239**	YS21JVJ	**242**	YS21JVH
234	YS21JUX	**237**	YS21JVA	**240**	YS21JVD	**243**	YS21OFA
235	YS21JVF	**238**	YS21JUT	**241**	YS21JVG		

244-255 Mercedes-Benz Sprinter L4 — EVM e-cityline — N17F — 2021

246	RJ21UYZ	**252**	RO21ODT	**254**	RX71TDZ	**255**	RX71TDV
249	RO21VKU	**253**	RO21WDN				

301-311 ADL E20D — ADL Enviro 200 — N29F — 2011-12

301	YX11CRK	**304**	YX11AGY	**307**	YX61DVT	**310**	YX12DME
302	YX11CRU	**305**	YX11AGZ	**308**	YX61DVU	**311**	YX12DMF
303	YX11AGK	**306**	YX11AHV	**309**	YX61DVV		

318	YX13EGC	ADL E20D	ADL Enviro 200	N29F	2013	
319	YX13EGD	ADL E20D	ADL Enviro 200	N29F	2013	
337	SK24CWA	ADL E20D 8.9m	ADL Enviro 200 MMC	N30F	2024	
338	SK24CWC	ADL E20D 8.9m	ADL Enviro 200 MMC	N30F	2024	
339	SK24XPN	ADL E20D 8.9m	ADL Enviro 200 MMC	N30F	2024	
351 w	BV19LPA	Volvo B8RLE	MCV eVoRa	N42F	2019	*Op for Transport for Wales*
352 w	BV19LPC	Volvo B8RLE	MCV eVoRa	N42F	2019	*Op for Transport for Wales*
354	CE72YRM	Yutong E12	Yutong Electric	NC38F	2017	*Op for Transport for Wales*
355	CE72YRL	Yutong E12	Yutong Electric	NC38F	2017	*Op for Transport for Wales*

4th May 2024 at Cleppa Park and Yutong U11DD 419, CK24AUO, works the main service between Newport and Cardiff. It is one of a pair that are the first with the provincial specification in Britain. *Richard Godfrey*

Like several operators in the country Newport have some vehicles that are used on the Transport for Wales services. Recently withdrawn for reallocation are two Volvo B8RLEs with BV19LPA illustrating them. It carried fleet number 351 while with Newport. *Steve Rice*

400-404		ADL E40D		ADL Enviro 400		N45/31F	2012	
400	SN62AOH	**402**	SN62AOP	**403**	SN62AOW		**404**	SN62AOX
401	SN62AOO							

405	SK70BUO	ADL E40D	ADL Enviro 400 MMC	NC51/35F	2021	
406	SK70BUP	ADL E40D	ADL Enviro 400 MMC	NC51/35F	2021	
407	YX70OLA	ADL E40D	ADL Enviro 400 MMC	NC51/35F	2021	
408	LK55KKO	ADL E40D	ADL Enviro 400	N41/26D	2006	Metroline, 2021
409	LJ56VTO	ADL E40D	ADL Enviro 400	N41/26D	2006	Candy Coaches, 2021
410	SK71CKL	ADL E40D	ADL Enviro 400 MMC	NC51/35F	2021	
411	YX72ONR	ADL E40D	ADL Enviro 400 MMC	NC51/35F	2023	
412	YJ09ZCL	Scania OmniCity N230 UD	Scania	N41/26F	2009	RATP, 2022
413	YJ59SFK	Scania OmniCity N230 UD	Scania	N41/26F	2009	RATP, 2022
414	YJ59SFV	Scania OmniCity N230 UD	Scania	N41/26F	2009	RATP, 2022
415	YJ59SGO	Scania OmniCity N230 UD	Scania	N41/26F	2009	RATP, 2022
416	YJ59SGU	Scania OmniCity N230 UD	Scania	N41/26F	2009	RATP, 2022
417	YX72ONU	ADL E40D	ADL Enviro 400 MMC	NC51/35F	2023	
418	CK24AUH	Yutong U11 DD	Yutong	NC41/29F	2024	
419	CK24AUO	Yutong U11 DD	Yutong	NC41/29F	2024	
420	LX51KXR	Dennis Trident	Plaxton President	N43/31F	2002	Metroline, 2013
421	LX51KXW	Dennis Trident	Plaxton President	N43/31F	2002	Metroline, 2013
422	LN51KXV	Dennis Trident	Plaxton President	N43/31F	2002	Metroline, 2013
424	LR02BAU	Dennis Trident	Plaxton President	N43/31F	2002	Metroline, 2013
425	LR02BBF	Dennis Trident	Plaxton President	N43/31F	2002	Metroline, 2013

426-440		Dennis Trident		Alexander ALX400		N43/24F	2002	Abellio, London 2017
426	KV02USM	**431**	KV02USH	**435**	KN52NEU		**438**	LR52LYC
427	KV02URS	**432**	KN52NDG	**436**	KN52NEY		**439**	LR52LWF
428	KV02URL	**433**	KN52NFA	**437**	KN52NEO		**440**	KV02URM
429	KV02USB	**434**	KN52NDY					

The latest pair of Transport for Wales buses allocated to Newport are Yutong E12s numbered 354 and 355. The latter, CE72YRL, is seen on TrawsCymru service T7 which links Magor, Chepstow and Bristol City Centre. *Steve Rice*

Fleet no.	Registration	Chassis	Body	Seating	Year	Previous owner
D20	KX72CWO	Isuzu/AOS Grand Toro	AOS	C35F	2022	
D21	VU19WNP	Yutong TC9	Yutong	C37F	2019	Creswell, Evesham, 2022
D22	W648RCG	Dennis Javelin	Berkhof Axial	C55F	2000	Travel Wright, 2022
D23	BF16XPN	Mercedes-Benz Tourismo	Mercedes-Benz	C53FT	2016	A-Line, Coventry, 2022
D24	BF16XPP	Mercedes-Benz Tourismo	Mercedes-Benz	C53FT	2016	A-Line, Coventry, 2022
D25	BF16XPO	Mercedes-Benz Tourismo	Mercedes-Benz	C53FT	2016	A-Line, Coventry, 2022
D26	YN06MXU	Volvo B12B 15m	Plaxton Panther	C65FT	2006	Woottens, Chesham, 2012
D27	YN06MXV	Volvo B12B 15m	Plaxton Panther	C65FT	2006	Woottens, Chesham, 2012
D28	SV59CHL	Volvo B12B 15m	Plaxton Panther	C65FT	2009	Stagecoach, 2017
D29	KX59DLU	Volvo B12B 15m	Plaxton Panther	C65FT	2009	Stagecoach, 2017
D30	YN10FZT	Volvo B9R	Plaxton Elite	S70F	2001	Cymru, Swansea, 2022
D31	WT54JAC	VDL SB4000	Van Hool T9 Alizée	S70F	2004	Eagle, Bristol, 2023
D32	CE23ZDK	Yutong TCe12	Yutong	C46F	2023	
D33	CE23ZDL	Yutong TCe12	Yutong	C46F	2023	
D34	CE23ZDJ	Yutong TCe12	Yutong	C46F	2023	
D35	CE23ZDM	Yutong TCe12	Yutong	C46F	2023	
D36	AB60MTB	Volvo B12M	Plaxton Panther	C53FT	2010	South Wales, Swansea, '23
D37	EB60MTB	Volvo B12M	Plaxton Panther	C53FT	2010	South Wales, Swansea, '23

D38-D45		Volvo 9700		Volvo		C53FT	2023
D38	BV23NNM	**D40**	BV23NNP	**D42**	BV23NNJ	**D44**	BV23NNR
D39	BV23NNH	**D41**	BV23NNG	**D43**	BV23NNO	**D45**	BV23NNU

Fleet no.	Registration	Chassis	Body	Seating	Year	Previous owner
D46	YN56FEX	Scania K94	irizar S-Kool	S70F	2006	Turners, Bristol, 2023
D47	BV16YNK	Mercedes-Benz Tourismo	Mercedes-Benz	C51FT	2016	Turners, Bristol, 2023
D48	BV16YNJ	Mercedes-Benz Tourismo	Mercedes-Benz	C51FT	2016	Turners, Bristol, 2023
D49	YN56FEV	Scania K94	irizar S-Kool	S70F	2006	Turners, Bristol, 2023
D50	CK73ATY	Yutong GT12	Yutong	C53FT	2024	
D51	FJ55DZL	Volvo B12B 15m	Plaxton Panther	C49FT	2006	Ashwood, Wycombe, 2024
D52	YN54OCE	Scania K94	irizar S-Kool	S70F	2005	Ashwood, Wycombe, 2024

D53-D59		Yutong GT12		Yutong		C53FT	2024
D53	CK73AVR	**D55**	CK73AWC	**D57**	CK73AWX	**D59**	CK73AWP
D54	CK73AVW	**D56**	CK73AWJ	**D58**	CK73AWR		

Earlier in 2024 Newport received eleven of the short Yutong E9L model. Illustrating this version as it works route R1 through Risca is Z50, CK24AWO. The E9 is an e-bus 8.94 metres long and 2.42 wide and equipped with 255 kWh batteries. *Richard Godfrey*

Z01	YK66CBC	Yutong E12		Yutong Electric	N38F	2017	Pelican demonstrator, 2020
Z02-Z15		Yutong E12		Yutong Electric	N38F	2020	
Z02	YD70CFE	**Z06**	YD70CFK	**Z10**	YD70CHH	**Z13**	YD70CHL
Z03	YD70CFF	**Z07**	YD70CFL	**Z11**	YD70CHJ	**Z14**	YD70CHN
Z04	YD70CFG	**Z08**	YD70CFM	**Z12**	YD70CHK	**Z15**	YD70CHO
Z05	YD70CFJ	**Z09**	YD70CHG				
Z16	YG18CVS	Yutong E10		Yutong	N32F	2018	Pelican demonstrator, 2022
Z17-Z32		Yutong E12*		Yutong	N37F*	2022	*Z21/3-31 E10 and N33F
Z17	CE22WXG	**Z21**	CE22WWL	**Z25**	CE22WWP	**Z29**	CE22WWM
Z18	CE22WXD	**Z22**	CE22WXB	**Z26**	CE22WWO	**Z30**	CE22WWJ
Z19	CE22WXA	**Z23**	CE22WWT	**Z27**	CE22WWR	**Z31**	CE22WWK
Z20	CE22WXC	**Z24**	CE22WWN	**Z28**	CE22WWH	**Z32**	CE22WXF
Z33-Z40		Yutong E10		Yutong	N33F	2023	
Z33	CE23ZGA	**Z35**	CE23ZGC	**Z37**	CE23ZGF	**Z39**	CE23ZGH
Z34	CE23ZGB	**Z36**	CE23ZGD	**Z38**	CE23ZGG	**Z40**	CE23ZGJ
Z41-Z44		Yutong E12		Yutong	N37F	2023	
Z41	CE23ZGK	**Z42**	CE23ZGL	**Z43**	CE23ZGM	**Z44**	CE23ZGN
Z45-Z55		Yutong E9L		Yutong	N26F	2024	
Z45	CK24AVL	**Z48**	CK24AWA	**Z51**	CK24AUN	**Z54**	CK24AVW
Z46	CK24AVP	**Z49**	CK24AWH	**Z52**	CK24AUU	**Z55**	CK24AVM
Z47	CK24AVV	**Z50**	CK24AWO	**Z53**	CK24AUY		

Anciliary vehicle:

61	YN53PZR	Scania OmniCity CN94 UB	Scania	tv	2003

Special event vehicle:

178	PDW484	Leyland Titan PD2/40	Longwell Green	B30/28R	1958

NOTTINGHAM CITY TRANSPORT

Nottingham City Transport - South Notts - Pathfinder

Nottingham City Transport Ltd, Lower Parliament Street, Nottingham, NG1 1GG

201-217			Yutong E12			Yutong		N39F	2023-24		
201	TB	YD73FSC	**206**	TB	YD73FSK	**210**	TB	YD73FSS	**214**	-	-
202	TB	YD73FSJ	**207**	TB	YD73FSL	**211**	TB	YD73FSU	**215**	-	-
203	TB	YD73FSE	**208**	TB	YD73FSO	**212**	TB	YD73FSV	**216**	-	-
204	TB	YD73FSF	**209**	TB	YD73FSP	**213**	-	-	**217**	-	-
205	TB	YD73FSG									

251-281			Yutong E10			Yutong		N31F	2023-24		
251	TB	YH24MFA	**259**	TB	YH24MFU	**267**	-	-	**275**	-	-
252	TB	YH24MFE	**260**	TB	YH24MFV	**268**	-	-	**276**	-	-
253	TB	YH24MFF	**261**	TB	YH24MFX	**269**	-	-	**277**	-	-
254	TB	YH24MFJ	**262**	TB	YH24MFY	**270**	-	-	**278**	-	-
255	TB	YH24MFK	**271**	-	-	**279**	-	-			
256	TB	YH24MFN	**264**	-	-	**272**	-	-	**280**	-	-
257	TB	YH24MFO	**265**	-	-	**273**	-	-	**281**	-	-
258	TB	YH24MFP	**266**	-	-	**274**	-	-			

301-309			ADL E20D 10.2m			ADL Enviro 200 MMC		N33F	2019		
301	TB	YX69NRE	**304**	TB	YX69NRK	**306**	TB	YX69NRN	**308**	TB	YX69NRU
302	TB	YX69NRF	**305**	TB	YX69NRL	**307**	TB	YX69NRO	**309**	TB	YX69NRV
303	TB	YX69NRJ									

330-353			Optare Solo M990			Optare		N33F	2011-12		
330	TB	YJ11OHA	**345**	TB	YJ61CGG	**348**	TB	YJ61CGU	**352**	TB	YJ61CGZ
342	TB	YJ61CFZ	**346**	TB	YJ61CGK	**350**	TB	YJ61CGX	**353**	TB	YJ61CHC
344	TB	YJ61CGF	**347**	TB	YJ61CGO	**351**	TB	YJ61CGY			

Nottingham City Transport is another operator to take the electric Yutong product with an order for forty-eight E12s currently in progress. Seen arriving in Wollaton is 205, YD73FSG. *Richard Godfrey*

354-365			Optare Solo M970			Optare		N33F	2012		
354	TB	YJ12GYN	**357**	TB	YJ12GYR	**360**	TB	YJ12GYU	**363**	TB	YJ12GYX
355	TB	YJ12GYO	**358**	TB	YJ12GYS	**361**	TB	YJ12GYV	**364**	TB	YJ12GYY
356	TB	YJ12GYP	**359**	TB	YJ12GYT	**362**	TB	YJ12GYW	**365**	TB	YJ12GYZ

399	TB	YX69NPJ	ADL E20D 10.2m	ADL Enviro 200 MMC	N33F	2019

401-453			Scania N280 UD Bio-gas			ADL Enviro 400 City		N42/30F	2017-18		
401	PS	YP17UFA	**415**	PS	YP17UGG	**428**	PS	YP17UFS	**441**	PS	YN18SVZ
402	PS	YP17UFB	**416**	PS	YP17UGH	**429**	PS	YP17UGA	**442**	PS	YN18SXA
403	PS	YP17UFC	**417**	PS	YP17UGJ	**430**	PS	YP17UGB	**443**	PS	YN18SXB
404	PS	YP17UFD	**418**	PS	YP17UFH	**431**	PS	YN18SVA	**444**	PS	YN18SXC
405	PS	YP17UFE	**419**	PS	YP17UGK	**432**	PS	YN18SVC	**445**	PS	YN18SXD
406	PS	YP17UFK	**420**	PS	YP17UGL	**433**	PS	YN18SVD	**446**	PS	YN18SXE
407	PS	YP17UFL	**421**	PS	YP17UGM	**434**	PS	YN18SVE	**447**	PS	YN18SXF
408	PS	YP17UFM	**422**	PS	YP17UGN	**435**	PS	YN18SVF	**448**	PS	YN18SXG
409	PS	YP17UFN	**423**	PS	YP17UGO	**436**	PS	YN18SVU	**449**	PS	YN18SXJ
410	PS	YP17UFO	**424**	PS	YP17UGR	**437**	PS	YN18SVV	**450**	PS	YN18SXK
411	PS	YP17UGC	**425**	PS	YP17UGT	**438**	PS	YN18SVW	**451**	PS	YN18SXL
412	PS	YP17UGD	**426**	PS	YP17UFJ	**439**	PS	YN18SVX	**452**	PS	YN18SXM
413	PS	YP17UGE	**427**	PS	YP17UFR	**440**	PS	YN18SVY	**453**	PS	YN18SXO
414	PS	YP17UGF									

454-520			Scania N280 UD Bio-gas			ADL Enviro 400 City		N42/30F	2019		
454	PS	YN19EEJ	**471**	PS	YN19EFE	**488**	PS	YN19EFZ	**505**	PS	YN69DPE
455	PS	YN19EEM	**472**	PS	YN19EFF	**489**	PS	YN19EGC	**506**	PS	YN69DPF
456	PS	YN19EEO	**473**	PS	YN19EFG	**490**	PS	YN19EGD	**507**	PS	YN69DPK
457	PS	YN19EEP	**474**	PS	YN19EFJ	**491**	PS	YN19EGE	**508**	PS	YN69DPO
458	PS	YN19EER	**475**	PS	YN19EFK	**492**	PS	YN19EGF	**509**	PS	YN69DPU
459	PS	YN19EES	**476**	PS	YN19EFL	**493**	PS	YN19EGJ	**510**	PS	YN69DPV
460	PS	YN19EET	**477**	PS	YN19EFM	**494**	PS	YN19EGK	**511**	PS	YN69DPX
461	PS	YN19EEU	**478**	PS	YN19EFN	**495**	PS	YN19EGX	**512**	PS	YN69DPY
462	PS	YN19EEV	**479**	PS	YN19EFP	**496**	PS	YN19EGY	**513**	PS	YN69DPZ
463	PS	YN19EEW	**480**	PS	YN19EFR	**497**	PS	YN19EHB	**514**	PS	YN69DRO
464	PS	YN19EEX	**481**	PS	YN19EFS	**498**	PS	YN19EHC	**515**	PS	YN69DRV
465	PS	YN19EEY	**482**	PS	YN19EFT	**499**	PS	YN19EHD	**516**	PS	YN69DRX
466	PS	YN19EEZ	**483**	PS	YN19EFU	**500**	PS	DD18GAS	**517**	PS	YN69DRZ
467	PS	YN19EFA	**484**	PS	YN19EFV	**501**	PS	YN19EHE	**518**	PS	YN69DSE
468	PS	YN19EFB	**485**	PS	YN19EFW	**502**	PS	YN69DOH	**519**	PS	YN69DSO
469	PS	YN19EFC	**486**	PS	YN19EFX	**503**	PS	YN69DOJ	**520**	PS	YN69DSU
470	PS	YN19EFD	**487**	PS	YN19EFY	**504**	PS	YN69DOU			

Nottingham is a keen user of different colours for selected routes. Purple route 89 is represented by Scania bio-gas bus 472, YN19EFF.
Alan Blagburn

521-543			Scania N280 UD Bio-gas			ADL Enviro 400 City			N42/30F	2022	
521	PS	YN71CYK	527	PS	YN22BMY	533	PS	YN22BNF	539	PS	YN22BNV
522	PS	YN22BLX	528	PS	YN22BMZ	534	PS	YN22BNJ	540	PS	YN22BNX
523	PS	YN22BLZ	529	PS	YN22BNA	535	PS	YN22BNK	541	PS	YN22BNY
524	PS	YN22BMO	530	PS	YN22BNB	536	PS	YN22BNL	542	PS	YN22BNZ
525	PS	YN22BMU	531	PS	YN22BND	537	PS	YN22BNO	543	PS	YN22BOF
526	PS	YN22BMV	532	PS	YN22BNE	538	PS	YN22BNU			

601-640			Scania N230 UD			ADL Enviro 400			N47/27F	2013-14	
601	PS	YP63WFA	611	PS	YN63WEC	621	PS	YN14MUB	631	PS	YN14MVC
602	PS	YP63WFB	612	TB	YN14MTJ	622	PS	YN14MUC	632	PS	YN14MVD
603	PS	YP63WFC	613	TB	YN14MTK	623	PS	YN14MUE	633	PS	YN14MVE
604	PS	YP63WFD	614	PS	YN14MTO	624	PS	YN14MUO	634	PS	YN14MVF
605	PS	YP63WFE	615	PS	YN14MTU	625	PS	YN14MUP	635	PS	YN14MVG
606	PS	YP63WFF	616	PS	YN14MTV	626	PS	YN14MUU	636	PS	YN14MVH
607	PS	YP63WFG	617	PS	YN14MTX	627	PS	YN14MUV	637	PS	YN14MVK
608	PS	YP63WFH	618	PS	YN14MTY	628	PS	YN14MUW	638	PS	YN14MVL
609	PS	YP63WFJ	619	PS	YN14MTZ	629	PS	YN14MUY	639	PS	YN14MVM
610	PS	YP63WFK	620	PS	YN14MUA	630	PS	YN14MVA	640	TB	YN14MVO

641-662			Scania N230 UD			ADL Enviro 400			N47/27F	2015	
641	TB	YN15EJA	647	TB	YN15EJK	653	PS	YN65XFM	658	PS	YN65XFU
642	TB	YN15EJC	648	TB	YN65XFG	654	PS	YN65XFO	659	PS	YN65XFV
643	TB	YN15EJD	649	PS	YN65XFH	655	PS	YN65XFP	660	PS	YN65XFW
644	TB	YN15EJE	650	PS	YN65XFJ	656	PS	YN65XFR	661	PS	YN65XFT
645	TB	YN15EJF	651	PS	YN65XFK	657	PS	YN65XFS	662	PS	YN65XFX
646	TB	YN15EJJ	652	PS	YN65XFL						

907	TB	YT61GOP	Scania N230 UD	Optare Omnidekka	N51/35F	2011

925-932			Scania N230 UD			Optare Omnidekka			N51/35F	2011	
925	PS	YT61FFM	927	PS	YT61FFO	929	PS	YT61FFR	931	PS	YT61FFU
926	PS	YT61FFN	928	PS	YT61FFP	930	PS	YT61FFS	932	PS	YT61FFV

Ancilliary vehicles:

375	PS	YX13AEU	ADL E20D 10.2m	ADL Enviro 200	N33F	2013
376	PS	YX13BNO	ADL E20D 10.2m	ADL Enviro 200	N33F	2013
T912	PS	YT61GPF	Scania N270 UD	Optare Omnidekka	N51/26F	2011
T913	PS	YT61GPJ	Scania N270 UD	Optare Omnidekka	N51/26F	2011
T914	PS	YT61GPK	Scania N270 UD	Optare Omnidekka	N51/26F	2011
T915	PS	YT61GPO	Scania N270 UD	Optare Omnidekka	N51/26F	2011
T916	PS	YT61GPU	Scania N270 UD	Optare Omnidekka	N51/26F	2011
T917	PS	YT61GPV	Scania N270 UD	Optare Omnidekka	N51/26F	2011

Depots: Parliament Street (PS) and Trent Bridge (TB)

Celebrating 125 years of public ownership, Scania N230 627, YN14MUV, is seen in a special livery. It was working route 10 through West Bridgford when seen.
Richard Godfrey

NOTTINGHAM COMMUNITY TRANSPORT

Sherwood Bus Depot, Mansfield Road, Nottingham, NG5 2JN

901-906		Ford Transit		Ford	M8	2015	
901	MJ65VVY	**903** MJ65VWC		**905** MJ65VWG		**906** MJ65VWK	
902	MJ65VWA	**904** MJ65VWE					
909	K25CTN	Mercedes-Benz Sprinter 513 cdi		Mercredes-Benz	M16	2013	
911	YP11SPV	Ford Transit		Ford	M8	2011	
914	GX14NHL	Ford Transit		Ford	M8	2014	
917	YK10WBM	Ford Transit		Ford	M8	2010	
918	DK18AEL	Peugeot Boxer		Peugeot	N16F	2018	
919	DK18AHZ	Peugeot Boxer		Peugeot	N16F	2018	
920	K26CTN	Mercedes-Benz Sprinter 513 cdi		Mercredes-Benz	M16	2013	
921-924		Optare Solo M880 SL		Optare	N28F	2008	Nottingham CC, 2009
921	K16CTN	**923** K18CTN		**924** K19CTN			
929	YJ10EZL	Optare Versa V1040 EV		Optare	N32F	2013	
930	YJ10EZM	Optare Versa V1040 EV		Optare	N32F	2013	
932	YJ10EZO	Optare Versa V1040 EV		Optare	N32F	2013	
977-989		BYD K9UR		BYD	N35F	2016	
977	LJ16LMK	**981** LJ16LMV		**984** LJ16LMZ		**987** LJ16LNC	
978	LJ16LMM	**982** LJ16LMX		**985** LJ16LNA		**988** LJ16LNE	
979	LJ16LMO	**983** LJ16LMY		**986** LJ16LNB		**989** LJ16LNF	
980	LJ16LMU						
994	KM21OXK	Mercedes-Benz Sprinter 45		Mercredes-Benz	N16F	2021	
995	KP21OZT	Mercedes-Benz Sprinter 45		Mercredes-Benz	N16F	2021	
996	KP21PCU	Mercedes-Benz Sprinter 45		Mercredes-Benz	N16F	2021	
1000	NK09FVL	Optare Versa V1110		Optare	N38F	2009	Go North East, 2023
1001	NK09FVH	Optare Versa V1110		Optare	N38F	2009	Go North East, 2023
1002	NK09FVJ	Optare Versa V1110		Optare	N38F	2009	Go North East, 2023
1003	K33CTN	Optare Solo M950		Optare	N33F	2008	Blackpool, 2019
1004	K44CTN	Optare Solo M950		Optare	N33F	2008	Blackpool, 2019
1005	K66CTN	Optare Solo M950		Optare	N33F	2009	Blackpool, 2019
1006	K40CTN	Optare Versa V1110		Optare	N40F	2010	GHA Buses, 2019
1007	K30CTN	Optare Versa V1110		Optare	N40F	2010	GHA Buses, 2019
1008	K20CTN	Optare Versa V1110		Optare	N40F	2010	GHA Buses, 2019
1009-1013		Optare Solo M950		Optare	N33F	2009	Blackpool, 2019
1009	K10CTN	**1011** K12CTN		**1012** K13CTN		**1013** K14CTN	
1010	K11CTN						
1014	YJ62FFB	Optare Versa V1170		Optare	N43F	2012	Go North East, 2023
1015	YJ62FLD	Optare Versa V1170		Optare	N43F	2012	Go North East, 2023
1020	DK19AWF	Peugeot Boxer		Peugeot	N16F	2019	
1021	UP63RWL	Ford Transit		Ford	M8	2013	
1022	YD24ERV	Yutong E10		Yutong	N39F	2024	
1023	YD24ESG	Yutong E10		Yutong	N39F	2024	

NOTTINGHAM LIGHT RAPID TRANSIT

The Greater Nottingham Light Rapid Transit Advisory Committee, Loxley House, Station Street, Nottingham. NG2 3NG

201-215		Bombardier Incentro		Bombardier		N62D	2004
201	**203**	**205**	**207**	**209**	**211**	**213**	**215**
202	**204**	**206**	**208**	**210**	**212**	**214**	

216-237		Alstrom Citadis 302		Alstrom		N62D	2013-14
216	**219**	**222**	**225**	**228**	**231**	**234**	**236**
217	**220**	**223**	**226**	**229**	**232**	**235**	**237**
218	**221**	**224**	**227**	**230**	**233**		

Tram depot: Wilkinson Street

Opened in 2004 and extended in 2015, the network covers all major employment sites, both Universities and Nottingham College as well as the main attractions within the city. Trams currently operate every seven to eight minutes on a daily service. Two models of tram are used, with 222, an Alstrom Citadis 302, pictured on Queen's Walk. *Mark Lyons*

PILKINGTONBUS

Pilkingtons, Argyle Garage, Argyle Street, Accrington, BB5 1DQ

1	PK16BUS	Optare Solo M790 SL	Optare	N29F	2016	
2	YJ64DSE	Optare Solo M780 SE	Optare	N27F	2014	Elite, Blackpool, 2016
3	KY63VTJ	Optare Solo M710 SE	Optare	N23F	2013	Stanley Taxis, Stanley, 2015
4	YJ60KFP	Optare Solo M710 SE	Optare	N23F	2013	A2B, Prenton, 2016
5	FM55NVH	Volvo B7TL	ADL ALX400	N49/27F	2006	Thandi, Smethwick, 2022
6	BC05RVO	Volvo B7TL	ADL ALX400	N49/27F	2006	Thandi, Smethwick, 2022
7	BC05RVJ	Volvo B7TL	ADL ALX400	N49/27F	2006	Thandi, Smethwick, 2022
8	BC05RVN	Volvo B7TL	ADL ALX400	N49/27F	2006	Thandi, Smethwick, 2022
9	SB58BUS	Optare Solo M780 SE	Optare	N27F	2008	Gem Travel, Rampton, 2020
11	BC05RVU	Volvo B7TL	ADL ALX400	N49/27F	2006	Thandi, Smethwick, 2022
12	LG02FCM	Dennis Trident 9.9m	Alexander ALX400	N43/24F	2002	M Travel, Normanton, 2017
14	R19PLK	Optare Solo M710 SE	Optare	N23F	2008	Stantons, Stoke, 2018
16	R18PLK	Dennis Trident 10.5m	Plaxton President	N47/25F	2001	Tyrers, Adlington, 2018
17	BR04AJV	Volvo B7TL	ADL ALX400	N49/27F	2006	Thandi, Smethwick, 2022
19	R20PLK	Dennis Trident 10.5m	Plaxton President	N47/25F	2001	Tyrers, Adlington, 2018
20	LG02FEO	Dennis Trident 9.9m	Alexander ALX400	N43/24F	2002	M Travel, Normanton, 2017
21	LG02FCU	Dennis Trident 9.9m	Alexander ALX400	N43/24F	2002	M Travel, Normanton, 2017
22	PK56AGO	Volvo B7TL	ADL ALX400	N49/27F	2006	Dublin Bus, 2019
23	BC05RVR	Volvo B7TL	ADL ALX400	N49/27F	2006	Thandi, Smethwick, 2022
25	LX06EZU	ADL Dart SLF 8.9m	ADL Pointer	N23F	2006	Go-Ahead London, 2016
27	R6PLK	Volvo B7TL	ADL ALX400	N49/27F	2006	Dublin Bus, 2019
28	R12PLK	TransBus Trident 9.9m	TransBus President	N45/28F	2003	Tyrers, Adlington, 2019
29	R14PLK	TransBus Trident 9.9m	TransBus President	N45/28F	2003	Tyrers, Adlington, 2019
30	R10PLK	Volvo B7TL	ADL ALX400	N49/27F	2006	Dublin Bus, 2019
31	MX09MKG	Optare Solo M890 SL	Optare	N28F	2009	Boultons, Cardington, 2019
36	MK63XAW	Optare Solo M720 SE	Optare	N19F	2014	Reays, Wigton, 2020
37	PK20BUS	Mercedes-Benz Sprinter 516 cdi	Mellor Strata	N21F	2020	
38	PK20BUZ	Mercedes-Benz Sprinter 516 cdi	Mellor Strata	N21F	2020	
44	NK56UCA	Volvo B7TL	ADL ALX400	N49/27F	2006	Dublin Bus, 2019
50	RO23ODT	Iveco Daily 70C21	Illesbus i-City	N23F	2023	
51	RO23OFP	Iveco Daily 70C21	Illesbus i-City	N23F	2023	

Representing the Pilkingtonbus operation is Optare Solo 4, YJ60KFP, the smallest of the Solo variants at 7.10 metres long and only 2.34 metres wide. The operation has served the local area around Accrington and since its inception in1967 has remained a family firm, headed by Alan, Vicky and John Pilkington.
John Birtwistle

REDLINE

Redline Buses, 8 Gatehouse Way, Aylesbury, HP19 8DB

V112LGC	Volvo B7TL	Alexander ALX400	N43/24F	2000	Go-Ahead London
V119LGC	Volvo B7TL	Alexander ALX400	N43/24F	2000	Go-Ahead London
V185OOE	Volvo B7TL	Alexander ALX400	N43/24F	2000	RATP, Cambridge
X154FBB	Volvo B7TL	Plaxton President	N41/22F	2000	Go-Ahead London
Y703TGH	Volvo B7TL	Plaxton President	N41/24F	2001	Go-Ahead London
Y734TGH	Volvo B7TL	Plaxton President	N41/24F	2001	Go-Ahead London
KF52NBN	Dennis Dart SLF 10.1m	Plaxton Pointer 2	N27D	2001	RATP, London
PN52XBP	Volvo B7TL	East Lancs Vyking	NC47/33F	2002	Richardson's, 2018
SK52MPU	Volvo B7TL	Alexander ALX400	N45/26F	2002	Transdev, London
LF52UPO	Volvo B7TL	Wrightbus Eclipse Gemini	N43/27F	2002	Arriva London
KM55KMH	ADL E300 12.5m	ADL Enviro 300	S60F	2005	Tonna Luxury Travel
LK55KKH	ADL Trident 2	ADL Enviro 400	N41/26D	2006	Metroline, 2019
LK55KKZ	ADL Trident 2	ADL Enviro 400	N41/26D	2006	Metroline, 2019
LK06FLB	ADL Trident 2	ADL Enviro 400	N41/26D	2006	Metroline, 2019
YN07EYK	Scania N270 UD	East lancs Omnidekka	N51/35F	2007	Nottinham CT, 2023
AE07DZB	ADL Dart 10.8m	MCV eVolution	N40F	2007	Jones, Acrefair, 2021
AE07DZC	ADL Dart 10.8m	MCV eVolution	N40F	2007	Jones, Acrefair, 2021
KB07OXF	Volvo B12B	Plaxton Panther	S70F	2007	Go-Ahead Oxford, 2014
YX08MDY	ADL Dart 8.9m	ADL Enviro 200	N29F	2008	RATP, London, 2019
PL08YLZ	Volvo B9TL	Optare Olympus	N51/31F	2008	Ensignbus, Purfleet, 2022
PL08YMA	Volvo B9TL	Optare Olympus	N51/31F	2008	Ensignbus, Purfleet, 2022
PO58NPJ	Volvo B9TL	Optare Olympus	N51/31F	2008	Ensignbus, Purfleet, 2022
PO58NPP	Volvo B9TL	Optare Olympus	N51/31F	2008	Ensignbus, Purfleet, 2022
LJ09KPL	ADL Dart 4 10.8m	ADL Enviro 200	N41F	2009	Arriva London, 2021
LJ09KPZ	ADL Dart 4 10.8m	ADL Enviro 200	N41F	2009	Arriva London, 2021
MX09HHL	ADL Dart 4 8.9m	ADL Enviro 200	N29F	2008	Maytree, Bolton
MX09HHN	ADL Dart 4 8.9m	ADL Enviro 200	N29F	2009	Maytree, Bolton
MX09HJN	ADL Dart 4 8.9m	ADL Enviro 200	N29F	2009	Maytree, Bolton
YX09FMD	ADL Dart 4 10.4m	ADL Enviro 200	N26F	2009	Metroline, London, 2020
MX60GXJ	ADL Dart 4 8.9m	ADL Enviro 200	N29F	2010	Mistral, Knutsford

Redline provides bus services in Aylesbury, Oxford and Slough having been founded in 1990s. Seen arriving in Oxford is Enviro 200 YX65RGV. Route X20 connects the university city with Aylesbury.
Mark Doggett

The sole Enviro 300 with Redline is the model marketed with sixty seats for school work. Registered KH55KMH, it was painted in schoolbus yellow when new, and is seen in its latest colours while in Oxford during May 2023. *Mark Doggett*

MX60GXK	ADL Dart 4 8.9m	ADL Enviro 200	N29F	2010	Mistral, Knutsford
YX10BFZ	ADL Dart 4 10.4m	ADL Enviro 200	N29D	2010	Abellio London
YX10FEF	ADL Dart 4 10.4m	ADL Enviro 200	N29D	2010	Metroline, 2019
YX10FFJ	ADL Dart 4 10.4m	ADL Enviro 200	N29D	2010	Abellio, London
MX61BAO	ADL Dart 4 8.9m	ADL Enviro 200	N29F	2011	Red Rose, Aylesbury, 2020
MX61BAU	ADL Dart 4 8.9m	ADL Enviro 200	N29F	2011	Red Rose, Aylesbury, 2020
YX12DKA	ADL Dart 4 10.4m	ADL Enviro 200	N29D	2012	Metroline, 2019
YX12AEW	ADL E20D 10.8m	ADL Enviro 200	N38F	2012	Yellow Buses, 2023
YX12AGY	ADL E20D 10.8m	ADL Enviro 200	N38F	2012	Yellow Buses, 2023
YX12AXU	ADL E20D 10.2m	ADL Enviro 200	N33F	2012	Yellow Buses, 2023
YX12AZN	ADL E20D 10.8m	ADL Enviro 200	N38F	2012	Yellow Buses, 2023
MX13BCF	ADL E20D 8.9m	ADL Enviro 200	N29F	2013	
MX13BCK	ADL E20D 8.9m	ADL Enviro 200	N29F	2013	
YX13BNV	ADL E20D 10.5m	ADL Enviro 200	N33F	2013	Nottingham CT, 2023
YX63LJE	ADL E20D 10.5m	ADL Enviro 200	N33F	2013	Nottingham CT, 2023
MK63XAR	ADL E20D 8.9m	ADL Enviro 200	N29F	2014	
MK63XAS	ADL E20D 8.9m	ADL Enviro 200	N29F	2014	
MK63XAT	ADL E20D 8.9m	ADL Enviro 200	N29F	2014	
YX65RGV	ADL E20D 10.8m	ADL Enviro 200	N37F	2015	
T25RRT	ADL E20D 8.9m	ADL Enviro 200	N29F	2016	Red Rose, Aylesbury, 2018
W25RRT	ADL E20D 8.9m	ADL Enviro 200	N29F	2016	Red Rose, Aylesbury, 2018
BV73MLX	Volvo B8RLE 10.8m	MCV eVoRa	N38F	2023	
BV73MLY	Volvo B8RLE 10.8m	MCV eVoRa	N38F	2023	
BV73MLZ	Volvo B8RLE 10.8m	MCV eVoRa	N38F	2023	
BV73MME	Volvo B8RLE 10.8m	MCV eVoRa	N38F	2023	
BV73MTE	Volvo B8RLE 10.8m	MCV eVoRa	N38F	2023	
BV73MTF	Volvo B8RLE 10.8m	MCV eVoRa	N38F	2023	
BV73MTJ	Volvo B8RLE 10.8m	MCV eVoRa	N38F	2023	
BV73MTK	Volvo B8RLE 10.8m	MCV eVoRa	N38F	2023	

RELIANCE

Reliance Motor Services Ltd, Reliance Garage, York Road, Sutton-on-the-Forest, York, YO61 1ES

1	YJ05UKR	Volvo B7RLE	Wrightbus Eclipse Urban	N43F	2005	
4	BF62UYO	Volvo B7RLE	Wrightbus Eclipse 2	N49F	2012	Volvo demonstrator
5	BA15BXS	Volvo B8RLE	Wrightbus Eclipse 3	N45F	2015	Volvo demonstrator
9	YX68URM	ADL E20D 10.8m	ADL Enviro 200 MMC	N41F	2018	
14	PJ02RDX	Volvo B7TL	Plaxton President	N41/23D	2002	York Pullman, 2019
15	Y445CUB	Volvo B7L	Wrightbus Eclipse	N41F	2001	First, 2020
16	YX19ONV	ADL E20D 10.8m	ADL Enviro 200 MMC	NC40F	2019	ADL demonstrator
17	YX19OWA	ADL E20D 11.5m	ADL Enviro 200 MMC	NC42F	2019	ADL demonstrator
18	BJ11EAE	Volvo B9TL	Wrightbus Gemini 2	N43/30F	2011	Tower Transit, 2020
20	YK54ENN	Volvo B7RLE	Wrightbus Eclipse 2	N43F	2005	First, 2021
22	AE12FGM	Volvo B7RLE	Wrightbus Eclipse 2	N44F	2012	York Pullman, 2021
23	SN57GNO	Volvo B9TL	Wrightbus Gemini 2	N48/32F	2007	Lothian Buses, 2021
24	SN59BFZ	Volvo B9TL	Wrightbus Gemini 2	N48/32F	2009	Lothian Buses, 2021
25	BV22HBH	Volvo B8RLE	MCV eVoRa	N46F	2022	
26	BV22HBJ	Volvo B8RLE	MCV eVoRa	N46F	2022	
27	AU07DXT	Volvo B7TL	Wrightbus Eclipse Gemini	N45/29F	2007	First, 2023
29	AU07DXS	Volvo B7TL	Wrightbus Eclipse Gemini	N45/29F	2007	First, 2023
30	G19REL	Volvo B7RLE	Wrightbus Eclipse Urban	N43F	2008	First, 2024
31	T10MCL	Volvo B7RLE	Wrightbus Eclipse Urban	N43F	2008	First, 2024

Web: www.reliancemotorservices.co.uk

Looking down on an Enviro 200 MMC we see Reliance 9, YX68URM, as it leaves York for Easingwold and Thirsk on route 30. One of three of the model, the other pair were formerly demonstration buses with Alexander Dennis. *John Birtwistle*

ROBERTS TRAVEL

Roberts Travel Group Ltd, The Limes, Midland Road, Hugglescote, Coalville, LE67 2FX

R403EOS	Volvo B10M-62	Van Hool T8 Alizée	C53F	1997	Ali, Worcester, 2004
X211HBT	Volvo B7TL	Alexander ALX400	N49/27F	2000	Helms, Bootle, 2018
X929YCC	Volvo B7TL	Alexander ALX400	N49/27F	2000	Helms, Bootle, 2018
RBZ494	Dennis Javelin	Plaxton Profile	S70F	2002	Mod, 2014
RBZ565	Volvo B7TL	Alexander ALX400	N49/27F	2002	Dublin Bus,
RBZ959	Volvo B7TL	Transbus ALX400	N49/27F	2003	Dublin Bus,
RBZ1664	Volvo B7TL	Alexander ALX400	N49/27F	2002	Dublin Bus,
RBZ3430	Volvo B7TL	Alexander ALX400	N49/27F	2002	Dublin Bus,
RBZ5544	Volvo B7TL	Alexander ALX400	N49/27F	2002	Dublin Bus,
SHZ2712	Dennis Javelin	Plaxton Profile	S70F	2003	Mod, 2015
SHZ3696	Dennis Javelin	Plaxton Profile	S70F	2003	Mod, 2015
SHZ3698	Dennis Javelin	Plaxton Profile	S70F	2003	Mod, 2015
SHZ3490	Volvo B7TL	Transbus ALX400	N49/27F	2003	Dublin Bus,
SHZ3492	Volvo B7TL	Transbus ALX400	N49/27F	2003	Dublin Bus,
FC03VEM	Volvo B7TL	Transbus ALX400	N49/27F	2003	Dublin Bus,
FC03VEY	Volvo B7TL	Transbus ALX400	N49/27F	2003	Dublin Bus,
FC03VFM	Volvo B7TL	Transbus ALX400	N49/27F	2003	Dublin Bus,
FC03VGN	Volvo B7TL	Transbus ALX400	N49/27F	2003	Dublin Bus,
FC03VGT	Volvo B7TL	Transbus ALX400	N49/27F	2003	Dublin Bus,
FF04JXS	Volvo B7TL	Transbus ALX400	N49/27F	2004	Dublin Bus,
FF04JXV	Volvo B7TL	Transbus ALX400	N49/27F	2004	Dublin Bus,
FB05KRE	Volvo B7TL	ADL ALX400	N49/27F	2005	Dublin Bus,
FB05KRF	Volvo B7TL	ADL ALX400	N49/27F	2005	Dublin Bus,
FB05KSK	Volvo B7TL	ADL ALX400	N49/27F	2005	Dublin Bus,
FB05KSN	Volvo B7TL	ADL ALX400	N49/27F	2005	Dublin Bus
RBZ9595	Volvo B7R	Plaxton Profile	S70F	2005	Bedford CC, 2015
C3BCP	Volvo B7R	Plaxton Profile	S70F	2006	Bedford CC, 2015
C6BCP	Volvo B7R	Plaxton Profile	S70F	2006	Medway, Birmingham, '15
YJ13HTN	Van Hool TX17 Astron	Van Hool	C61FT	2013	
OO05RTG	Neoplan Tourliner N2216/23 SHDL	Neoplan	C61FT	2013	
OO06RTG	Neoplan Tourliner N2216/23 SHDL	Neoplan	C61FT	2013	
BU14EFV	Volvo B11R	VDL Jonckheere SHV	C53F	2014	
J200RTG	Mercedes-Benz Tourismo	Mercedes-Benz	C53FT	2015	
J300RTG	Mercedes-Benz Tourismo	Mercedes-Benz	C53FT	2015	
RBZ913	Mercedes-Benz Tourismo	Mercedes-Benz	C53FT	2016	
YJ16UTR	Yutong TC9	Yutong	C36F	2016	

Electric buses were introduced on the park and ride services in Leicester May 2021, and Yutong YD21NFL, was one of the initial batch for the service. *Steve Rice*

Operating in conjunction with Leicestershire County Council, Roberts Travel operates its park and ride buses. Parking is free for bus service users at each of the Leicester Park & Ride sites, located at Enderby, Birstall and Meynell's Gorse. Seen on the Birstall service is YD21NFK. *Steve Rice*

GJ17FWA	Volkswagen Transporter	Volkswagen	M8	2017	
OO10RTG	Neoplan Tourliner N2216/23 SHDL	Neoplan	C61FT	2017	
OO09RTG	Mercedes-Bemz Tourismo	Mercedes-Benz	C53FT	2018	
RV68YLZ	Mercedes-Bemz Sprinter 516 cdi	EVM X-lusive	C16F	2018	
OO07RTG	ADL E40D	ADL Enviro 400 MMC	NC49/37F	2018	Beestons, Hadleigh, 2020
OO08RTG	Volvo B11R	VDL Jonckheere SHV	C53F	2018	
YD19HHR	Yutong TC9	Yutong	C35F	2019	
BV19YHS	Mercedes-Bemz Tourismo M2	Mercedes-Benz	C48FT	2019	
BV19YHT	Mercedes-Bemz Tourismo M2	Mercedes-Benz	C48FT	2019	
BV69LME	Mercedes-Bemz Tourismo M2	Mercedes-Benz	C48FT	2019	Shearings, Wigan, 2021
BV69LMJ	Mercedes-Bemz Tourismo M2	Mercedes-Benz	C48FT	2019	Shearings, Wigan, 2021
BV69LNW	Mercedes-Bemz Tourismo M3	Mercedes-Benz	C57FT	2019	Redwing, Croydon, 2022
BV69LNX	Mercedes-Bemz Tourismo M3	Mercedes-Benz	C57FT	2019	Redwing, Croydon, 2022
BV69LNY	Mercedes-Bemz Tourismo M3	Mercedes-Benz	C57FT	2019	Redwing, Croydon, 2022
BV69LNZ	Mercedes-Bemz Tourismo M3	Mercedes-Benz	C57FT	2019	Redwing, Croydon, 2022
BV20HOA	Mercedes-Bemz Tourismo M3	Mercedes-Benz	C57FT	2020	
BV20UZK	Ford Transit	Ford	M8	2020	
YD21NFF	Yutong E12	Yutong	N37F	2021	
YD21NFG	Yutong E12	Yutong	N37F	2021	
YD21NFH	Yutong E12	Yutong	N37F	2021	
YD21NFJ	Yutong E12	Yutong	N37F	2021	
YD21NFK	Yutong E12	Yutong	N37F	2021	
YD21NFL	Yutong E12	Yutong	N37F	2021	
YD21NFM	Yutong E12	Yutong	N37F	2021	
YD21NFN	Yutong E12	Yutong	N37F	2021	
YD21NFO	Yutong E12	Yutong	N37F	2021	
YD21NFP	Yutong E12	Yutong	N37F	2021	
YD21NFR	Yutong TC9	Yutong	C37F	2021	
PO71MXH	Ford Transit	Ford	M16	2021	
PO71MXM	Ford Transit	Ford	M16	2021	
YX71LVD	Volvo B8R	Plaxton Leopard	S72F	2021	
YX71LVE	Volvo B8R	Plaxton Leopard	S72F	2021	
YX23OSK	ADL E40D	ADL Enviro 400 MMC	NC51/34F	2023	
YD73FRL	Yutong TC9	Yutong	C37F	2023	
YD73FRN	Yutong TC12	Yutong	C50D	2023	
YD24ETR	Yutong GT12	Yutong	C53FT	2024	
YX24MBF	Volvo B8R	Plaxton Leopard	S72F	2024	
BF24AJU	Mercedes-Bemz Tourismo M2	Mercedes-Benz	C53FT	2024	
BF24AJV	Mercedes-Bemz Tourismo M2	Mercedes-Benz	C53FT	2024	
BF24AKJ	Mercedes-Bemz Tourismo M2	Mercedes-Benz	C53FT	2024	
BF24AKK	Mercedes-Bemz Tourismo M2	Mercedes-Benz	C53FT	2024	
BF24AOA	Mercedes-Bemz Tourismo M3	Mercedes-Benz	C61FT	2024	
YY24HCV	ADL E40D	ADL Enviro 400 MMC	NC51/34F	2024	

SAFEGUARD

Safeguard Coaches - Farnham Coaches

Safeguard Coaches Ltd, Safeguard House, Clay Lane, Guildford, GU4 7NZ

w	VU02TTJ	Dennis Dart SLF	Plaxton Pointer	N29F	2002	
	247FCG	Volvo B12M	Plaxton Paragon	C53FT	2004	Logan, Dunloy, 2005
	YJ06FXM	Optare Tempo X1130	Optare	N37F	2006	
	WA57CYY	Volvo B12B	Van Hool T9 Alizée	C57F	2007	
	WA07KXX	Volvo B12B	Van Hool T9 Alizée	C53F	2007	
	YJ58CEY	Optare Tempo X1060	Optare	N34F	2008	Lynx, Kings Lynn
	WA58EOO	Volvo B12B	Van Hool T9 Alizée	C49FT	2008	
	SN09JUV	Volvo B12B	Van Hool T9 Alizée	C49FT	2009	AAA, Edinburgh, 2011
	SN09JUX	Volvo B12B	Van Hool T9 Alizée	C49FT	2009	AAA, Edinburgh, 2011
	YJ10EZT	Optare Versa V1100	Optare	N38F	2010	
	SN60FMO	Volvo B7R	Plaxton Profile	S70F	2010	Allan, Gorebridge, 2014
	YJ60LRO	Optare Versa V1100	Optare	N37F	2011	
	YD63UZJ	Optare Versa V1100	Optare	N37F	2013	
	GU64SAF	VDL Futura FHD2-129.365	VDL	C57F	2014	
	AA64SAF	VDL Futura FHD2-129.365	VDL	C57F	2014	
	YJ64DVY	Optare Versa V1100	Optare	N37F	2015	
	YX15OVT	Volvo B8R	Plaxton Leopard	S70F	2015	
	AA16SAF	Volvo B8R	Plaxton Leopard	S70F	2016	

Safeguard Coaches has operated from a base in Guildford for over a hundred years, celebrating its centenary during 2024. The fleet currently includes five of the MCV-bodied Volvo B8RLE model that joined the fleet in 2022-23. Pictured in Bellfields, while operating route 3 from Guildford, the type is represented by BV23NUJ. *Richard Godfrey*

Taking a trip around the Bransbury Estate is classic Enviro 200 YX18KOD pictured shortly after its arrival with Safeguard in 2023. The vehicle first entered service in 2018 at Glasgow Airport. *Richard Godfrey*

AA16FAR	VDL Futura FHD2-129.365	VDL	C57F	2016	
AC16FAR	VDL Futura FHD2-129.365	VDL	C57F	2016	
YJ17FZE	Optare MetroCity V1080 MC	Optare	N37F	2017	
YJ67FYX	Optare MetroCity V1080 MC	Optare	N37F	2017	
YX18KOD	ADL E20D 8.9m	ADL Enviro 200	N29F	2018	Glasgow Airport, 2023
YX18LHD	Volvo B8R	Plaxton Leopard	S70F	2018	
YX71LTN	Volvo B8R	Plaxton Panther	C53FT	2021	
YX71LTO	Volvo B8R	Plaxton Panther	C53FT	2021	
BV72KOD	Volvo B8RLE	MCV eVoRa	N38F	2022	
LF72DUV	Volvo B8RLE	MCV eVoRa	N38F	2022	
BV23NUJ	Volvo B8RLE	MCV eVoRa	N38F	2023	
BV23NUM	Volvo B8RLE	MCV eVoRa	N38F	2023	
BV23NUP	Volvo B8RLE	MCV eVoRa	N38F	2023	
SA24SAF	Volvo B8R	Plaxton Leopard	S70F	2024	
SG24SAF	Volvo B8R	Plaxton Leopard	S70F	2024	

Special event vehicles:

200APB	AEC Reliance MU3RV	Burlingham	B44F	1956
644HAA	Bedford J2	Plaxton Embassy	C18F	1963

Web: www.safeguardcoaches.co.uk; www.farnhamcoaches.co.uk;

Depots: Clay Lane, Guildford and Odiham Road, Farnham

SANDERS

Sanders Coaches Ltd, Heath Drive, Hempstead Road, Holt, NR25 6JU

1	NS17GAS	Yutong TC9	Yutong	C32FT	2017	
2	WF63LVH	Mercedes-Benz Vario 0816	Sitcar Beluga 3	C25F	2014	London Mini
3	HV20HRV	Yutong TC9	Yutong	C33FT	2020	
4	ED22WRD	Yutong TC9	Yutong	C37F	2022	
5	E19SCL	Mercedes-Benz Sprinter 516 cdi	Car-bus Spica	C19F	2016	Watts, Sutton, 2024
6	MB71LUX	Mercedes-Benz Sprinter 516 cdi	EVM Grand Tourer	C19F	2021	EPL Cars, Bedford, 2024
113	YN54AFU	Scania N94 UD	East Lancs Omnidekka	NC51/39F	2004	Reading Buses, 2011
114	YN54AFV	Scania N94 UD	East Lancs Omnidekka	NC51/39F	2004	Reading Buses, 2011
115	YN53CFF	Scania N94 UD	East Lancs Omnidekka	N51/39F	2003	Nottingham Transport, '18
116	YN53CFZ	Scania N94 UD	East Lancs Omnidekka	N51/39F	2003	Nottingham Transport, '18
117	YN06JWC	Scania N94 UD	East Lancs Omnidekka	NC47/33F	2006	Reading Buses, 2015
118	YN06JWF	Scania N94 UD	East Lancs Omnidekka	NC47/33F	2006	Reading Buses, 2015
119	YN06JWP	Scania N94 UD	East Lancs Omnidekka	NC47/33F	2006	Reading Buses, 2015
123	YN07EYY	Scania N94 UD	East Lancs Omnidekka	N51/29F	2007	Nottingham Transport, '18
124	YN07EYX	Scania N94 UD	East Lancs Omnidekka	N51/29F	2007	Nottingham Transport, '18
125	SA71SAN	Volvo B5TL	Wrightbus Gemini 3	NC51/30F	2021	
126	LL71SHA	Volvo B5TL	Wrightbus Gemini 3	NC51/30F	2021	
127	ED23SAN	Volvo B8L 14m	MCV eVoSeti	NC55/35F	2023	
128	PC23SAN	Volvo B8L 14m	MCV eVoSeti	NC55/35F	2023	
129	EC23SHA	Volvo B8L 14m	MCV eVoSeti	NC55/35F	2023	
130	HM24SAN	ADL E40D	ADL Enviro 400 MMC	NC51/35F	2024	
131	VR24VAR	ADL E40D	ADL Enviro 400 MMC	NC51/35F	2024	
132	TJ24TJH	ADL E40D	ADL Enviro 400 MMC	NC51/35F	2024	
222	RX22SKU	Mercedes-Benz Sprinter 516 cdi	EVM Cityline	N17F	2022	
316	YN05GXX	Scania L94UB	Wrightbus Solar	N43F	2005	Reading Buses, 2013
317	YN06NXS	Scania L94UB	Wrightbus Solar	N43F	2006	Reading Buses, 2013
318	YN06NXR	Scania L94UB	Wrightbus Solar	N43F	2006	Reading Buses, 2013

Volvo B5TL 126, LL71SHA, heads for Sheringham, one of a pair with Wrightbus Gemini bodywork added to the fleet in 2021. Sanders Coaches was formed in 1975 by Norman and Gladys Sanders with just five buses though now owned by their sons Paul and Charles Sanders and the fleet has increased to over ninety vehicles. *Mark Doggett*

Like many of the independent operators, Saunders has selected the MCV-bodied Volvo B8RLE for its single-deck needs. Representing the type is 521, BV21OOD, one of four from 2021 that are fitted with high-back seating. *Mark Doggett*

319w	YN57FWJ	Scania K230 UB	Wrightbus Solar	N43F	2007	Reading Buses, 2013
320	YN57FWH	Scania K230 UB	Wrightbus Solar	N43F	2007	Reading Buses, 2013
324	WX06JYA	Scania L94 UB	Wrightbus Solar	N43F	2006	Cardiff Bus, 2024
400	YJ64FWF	VDL SB200	Wrightbus Pulsar 2	N44F	2014	Fishwicks, Leyland, 2015
401	YH63CXE	VDL SB200	Wrightbus Pulsar 2	N44F	2013	Fishwicks, Leyland, 2015
402	YH63CXF	VDL SB200	Wrightbus Pulsar 2	N44F	2013	Fishwicks, Leyland, 2015
404	YJ10DJV	VDL SB200	Wrightbus Pulsar 2	N37F	2010	Manchester Airport, 2015
406	YJ59AZN	VDL SB200	Wrightbus Pulsar 2	N44F	2010	Arrive Bus & Coach, 2015
407	YJ59AYY	VDL SB200	Wrightbus Pulsar 2	N44F	2009	Arrive Bus & Coach, 2015
409	YX63LJA	ADL E20D	ADL Enviro 200	N33F	2013	Nottingham CT, 2024
410	YX63LJC	ADL E20D	ADL Enviro 200	N33F	2013	Nottingham CT, 2024
501	DK09DZD	Volvo B7RLE	Wrightbus Eclipse Urban	N49F	2009	GHA, Ruabon, 2017
502	DK09DZH	Volvo B7RLE	Wrightbus Eclipse Urban	N49F	2009	GHA, Ruabon, 2017

503-514		Volvo B7RLE	Wrightbus Eclipse Urban	N40F	2004	Go-South Coast, 2018

503w	HF54HFO	**506**	HF54HHB	**509**	HF54HGX	**513**	HF54HGA
504	HF54HFP	**507**	HF54HGJ	**511**	HF54HHM	**514**	HF54HGC
505	HF54HHA	**508w**	HF54HGN	**512**	HF54HHE		

515	FJ57CZN	Volvo B7RLE	Wrightbus Eclipse Urban	NC44F	2007	Transdev, 2019
516	FJ57CZM	Volvo B7RLE	Wrightbus Eclipse Urban	NC44F	2007	Transdev, 2019
517	BX07AZJ	Volvo B7RLE	Wrightbus Eclipse Urban	N45F	2007	Transdev, 2019
518	BV21OOA	Volvo B8RLE	MCV eVoRa	NC37F	2021	
519	BV21OOB	Volvo B8RLE	MCV eVoRa	NC37F	2021	
520	BV21OOC	Volvo B8RLE	MCV eVoRa	NC37F	2021	
521	BV21OOD	Volvo B8RLE	MCV eVoRa	NC37F	2021	
522	SK07CFX	Volvo B7RLE	Wrightbus Eclipse Urban	N45F	2007	Lothian Buses, 2022
523	SK07CGG	Volvo B7RLE	Wrightbus Eclipse Urban	N45F	2007	Lothian Buses, 2022
524	BV22HBN	Volvo B8RLE	MCV eVoRa	NC37F	2022	
525	BV22HBO	Volvo B8RLE	MCV eVoRa	NC37F	2022	
526	BV72KKA	Volvo B8RLE	MCV eVoRa	N46F	2023	
527	BV72KKB	Volvo B8RLE	MCV eVoRa	N46F	2023	
528	BV72KKC	Volvo B8RLE	MCV eVoRa	N46F	2023	
529	BV72KKD	Volvo B8RLE	MCV eVoRa	N46F	2023	
530	BV23NNZ	Volvo B8RLE	MCV eVoRa	NC37F	2023	
531	BV23NUU	Volvo B8RLE	MCV eVoRa	NC37F	2023	
532	BV23NUW	Volvo B8RLE	MCV eVoRa	NC37F	2023	
533	SW63TAV	Volvo B8RLE	MCV eVolution	N46F	2014	Leasks, Lerwick. 2023
534	KP12BUS	Volvo B8RLE	MCV eVolution	N46F	2014	Hulley's Baslow. 2024
540	BP24GWW	Volvo B8RLE	MCV eVoRa	NC38F	2024	
541	BP24GWX	Volvo B8RLE	MCV eVoRa	NC38F	2024	

With Norwich's historic Maids Head Hotel in the background, Volvo B5L 129, EC23SHA, works route 44A towards Holt. It is one of three in the fleet with MCV eVoSeti styling from the 2023 vehicle deliveries.
Mark Doggett

800	WH11CHR	Van Hool T915 Alicron	Van Hool	C48D	2011	
901	RDV903	Volvo B12B	VDL Jonckheere SHV	C57FT	2007	Lochs and Glens, 2023
902	OGR647	Volvo B12B	VDL Jonckheere SHV	C57FT	2008	Lochs and Glens, 2023
903	YN07DUU	Volvo B12M 12.8m	Plaxton Panther	S70F	2007	Phillips, Bewdley, 2016
904	SGF965	Volvo B12M 12.8m	Plaxton Panther	C53F	2006	Parks, Hamilton, 2010
905	YN05VSG	Volvo B12M	Plaxton Panther	S60F	2006	Eddie Brown, Barnsley
906	3990ME	Volvo B9R	Caetano Levanté	S70F	2011	National Express, 2019
907	WOA521	Volvo B9R	Caetano Levanté	S70F	2011	National Express, 2019
908	6542FN	Volvo B9R	Caetano Levanté	S70F	2011	Edwards, 2019
909	6546FN	Volvo B9R	Caetano Levanté	S70F	2011	National Express, 2019
912	PVF377	Volvo B9R	Plaxton Elite	C51F	2012	Parks, Hamilton, 2015
913	259VYC	Volvo B9R	Plaxton Elite	C51F	2012	Parks, Hamilton, 2015
914	E21AMX	Volvo B7R	Plaxton Profile	S70F	2009	GHA, Ruabon, 2017
915	E21APY	Volvo B7R	Plaxton Profile	S70F	2009	GHA, Ruabon, 2017
916	WSV503	Volvo B9R	Plaxton Elite	C48FT	2011	Parks, Hamilton, 2018
917	YVJ677	Volvo B9R	Plaxton Elite	C48FT	2011	Parks, Hamilton, 2018
918	354TRT	Volvo B9R	Plaxton Elite	C48FT	2011	Parks, Hamilton, 2018
919	BT14DLX	Volvo B13R	Jonckheere SHV	C57FT	2014	Lochs & Glens, 2018
920	BT14DLZ	Volvo B13R	Jonckheere SHV	C57FT	2014	Lochs & Glens, 2018
921	536FN	Volvo B9R	Caetano Levanté	S70F	2011	National Express, 2019
922	537FN	Volvo B9R	Caetano Levanté	S70F	2011	National Express, 2019
923	538FN	Volvo B9R	Caetano Levanté	S70F	2011	National Express, 2019
924	OC21SAN	Volvo B8R	Plaxton Panther	C49FT	2021	
925	SC23NJS	Volvo 9700	Volvo	C53FT	2023	
926	PF24SAN	Volvo B8R	Plaxton Leopard	S72F	2024	
927	OE24SAN	Volvo B8R	Plaxton Panther	C49FT	2024	
1107	YN62AAE	Mercedes-Benz Vario 0816	Plaxton Cheetah	C29F	2012	
1108	YN13AVX	Mercedes-Benz Vario 0816	Plaxton Cheetah	C29F	2013	
1110	WA18DDY	Peugeot Boxer	GM Coachworks	M14	2018	
1112	AP66ELV	Ford Transit	Ford	M16	2017	
1113	AU66JAK	Ford Transit	Ford	M16	2017	
2000	AD09POF	Mercedes-Bemz Sprinter 111 cdi	Mercedes-Benz	M8	2009	
2001	AV62AUA	Mercedes-Bemz Sprinter 111 cdi	Mercedes-Benz	M8	2012	
2002	WX66EGE	Ford Tourneo	Ford	M8	2017	
2003	NX18XYW	Ford Tourneo	Ford	M8	2018	
2004	NX18NCZ	Ford Tourneo	Ford	M8	2018	

Depots: Heath Drive, Holt; Cornish Way, North Walsham and Claypit Lane, Fakenham.

Web: www.sanderscoaches.com

SARGEANTS

Sargeant Brothers Ltd, Mill Street, Kington, HR5 3AL

FJ04SNV	Volvo B12B	Caetano Enigma	S70F	2004	Bay, Cowdenbeath, 2023
T900NTS	Volvo B9TL	Wrightbus Eclipse Gemini	N48/33F	2006	Lothian Buses, 2021
MX55BXU	Optare Solo M880 SL	Optare	N27F	2006	James Bevan, Lydney, 21
YJ06FYO	Optare Solo M780 SL	Optare	N27F	2006	Warwickshire CC, 2021
YJ06FYU	Optare Solo M850 SL	Optare	N25F	2006	County, Newton Abbot, 21
MX58ABF	Optare Versa V1110	Optare	N39F	2008	Safeguard, Guildford, 2023
YJ10MHU	Optare Solo M950 SL	Optare	N33F	2010	D.Jones, Wrexham, 2018
YJ12GVF	Optare Solo M950 EV	Optare	N32F	2012	Trent-Barton, 2021
YJ12GVG	Optare Solo M950 EV	Optare	N32F	2012	Trent-Barton, 2021
YJ62FVT	Optare Solo M970	Optare	N33F	2012	Coastal, Warton, 2022
YJ62FXK	Optare Solo M970	Optare	N33F	2012	Coastal, Warton, 2022
YJ62FZO	Optare Solo M960	Optare	N34F	2012	EVE, Dunbar, 2020
YJ62FZR	Optare Solo M960	Optare	N34F	2012	EVE, Dunbar, 2020
YD63VDZ	Optare Solo M960	Optare	N33F	2014	
OP14ARE	Optare Solo M8570 SL	Optare	N28F	2014	Switch demonstrator, 2023
YJ14BGK	Optare Solo M900	Optare	N34F	2014	RATP, London, 2021
YJ14BGO	Optare Solo M900	Optare	N34F	2014	RATP, London, 2021
YJ16DDA	Optare Solo M9250 SR	Optare	N31F	2014	Taff Valley, 2022
YJ16DFG	Optare Metrodecker MD1114	Optare	N51/32F	2016	Optare demonstrator, 2020
YJ66AOO	Optare Metrocity V1010 MC	Optare	N33F	2016	
YJ66APZ	Optare Metrocity V1080 MC	Optare	N40F	2016	BL Travel, Wakefield, 2022
YJ67GEK	Optare Solo M7800 SL	Optare	N24F	2017	Optare demonstrator, 2020
YJ67FYV	Optare Solo M7800 SL	Optare	N24F	2017	McNairn, Coatbridge, 2021
YJ18CZL	Optare Solo M9250 SR	Optare	N30F	2018	Coastline, Rhyl, 2021
YJ18CZG	Optare Metrocity V1152 MC	Optare	N40F	2018	Coastline, Rhyl, 2021
YJ18DKY	Optare Metrocity V1152 MC	Optare	N40F	2018	Proctor, Leeming Bar, 2010
YJ68FTO	Optare Metrocity V1152 MC	Optare	N37F	2018	iGo, Droitwich, 2021
YJ71GSY	Optare Solo M9250 SR	Optare	N32F	2021	
YJ72ETZ	Optare Solo M9250 SL	Optare	N29F	2022	
YJ72EUM	Optare Solo M9250 SR	Optare	N32F	2021	
YJ72EUN	Optare Solo M9250 SR	Optare	N32F	2021	

Sargeants Brothers started out back in the 1920's as Sargeants Motors Ltd and continues today from its base in Knighton. Knighton was originally an Anglo-Saxon settlement straddling the border between Powys and Shropshire. Services run into Hereford, Llandrindod as well as local routes. Optare Metrocity YJ68FTO is seen heading for Llandrindod as it passes through the Herfordshire village of Weobley. *Richard Godfrey*

STOTTS

Stotts Tours (Oldham) Ltd, 142b Lees Road, Oldham, Lancashire, OL4 1HT

MX08MYJ	Optare Solo M810 SL	Optare	N22F	2008	Jacksons, Silsden, 2010
EU08WNE	Optare Solo M880	Optare	N29F	2008	Nottingham CC, 2010
MX60BWY	ADL Dart 4 8.9m	ADL Enviro 200	N29F	2010	ACE Travel, Aintree, 2014
MX60BWZ	ADL Dart 4 8.9m	ADL Enviro 200	N29F	2010	WMSNT, Aston, 2010
BN61MXJ	Volvo B7TL	Wrightbus Eclips Gemini	N41/29F	2011	Arriva London, 2023
BN61MXM	Volvo B7TL	Wrightbus Eclips Gemini	N41/29F	2011	Arriva London, 2023
BN61MXR	Volvo B7TL	Wrightbus Eclips Gemini	N41/29F	2011	Arriva London, 2023
BN61MXU	Volvo B7TL	Wrightbus Eclips Gemini	N41/29F	2011	Arriva London, 2023
BN61MXY	Volvo B7TL	Wrightbus Eclips Gemini	N41/29F	2011	Arriva London, 2023
BN61MYA	Volvo B7TL	Wrightbus Eclips Gemini	N41/29F	2011	Arriva London, 2023
BG61SXK	Volvo B7TL	Wrightbus Eclips Gemini	N41/29F	2011	Arriva London, 2023
YJ62FEH	Optare Solo M890	Optare	N31F	2012	Courtney, Bracknell,2019
YJ62FET	Optare Solo M890	Optare	N31F	2012	Courtney, Bracknell,2019
YJ62FEU	Optare Solo M890	Optare	N31F	2012	Transdev, 2019
YJ62FYB	Optare Solo M890	Optare	N31F	2012	Transdev, 2019
BK13NZM	Volvo B7RLE	Wrightbus Eclipse 2	N44F	2013	Rotala, 2021
BK13NZR	Volvo B7RLE	Wrightbus Eclipse 2	N44F	2013	Rotala, 2021
BK13NZS	Volvo B7RLE	Wrightbus Eclipse 2	N44F	2013	Rotala, 2021
BK13NZU	Volvo B7RLE	Wrightbus Eclipse 2	N44F	2013	Rotala, 2021
YJ14BGZ	Optare Solo M900	Optare	N32F	2014	Coutrtney, Bracknell, 2020
KX15BLN	Optare Solo M900 SR	Optare	N32F	2015	Big Lemon, Brighton, 2021
SN67XBJ	ADL E20D 8.9m	ADL Enviro 200 MMC	N30F	2017	CT Plus, 2023
SN67XBL	ADL E20D 8.9m	ADL Enviro 200 MMC	N30F	2017	CT Plus, 2023
SK68LZF	ADL E20D 8.9m	ADL Enviro 200 MMC	N30F	2018	Manchester CT, 2021
SK68LZG	ADL E20D 8.9m	ADL Enviro 200 MMC	N30F	2018	Manchester CT, 2021
SK68LZN	ADL E20D 8.9m	ADL Enviro 200 MMC	N30F	2018	Meridian, Atheton, 2020
SK68LZO	ADL E20D 8.9m	ADL Enviro 200 MMC	N30F	2018	Selwyns, Runcorn, 2020
YX19OUU	ADL E20D 8.9m	ADL Enviro 200 MMC	N30F	2019	PK Travel, Bushmills, 2020
YX19OUV	ADL E20D 8.9m	ADL Enviro 200 MMC	N30F	2019	PK Travel, Bushmills, 2020
YX20OCO	ADL E20D 8.9m	ADL Enviro 200 MMC	N30F	2020	
YX20OCP	ADL E20D 8.9m	ADL Enviro 200 MMC	N30F	2020	
YX22BVB	ADL E20D 8.9m	ADL Enviro 200 MMC	N30F	2022	
YX22BVC	ADL E20D 8.9m	ADL Enviro 200 MMC	N30F	2022	
YX22BVD	ADL E20D 8.9m	ADL Enviro 200 MMC	N30F	2022	

Pictured in Hazel Grove, Stotts Enviro 200 MMC SK22BVD is one of thirteen in the fleet currently used on services in Greater Manchester. 364 is a circular route based on Stockport that serves Hazel Grove and Offerton. *John Young*

TANAT VALLEY COACHES

RE Morris & Sons Ltd, The Garage, Llanrhaeadr-ym-Mochnant, SY10 0AD

112	L	DU12NCY	Ford Transit	Ford	M16	2012	
116	L	MC16PYT	Ford Transit	Ford	C17F	2016	
161	L	YT66HCJ	Ford Transit	Ford	M16	2016	
162	L	YT66NPG	Ford Transit	Ford	C18F	2017	
163	L	HN15UZU	Ford Transit	Ford	C18F	2017	
206	L	MX57CDN	Optare Solo M950	Optare	N31F	2007	Maynes, Buckie, 2013
207	L	MX07BBK	Optare Solo M950	Optare	NC31F	2007	Alton Towers, 2009
229	L	YX24PLJ	ADL E20D 9.7m	ADL Enviro 200 MMC	NC33F	2024	
230	L	YX23OXD	ADL E20D 8.9m	ADL Enviro 200 MMC	NC30F	2023	
231	L	YX72OMV	ADL E20D 8.9m	ADL Enviro 200 MMC	NC30F	2023	
232	L	YX73OMJ	ADL E20D 8.9m	ADL Enviro 200 MMC	NC30F	2023	
233	W	BV23NTA	Volvo B8RLE	MCV eVoRa	NC38F	2023	
234	W	BV23NTX	Volvo B8RLE	MCV eVoRa	NC38F	2023	
235	W	BV73MHX	Volvo B8RLE	MCV eVoRa	NC38F	2023	
236	L	BV73MHY	Volvo B8RLE	MCV eVoRa	NC38F	2023	
237	W	BV73MUY	Volvo B8RLE	MCV eVoRa	NC38F	2023	
240	W	YJ60GDO	VDL SB180	MCV eVolution	N36F	2011	Galloway, Stowmarket, '22
241	W	YJ60GFA	VDL SB180	MCV eVolution	N36F	2011	Galloway, Stowmarket, '22
255	L	SN55HSF	ADL Enviro 300	ADL Enviro 300	S60F	2005	Yelloway, 2023
257	W	YJ09CVF	VDL SB200	Wrightbus Pulsar 2	N44F	2009	Isle, Scunthorpe, 2023
259	W	YJ59AZA	VDL SB200	Wrightbus Pulsar 2	N44F	2010	Sanders, Holt, 2022
262	W	YJ62JZT	VDL SB200	Wrightbus Pulsar 2	N44F	2012`	Isle, Scunthorpe, 2022
263	L	YD63UZB	Optare Versa V1040	Optare	N34F	2013	Caelloi, Pwllheli, 20
271	L	YJ57YCB	Optare Versa V1110	Optare	N38F	2008	Webberbus, 2016
272	L	YJ58CEK	Optare Versa V1110	Optare	N38F	2008	Webberbus, 2016
281	L	SP58DPE	Optare Versa V1110	Optare	N38F	2008	Maytree, Bolton, 2013
282	L	SP58DPF	Optare Versa V1110	Optare	N38F	2008	Smith, Coupar Angus, 2013
373	L	CN71HFO	Mercedes-Benz Sprinter 45	Mercedes-Benz	N20F	2021	Reay's, Wigton, 2022
374	W	CN71HFM	Mercedes-Benz Sprinter 45	Mercedes-Benz	N20F	2021	Reay's, Wigton, 2022
375	W	CN71HFP	Mercedes-Benz Sprinter 45	Mercedes-Benz	N20F	2021	Reay's, Wigton, 2022
376	L	RF72ZFO	Iveco Daily 70C21	Illesbus i-City Max	N26F	2023	

Four Alexander Dennis Enviro 200 MMCs fitted with high-back seating arrived in 2023. Seen while working the main service to Shrewsbury is 230, YX23OXD, an 8.9 metre version. *Chris Clegg*

2020 marked one hundred years since its founder, William Williams, bought his first motor car and began to take passengers to places where the train did not go. Llanrhaeadr-ym-Mochnant is a village in the north of Powys around six miles from the England border and nine miles west of the Shropshire town of Oswestry. Buses allocated L are licensed in Wales while those marked W are at Welshpool and licenced in England. Several buses are operated for TrawsCymru. Frequently found on route T12 that plies between Machynlleth and Wrexham via Newtown and Welshpool is Volvo B8RLE 236, BV73MHY. *Chris Clegg*

401	L	TC09TVC	Yutong TC9	Yutong	C35F	2018	Roy McCarthy, Maccesfield
407	L	YN07EAX	MAN 18.360	Plaxton Panther	S70F	2007	Greys, Petersfield, 2023
411	L	TC08TVC	Volvo B9R	Jonckheere JHV	C34F	2006	Smiths, Tring, 2021
416	L	A16TVC	Volvo B12B	Plaxton Panther	S70F	2006	Humphries, Thatcham, '23
417	L	YX17OGS	Volvo B11R	Plaxton Panther	C48FT	2017	Logan, Dunloy, 2021
418	L	PG17KMY	Scania OmniExpress K410 EB4	Scania	C53FT	2017	Lucketts, 2024
419	L	PG17KMZ	Scania OmniExpress K410 EB4	Scania	C53FT	2017	Lucketts, 2024
420	L	T12TVC	Scania K410 EB6	Higer Touring	C57FT	2015	Tranzcare Travel, 2024
427	L	YX17OGR	Volvo B11R	Plaxton Panther	C48FT	2017	Logan, Dunloy, 2021
437	L	MP21MPT	Volvo B11R	Plaxton Panther	C48FT	2021	MP Travel, Warrington, '22
447	L	TC10TVC	Mercedes-Benz Tourismo	Mercedes-Benz	S72F	2014	Hatton, St Helens, 2023
466	L	T11TVC	Volvo B12B	Plaxton Panther	C57F	2001	Shelton, Guisborough, 2024
467	L	TC06TVC	Volvo B11R	Plaxton Panther	C57F	2017	
474	L	T10TVC	Volvo B12B	Plaxton Panther	S70F	2005	Yelloway, Chadderton
475	L	TC03TVC	Volvo B12B	Plaxton Panther	S70F	2005	Yelloway, Chadderton
476	L	TC02TVC	Volvo B12R	Van Hool	S71F	2004	Yelloway, Chadderton
487	L	A15TVC	Volvo B12R	Plaxton Panther	S71F	2007	Yelloway, Chadderton
496w	L	757FFR	Volvo B10M-62	Van Hool Alizée HE	S70F	1996	Cookson Travel, Hope, '23
497w	L	M77GGT	Volvo B10M-62	Van Hool Alizée HE	C55F	1997	Cookson Travel, Hope, '23
501	W	LJ59LVX	VDL DB300	Wrightbus Gemini 2	N41/24D	2009	Arriva London, 2023
502	W	BN61MXE	Volvo B9TL	Wrightbus Gemini 2	N43/30F	2011	Atlantic Bolton, 2023
713	L	FY13FYE	Peugeot Boxer	Peugeot	M8	2013	
714	L	SA14JHH	Vauxhall Vivaro	Vauxhall	M8	2014	
715	L	ML68FCV	Ford Tourneo	Ford	M8	2018	

Special event vehicle:

194	YRC194	Leyland Tiger Cub PSUC1/1	Alexander	DP41F	1962

Depots: Llanrhaeadr-ym-Mochnant, SY10 0AD (L); Pentrefelin, Llangedwyn, SY10 9LE in Wales and Bittington Cross, Welshpool, SY21 8SR (W).

TOWNLYNX

Town Lynx Ltd, Greenfield Business Park, 1 Bagillt Road, Greenfield, Holywell, CH8 7GJ

	S260KLG	Volvo Olympian	Alexander RH	B47/31F	1998	Dublin Bus, 2010
	YM51WGG	Dennis Javelin 12m	Plaxton Prima	C55F	2001	MoD, 2014
u	YM51WGU	Dennis Javelin 12m	Plaxton Prima	C55F	2001	MoD, 2014
u	YO02PCV	Dennis Javelin 12m	Plaxton Prima	S70F	2002	MoD, 2014
	KU02YBP	Dennis Trident	Aleander ALX400	N43/26F	2002	Abellio, London, 20
	KV02URY	Dennis Trident	Aleander ALX400	N43/26F	2002	Abellio, London, 20
	LX03OTG	Dennis Trident	Aleander ALX400	N43/26F	2002	Stagecoach, 2022
	LX03OSY	Dennis Trident	Aleander ALX400	N43/26F	2002	Stagecoach, 2022
	YO52FHD	Dennis Javelin 12m	Plaxton Prima	C55F	2002	MoD, 2014
	ET03WAE	Dennis Javelin 12m	Plaxton Profile	S70F	2003	Blue Fox, Peterborough, 16
	OX53ORU	Dennis Javelin 12m	Plaxton Profile	S70F	2003	Blue Fox, Peterborough, 16
	AW53GBE	Dennis Javelin 12m	Plaxton Profile	C53F	2003	Blue Fox, Peterborough, 16
	DK04NNB	TransBus Dart 8.8m	TransBus Pointer	N29F	2004	
	CN04NLL	TransBus Dart 8.8m	TransBus Pointer	N29F	2004	GHA, Ruabon, 2016
	SV55FJP	Volvo B7R	Plaxton Profile	S70F	2006	Swift, Barhead, 2020
	LJ07ECX	ADL E20D 9.3m	ADL Enviro 200	N24D	2007	Arriva London, 2023
	LK07BEV	ADL E20D 8.9m	ADL Enviro 200	N26F	2007	Vision, Bolton, 2023
	LK07ELJ	ADL E20D 8.9m	ADL Enviro 200	N26F	2007	Vision, Bolton, 2023
	BX07OOH	BMC Falcon 1100FE	BMC	S55F	2007	GHA, Ruabon, 2016
	BX07OPH	BMC Falcon 1100FE	BMC	S55F	2007	APT, Rayleigh, 2015
	BX07OPW	BMC Falcon 1100FE	BMC	S55F	2007	
	YJ64DZS	Optare Solo M890 EV	Optare	N31F	2012	Nottingham CT, 2021
	YX17NZB	ADL E20D 10.8m	ADL Enviro 200 MMC	N41F	2017	
	BL24FEG	Volvo B8RLE	MCV eVoRa	N38F	2024	

Depots: Greenfield Business Park, Holywell, CH8 7GJ and Northop Road, Milwr, Holywell, CH8 8BE.

Representing the Travelmasters fleet is YJ55KZR, a VDL SB200 with Wrightbus Commander bodywork. It was pictured in Minster while heading towards Sheerness from Sittingbourne. *Richard Godfrey*

TRAVELMASTERS

Travelmasters, Dorset Road Industrial Estate, Dorset Road, Sheerness, ME12 1LT

LF52ZNZ	Volvo B7TL	Wrightbus Eclipse Gemini	N41/27F	2003	Arriva London, 2015
YJ53VDV	DAF SB200	Wrightbus Commander	N44F	2004	Fishwicks, Leyland, 2016
YJ55KZR	VDL SB200	Wrightbus Commander	N44F	2005	Fishwicks, Leyland, 2016
	Volvo B9TL 13m	ADL Enviro 500	N57/34F	2005	Dublin Bus, 2020
LW55AHF	LW55AHZ	LW55AJX			LW55AJW
SN56AXA	ADL Dart 4	ADL Enviro 200	N29F	2006	Wigan Buses, 2021
MX07BVE	Volvo B9TL	Wrightbus Eclipse Gemini	NC45/29F	2007	Stagecoach, 2018
	Volvo B9TL	Wrightbus Eclipse Gemini	NC44/26F	2007	Rotala, 2017
EY07AXH	EY07AXJ	EY07AXK			EY07AXM
FJ08FYK	Volvo B9TL	Wrightbus Eclipse Gemini	NC44/26F	2008	Marshall, Sutton-on-Trent
AY58CYJ	ADL Trident 2 10.5m	ADL Enviro 400	N47/33F	2008	Carters, Capel St Mary, '15
SN58ENU	ADL Trident 2 10.5m	ADL Enviro 400	N47/33F	2008	
VE58XKX	ADL Dart 4 8.9m	ADL Enviro 200	N29F	2008	Aintree Coachlines, 2018
WX09TCK	ADL Dart 4 8.9m	ADL Enviro 200	N29F	2009	Aintree Coachlines, 2018
GD09JHX	Volvo B9TL	Wrightbus Gemini 2	NC41/30F	2009	Bus Vannin, 2018
FX09YKF	Mercedes-Benz Sprinter 515 cdi	Ferqui Soroco	C23F	2009	Lab Travel services
BK10MFU	Volvo B9TL	Wrightbus Gemini 2	N44/30F	2010	Yourbus, Heanor, 2017
BK10MFV	Volvo B9TL	Wrightbus Gemini 2	N44/30F	2010	Yourbus, Heanor, 2017
LX60DXD	Volvo B9TL	Wrightbus Gemini 2	N43/30F	2011	Go-Ahead London, 2019
LX60DXE	Volvo B9TL	Wrightbus Gemini 2	N43/30F	2011	Go-Ahead London, 2019
BJ11DUA	Volvo B9TL	Wrightbus Gemini 2	N43/30F	2011	Tower Transit, 2019
BJ11DVC	Volvo B9TL	Wrightbus Gemini 2	N43/30F	2011	Tower Transit, 2019
FJ61EYL	Volvo B9R	Caetano Levanté	C48FT	2012	RATP, London, 2019
BX12CVL	Volvo B9TL	Wrightbus Gemini 2	N43/30F	2012	RATP, London, 2019
BX12CVP	Volvo B9TL	Wrightbus Gemini 2	N43/30F	2012	RATP, London, 2019
BF63ZRL	Volvo B9R	Caetano Levanté	S70F	2013	Bennets, Gloucester, 2020
YX64VPR	Volvo B11R	Jonckheere SHV	C53FT	2014	Reading Buses, 2019
BF65WHU	Volvo B11R	Jonckheere SHV	C53FT	2015	Beestons, Hadliegh, 2021
SW16LOW	Volvo B11R	Jonckheere SHV	C53FT	2016	Swallow, Rainham, 2021
YG16LGF	Yutong ZK6938HQ (D12)	Yutong	C53F	2016	Belle, Newcaste, 2020
YX67UYG	ADL E40D 11.5m	ADL Enviro 400 MMC	NC49/37F	2017	Imperial, Colnbrook, 2020
YX67UYK	ADL E40D 11.5m	ADL Enviro 400 MMC	NC49/37F	2017	Imperial, Colnbrook, 2020
KT17YKS	Mercedes-Benz Sprinter 516 cdi	EVM Avantgarde	M16	2017	Highland Experience, 2022
YX20OGW	ADL E20D 10.8m	ADL Enviro 200 MMC	N36F	2020	Go Goodwins, 2023
RE71OWP	Iveco Daily 70C21	Illesbus i-City Max	N29F	2022	

Ancilliary vehicles:

RN52FPA	Dennis Dart SLF	Caetano Nimbus	N36D	2002	Abellio, London
NA52AWR	Dennis Mini Pointer Dart	Plaxton Pointer	N25F	2002	Go North East, 2023

Special event vehicle:

SMK725F	AEC Routemaster R2RH/1	Park Royal	B40/32R	1967	London Transport

TYRERS

Tyrers Coaches, Tyrer House, Bloomfield Road, Farnworth, Bolton, BL4 9LP

Registration	Chassis	Body	Seating	Year	Previous owner
	DAF DB250	Alexander ALX400	N47/25F	2003	Arriva London, 2015
JRZ3262	JRZ3268	JRZ8513			SHZ8495
JRZ3263	JRZ3269	JRZ8514			SHZ8496
JRZ3267					
808TYR	Volvo B9TL	East Lancs Nordic	NC63/39F	2005	Weavaway, 2010
	Scania OmniCity CN230 UB	Scania	N41F	2006	Nottingham, 2018
YN56FAK	YN56FAM	YN56FAO			YN56FAU
	Scania N94UD	East Lancs Omnidekka	N51/39F	2007	Nottingham, 2018
BIG9781	BIG9782	BIG9783			BIG9784
FX57GUF	Irisbus 150E24	Vehixel Scolabus 24	S67F	2007	Olympia, Hindley, 2019
TYR12R	Van Hool T915 Alicron	Van Hool	C48FT	2007	Eavesway, 2014
TYR2R	Volvo B12B	Van Hool T9 Alizée	C53FT	2007	Lothian Buses, 2020
FX57LKM	Irisbus 150E24	Vehixel Scolabus 24	S67F	2008	Olympia, Hindley, 2019
P3TYR	Volvo B7RLE	Plaxton Centro	NC45F	2008	Yellow Buses, 2018
4312FM	Volvo B7RLE	Plaxton Centro	NC45F	2008	Yellow Buses, 2018
SIL4054	Volvo B7RLE	Plaxton Centro	NC45F	2008	Yellow Buses, 2018
TYR25R	Volvo B9TL	Optare Olympus	NC61/39F	2009	
TYR26R	Volvo B9TL	Optare Olympus	NC61/39F	2009	
	Scania OmniCity CN230UD	Scania	N41/30F	2009	Stagecoach, 2017
LX59CME	LX59CMF	LX59CMZ			LX59CNV
YP59ODU	Scania OmniCity CN230 UD	Scania	NC47/30F	2009	RATP, 2019
YP59ODV	Scania OmniCity CN230 UD	Scania	NC47/30F	2009	RATP, 2019
YP59ODW	Scania OmniCity CN230 UD	Scania	NC47/30F	2009	RATP, 2019
TYR31R	Dennis Javelin 12m	Plaxton Profile	S70F	2009	GHA, Ruabon
TYR7R	Volvo B12B 13m	Van Hool T9 Acron	C53FT	2009	Lothian Buses, 2020
TYR8R	Volvo B12B 13m	Van Hool T9 Acron	C53FT	2010	Lothian Buses, 2020
TYR14R	Volvo B12B 13m	Van Hool T9 Acron	C53FT	2010	Lothian Buses, 2020
YN10GBO	Mercedes-Benz Vito 111 cdi	Mercedes-Benz	M8	2010	
	Volvo B9TL	Wrightbus Gemini 2	N43/30F	2011	Go-Ahead London, 2018
LX11CVN	LX11CVV	LX11CWE			LX11CWL
LX11CVO	LX11CVZ	LX11CWG			LX11CWM
LX11CVP	LX11CWC	LX11CWJ			LX11CWN
LX11CVU	LX11CWD	LX11CWK			
BJ11DSX	Volvo B9TL	Wrightbus Gemini 2	N43/30F	2011	Tower Transit, 2021
BJ11D2Z	Volvo B9TL	Wrightbus Gemini 2	N43/30F	2011	Tower Transit, 2021
BJ11EAO	Volvo B9TL	Wrightbus Gemini 2	N43/30F	2011	Tower Transit, 2021
BJ11EBL	Volvo B9TL	Wrightbus Gemini 2	N43/30F	2011	Tower Transit, 2021
YJ61CKA	Optare Versa V1210 H	Optare	S57F	2011	Olympia, Hindley, 2018
YJ61CKC	Optare Versa V1210 H	Optare	S57F	2011	Olympia, Hindley, 2018
YJ61JHL	Optare Versa V1210 H	Optare	S57F	2011	*operated for TfGM*
YJ61JHO	Optare Versa V1210 H	Optare	S57F	2011	*operated for TfGM*
TYR4R	Volvo B9R	Caetano Levanté	C75F	2011	Holmeswood Coaches, '20
TYR22R	Volvo B9R	Caetano Levanté	C49FT	2011	Lothian Buses, 2019
TYR23R	Volvo B9R	Caetano Levanté	C48FT	2011	Lothian Buses, 2019
TYR24R	Volvo B9R	Caetano Levanté	S70F	2011	Lothian Buses, 2019
TYR27R	Volvo B13R 13m	Van Hool T9 Acron	C53FT	2011	Lothian Buses, 2020
TYR28R	Volvo B13R 13m	Van Hool T9 Acron	C53FT	2011	Lothian Buses, 2020
	Volvo B9TL	Wrightbus Gemini 2	N43/30F	2011	Tower Transit, 2021
BN61MXC	BN61MXF	BN61MXG			BN61MXL
w YJ61JDO	Optare Solo M890 SR	Optare	N27F	2012	*operated for TfGM*
YJ12GXU	Optare Versa V1270 H	Optare	S57F	2012	*operated for TfGM*
YJ12GXV	Optare Versa V1270 H	Optare	S57F	2012	*operated for TfGM*

Since the reallocation of services in Greater Manchester, Tyrers now mostly provide services to schools, colleges, businesses, groups and associations in the area plus some routes in Lancashire. Showing fleet colours is tri-axle 808TYR, a Volvo B9TL with East Lancs Nordic bodywork. *Richard Godfrey*

Registration	Chassis	Body	Seating	Year	Notes
YJ12GXW	Optare Versa V1270 H	Optare	S57F	2012	*operated for TfGM*
YJ12GXZ	Optare Versa V1270 H	Optare	S57F	2012	*operated for TfGM*
	Volvo B9TL	Wrightbus Gemini 2	N43/30F	2012	Tower Transit, 2021
BF62UYA	BF62UYC	BF62UYE			BF62UYG
BF62UYB	BF62UYD				
TYR20R	VDL Futura FHD2-122.370	VDL	C49FT	2013	Anderson, Bermondsey, 17
TYR21R	VDL Futura FHD2-122.370	VDL	C49FT	2013	Anderson, Bermondsey, 17
MM14DWX	ADL E20D 8.9M	ADL Enviro 200	N29F	2014	Jim Stones, Leigh, 2020
YJ64DXZ	Optare Versa V1270 H	Optare	S57F	2014	*operated for TfGM*
YJ64DYA	Optare Versa V1270 H	Optare	S57F	2014	*operated for TfGM*
YJ64DYX	Optare Versa V1210 H	Optare	S57F	2014	*operated for TfGM*
TYR15R	VDL Futura FHD2-129.370	VDL	C53FT	2015	
TYR16R	VDL Futura FHD2-129.370	VDL	C53FT	2015	
TYR17R	VDL Futura FHD2-129.370	VDL	C53FT	2015	
	ADL E20D 8.9m	ADL Enviro 200	N29F	2015-17	Jim Stones, Leigh, 2020
MH15LHR	MT66MTE	MH17EGJ			MH17EGK
TYR19R	VDL Futura FHD2-129.370	VDL	C53FT	2016	
TYR29R	ADL E40D 11.5m	ADL Enviro 400 MMC	NC51/35F	2017	
TYR30R	ADL E40D 11.5m	ADL Enviro 400 MMC	NC51/35F	2017	
TYR18R	VDL Futura FHD2-129.370	VDL	C53FT	2018	
TYR311R	Mercedes-Benz Sprinter 516 cdi	Carbus	M19	2018	Black Roads, London, '21
TJ69XWG	Mercedes-Benz Sprinter 516 cdi	Ferqui Soroco	M19	2019	Black Roads, London, '21
TYR10R	Van Hool EX16 M	Van Hool	C57FT	2019	YPiJ of Hayes, 2021
TYR11R	Van Hool EX16 M	Van Hool	C57FT	2019	YPiJ of Hayes, 2021
TYR5R	Van Hool EX16 M	Van Hool	C57FT	2022	
TYR6R	Van Hool EX16 M	Van Hool	C57FT	2022	
OY73BJV	Neoplan Tourliner N2216 SHDC	Neoplan	C57FT	2023	
BL24YFY	Volvo B8L	MCV eVoSeti	NC60/38F	2024	
BL24YFZ	Volvo B8L	MCV eVoSeti	NC60/38F	2024	

Depots: Bloomfield Road, Farnworth, Bolton, BL4 9LP and Crosse Hall Street, Chorley, PR6 0UH

UNO

UnÜ Buses Ltd; Universitybus Ltd, Gypsy Moth Avenue, Hatfield, AL10 9BS

31	H	YE73	Mercedes-Benz Sprinter 516 cdi	EVM Cityline	N16F	2023	
32	H	YE73PYG	Mercedes-Benz Sprinter 516 cdi	EVM Cityline	N16F	2023	
39	H	YE73PZZ	Mercedes-Benz Sprinter 516 cdi	EVM Cityline	N16F	2024	
40	H	YJ23CWS	Mercedes-Benz Sprinter 516 cdi	EVM Cityline	N16F	2023	
41	H	RE21LRJ	Mercedes-Benz Sprinter 516 cdi	EVM Cityline	N16F	2021	
42	H	RJ21XDB	Mercedes-Benz Sprinter 516 cdi	EVM Cityline	N16F	2021	
43	H	RJ21YNL	Mercedes-Benz Sprinter 516 cdi	EVM Cityline	N16F	2021	
44	H	RX72SZT	Mercedes-Benz Sprinter 516 cdi	Atlas	M16	2022	
45	H	GX72BGK	Mercedes-Benz Sprinter 516 cdi	Atlas	M16	2022	
46	H	SN64CVA	Wrightbus StreetLite WF 8.8m	Wrightbus	N28F	2015	Go-Ahead London, 2020

51-54 Wrightbus StreetLite WF 9.5m — Wrightbus — N37F — 2012

51	H	MX12CFL	**52**	C	MX12CFM	**53**	H	MX12CFN	**54**	H	MX12CFO

56-60 Wrightbus StreetLite DF 10.8m — Wrightbus — N41F — 2018

56	C	SK68TNL	**58**	C	SK68TNO	**59**	C	SK68TNU	**60**	C	SK68TNV
57	C	SK68TNN									

201-205 Volvo B8L — MCV eVoSeti — N45/29F — 2024

201	H	-	**203**	H	-	**203**	H	-	**204**	H	-
202	H	-									

250-255 ADL E40D 10.5m — ADL Enviro 400 City — N45/29F — 2017

250	H	YX17NPZ	**252**	H	YX17NRE	**254**	H	YX17NRJ	**255**	H	YX17NRK
251	H	YX17NPY	**253**	H	YX17NRF						

256-262 ADL E40D 10.9m — ADL Enviro 400 MMC — N47/32F — 2017

256	H	YX67VFW	**258**	H	YX67VFR	**260**	H	YX67VFT	**262**	H	YX67VFV
257	H	YX67VFY	**259**	H	YX67VFS	**261**	H	YX67VFU			

263	C	SK72CWE	ADL E40D 11.5m	ADL Enviro 400 MMC	N51/34F	2022	
264	C	SK72CWF	ADL E40D 11.5m	ADL Enviro 400 MMC	N51/34F	2022	
265	C	SK72CWG	ADL E40D 11.5m	ADL Enviro 400 MMC	N51/34F	2022	
285	H	C14UNO	Volvo B9TL	Wrightbus Eclipse Gemini	N45/29F	2007	First, 2017
301	H	BX56VSJ	Mercedes-Benz Citaro O530	Mercedes-Benz	N27D	2006	
303	C	BX56VSL	Mercedes-Benz Citaro O530	Mercedes-Benz	N27D	2006	
304	C	BX56VSM	Mercedes-Benz Citaro O530	Mercedes-Benz	N27D	2006	
305	C	BX56VSN	Mercedes-Benz Citaro O530	Mercedes-Benz	N27D	2006	

306-322 Mercedes-Benz Citaro O530 — Mercedes-Benz — N42F — 2007-10

306	H	BV57VHE	**311**	H	BN58BJJ	**315**	H	BF59NHX	**320**	H	BF59NJK
307	H	BV57VHF	**312**	H	BN58BJK	**316**	H	BF59NHY	**321**	H	BF59NJN
309	w	BV57VHH	**313**	H	BN58BJO	**317**	H	BF59NHZ	**322**	H	BF59NJO
310	H	BV57VHJ	**314**	H	BF59NHV	**319**	H	BF59NJJ			

358	H	BV21ONO	Volvo B8RLE	MCV eVoRa	N43F	2021
359	H	BV21ONU	Volvo B8RLE	MCV eVoRa	N43F	2021

360-365 Volvo B8RLE — MCV eVoRa — N43F — 2018

360	H	LF18AWH	**362**	H	LF18AWM	**364**	H	LF18AWR	**365**	H	LF18AWP
361	H	LF18AWJ	**363**	H	LF18AWN						

366-377 Volvo B7RLE — Wrightbus Eclipse 2 — N43F — 2014 — Somerset PS, 2019

366	H	BG14OOH	**369**	H	BG14OPA	**372**	H	BG14OPF	**375**	H	BD14KXT
367	H	BG14OOX	**370**	H	BG14OPC	**373**	H	BD14KXR	**376**	H	BD14KXV
368	H	BG14OOY	**371**	H	BG14OPD	**374**	H	BD14KXS	**377**	H	BD14KXW

501-504 ADL Dart 4 10.8m — ADL Enviro 200 — N35F — 2011 — Connex, Jersey, 2013

501	H	T21UNO	**502**	H	T22UNO	**503**	H	T23UNO	**504**	H	T24UNO

Uno is owned by the University of Hertfordshire and began running buses in 1992 (then called University Bus) though services are provided for the general public. Its pink and navy livery is shown on MCV-bodied Volvo B8RLE 362, LF18AWM, pictured at Potters Bar while heading for Luton rail station. *Richard Godfrey*

513-517			ADL E20D 10.8m	ADL Enviro 200	N37F*	2015-17	*523-9 are N39F

513	H	SN65ZGU	**515**	H	SN65ZGW	**516**	H	SN65ZGX	**517**	H	SN65ZGY
514	H	SN65ZGV									

601-604			ADL E20D 8.9m	ADL Enviro 200	N25F	2015	

601	H	YY15NKA	**602**	H	YY15NKC	**603**	H	YY15NKD	**604**	H	YY15NKE

605	H	C17UNO	ADL Dart 4 8.9m	ADL Enviro 200	N26F	2007	RATP, London, 2019
606	H	LJ12BYW	ADL Dart 4 8.9m	ADL Enviro 200	N26F	2012	RATP, London, 2019
1468	H	LD72XZS	ADL/BYD D8UR	ADL Enviro 400 EV	N38/20D	2022	ADL demonstrator, 2024
1469	H	LF69UXJ	ADL/BYD D8UR	ADL Enviro 400 EV	N41/25D	2019	ADL demonstrator, 2023
1472	H	LJ16EZN	ADL/BYD K8SR	BYD	N37/22D	2016	Metroline, 2020
1474	H	LJ16EZP	ADL/BYDK8SR	BYD	N37/22D	2016	Metroline, 2020
1475	H	LJ16EZR	ADL/BYD K8SR	BYD	N37/22D	2016	Metroline, 2020
1476	H	SN12ARU	ADL E40H	ADL Enviro 400	N41/24D	2012	Tower Transit, 2023
1477	H	SN12ASO	ADL E40H	ADL Enviro 400	N41/24D	2012	Tower Transit, 2023
1478	H	SN65ZGO	ADL E40H	ADL Enviro 400	N41/24D	2015	Tower Transit, 2023
1479	H	YY64GXG	ADL E40D 10.5m	ADL Enviro 400 MMC	N41/25D	2014	ADL demonstrator, 2018

1481-1486			ADL E40D 10.5m	ADL Enviro 400	N41/25D	2012	RATP, 2023

1481	H	YX62BUA	**1483**	H	YX62BHD	**1485**	H	YX62BJF	**1486**	H	YX62BJU
1482	H	YX62BUE	**1484**	H	YX62BHW						

1487	H	LK60AFY	ADL E40H	ADL Enviro 400	N41/24D	2010	Comfortdelgro, 2023
1488	H	LK60AGY	ADL E40H	ADL Enviro 400	N41/24D	2010	Comfortdelgro, 2023

14xx-14xx			Volvo B8L	MCV eVoSeti	NC60/38F	2024	

14xx	H	BV24LUL	**14xx**	H	BV24LUP	**14xx**	H	BV24LUT	**14xx**	H	BV24LUW
14xx	H	BV24LUO									

1501	H	YR10FFX	Scania OmniCity N230 UD	Scania	N41/22D	2010	RATP, 2023
1502	H	YR10FGC	Scania OmniCity N230 UD	Scania	N41/22D	2010	RATP, 2023
1503	H	YR10FGF	Scania OmniCity N230 UD	Scania	N41/22D	2010	RATP, 2023
1504	H	YR10FGM	Scania OmniCity N230 UD	Scania	N41/22D	2010	RATP, 2023

Ancillary vehicles:

-	H	LK08DWV	ADL E20D	ADL Enviro 200	TV	2008	Metroline, 2023
116	H	C16UNO	Dennis Dart SLF 10.1m	Plaxton Pointer	N27D	2002	Metroline, 2015
207	H	PN08SWF	Scania N230 UD	East Lancs Olympus	N51/25F	2008	

Depots: Cranfield (C) and Hatfield (H)

VECTARE

Central Connect - Galleon Travel - Vectare

Vectare Ltd, 21 Jubilee Drive, Loughborough, LE11 5XS

-	V	GX68LNE	Ford Transit	Ford	M16	2018	
-	V	WP20LDO	Ford Transit	Ford	M16	2020	
-	V	HV22HLX	Ford Transit	Ford	M16	2022	
-	V	HV22HNG	Ford Transit	Ford	M16	2022	
197	V	RX71SYW	Mercedes-Benz Sprinter 516 cdi	EVM Cityline	N22F	2021	
198	V	EN16WKT	Ford Transit	Ford	M16	2016	
199	V	HY68AYS	Ford Transit	Ford	M16	2018	
200	C	WN69FYL	Mercedes-Benz Sprinter 516 cdi	EVM Cityline	N16F	2020	
201	C	RX20RJV	Mercedes-Benz Sprinter 516 cdi	EVM Cityline	N16F	2020	
202	C	WV20VDO	Mercedes-Benz Sprinter 516 cdi	EVM Cityline	N16F	2020	
203	C	RX20RDV	Mercedes-Benz Sprinter 516 cdi	EVM Cityline	N16F	2020	
204	C	RX70SKE	Mercedes-Benz Sprinter 516 cdi	EVM Cityline	N16F	2020	
205	V	RE70EZU	Mercedes-Benz Sprinter 516 cdi	EVM Cityline	N16F	2020	
206	V	RX71TGK	Mercedes-Benz Sprinter 516 cdi	EVM Cityline	N16F	2020	
207	V	RX72TWP	Mercedes-Benz Sprinter 516 cdi	EVM Cityline	N16F	2020	
208	V	RX23TFK	Mercedes-Benz Sprinter 519 cdi	EVM Cityline	N15F	2021	
209	V	RX18LNT	Mercedes-Benz Sprinter 516 cdi	EVM Cityline	N16F	2023	Arriva, 2023
210	V	RX68FLV	Mercedes-Benz Sprinter 516 cdi	EVM Cityline	N16F	2020	Arriva, 2023
211	V	RF68FMC	Mercedes-Benz Sprinter 516 cdi	EVM Cityline	N16F	2020	Arriva, 2023
212	V	RF68FLN	Mercedes-Benz Sprinter 516 cdi	EVM Cityline	N16F	2020	Arriva, 2023
213	V	RF68FMA	Mercedes-Benz Sprinter 516 cdi	EVM Cityline	N16F	2020	Arriva, 2023
214	V	RX23TKV	Mercedes-Benz Sprinter 516 cdi	EVM Cityline	N16F	2020	
215	V	RX23TFJ	Mercedes-Benz Sprinter 516 cdi	EVM Cityline	N16F	2020	
216	V	RX23TUU	Mercedes-Benz Sprinter 516 cdi	EVM Cityline	N16F	2020	
217	V	RX23TUV	Mercedes-Benz Sprinter 516 cdi	EVM Cityline	N16F	2020	
218	V	RX23TUW	Mercedes-Benz Sprinter 516 cdi	EVM Cityline	N16F	2020	
219	V	RX23TUY	Mercedes-Benz Sprinter 516 cdi	EVM Cityline	N16F	2020	
220	V	RX23TVD	Mercedes-Benz Sprinter 516 cdi	EVM Cityline	N16F	2020	
221	V	RX23TVE	Mercedes-Benz Sprinter 516 cdi	EVM Cityline	N16F	2020	
222	V	RX23TVF	Mercedes-Benz Sprinter 516 cdi	EVM Cityline	N16F	2020	
223	C	CC04GAL	Mercedes-Benz Sprinter 519 cdi	EVM Elegance	M16	2019	
251	V	RE22ERJ	Iveco Daily 70C21	Illesbus i-City	N31F	2022	
252	V	RE22ETZ	Iveco Daily 70C21	Illesbus i-City	N31F	2022	
305	V	YX69NWB	ADL E20D 10.8m	ADL Enviro 200 MMC	N41F	2019	

306-315 ADL E20D 10.8m — ADL Enviro 200 MMC — N39F — 2022

306	V	YX22OGR	**309**	V	YX22OGU	**312**	V	YX22OGY	**314**	V	YX22OHA
307	V	YX22OGS	**310**	V	YX22OGV	**313**	V	YX22OGZ	**315**	V	YX22OHB
308	V	YX22OGT	**311**	V	YX22OGW						

316	C	YX16OBO	ADL E20D 10.8m	ADL Enviro 200 MMC	N40F	2016	Abellio, London, 2023
317	C	YX16OBS	ADL E20D 10.8m	ADL Enviro 200 MMC	N40F	2016	Abellio, London, 2023
318	V	SN16OVM	ADL E20D 8.9m	ADL Enviro 200 MMC	N29F	2016	Britannia Parking
319	V	SN16OVO	ADL E20D 8.9m	ADL Enviro 200 MMC	N29F	2016	Britannia Parking
320	V	SN16OVP	ADL E20D 8.9m	ADL Enviro 200 MMC	N29F	2016	Britannia Parking
321	V	SN16OVR	ADL E20D 8.9m	ADL Enviro 200 MMC	N29F	2016	Britannia Parking
322	C	YX73OVM	ADL E20D 10.8m	ADL Enviro 200 MMC	N40F	2023	
323	C	YX73OVN	ADL E20D 10.8m	ADL Enviro 200 MMC	N40F	2023	
324	C	YX73OVO	ADL E20D 10.8m	ADL Enviro 200 MMC	N40F	2023	
325	V	YX73OVP	ADL E20D 10.8m	ADL Enviro 200 MMC	N40F	2023	
326	C	YX22OJJ	ADL E20D 10.8m	ADL Enviro 200 MMC	N39F	2023	LB of Redbridge
327	V	CC21GAL	ADL E20D 9.7m	ADL Enviro 200 MMC	N34F	2021	
328	V	CE21GAL	ADL E20D 9.7m	ADL Enviro 200 MMC	N34F	2021	
329	V	CC71GAL	ADL E20D 9.7m	ADL Enviro 200 MMC	N34F	2021	
330	V	CE71GAL	ADL E20D 9.7m	ADL Enviro 200 MMC	N34F	2021	
337	C	YX72ONB	ADL E20D 9.7m	ADL Enviro 200 MMC	N34F	2022	
339	C	YX72OND	ADL E20D 9.7m	ADL Enviro 200 MMC	N34F	2022	
340	C	YX72ONE	ADL E20D 9.7m	ADL Enviro 200 MMC	N34F	2022	
344	C	JW16BUS	ADL E20D 10.8m	ADL Enviro 200 MMC	N41F	2016	Red Rose, Aylesbury, 2024

Vectare has a growing fleet based in Loughborogh and provides vehicles for the services latterly run as Central Connect and Galleon Travel. Undertaking a duty on Chelmsford park and ride is Enviro 200 MMC 309, YX22OGU. *Mark Doggett*

345	C	WH66BUS	ADL E20D 10.8m	ADL Enviro 200 MMC	N41F	2016	Red Rose, Aylesbury, 2024
346	C	SW16BUS	ADL E20D 10.8m	ADL Enviro 200 MMC	N41F	2016	Red Rose, Aylesbury, 2024
347	V	SK73CNO	ADL E20D 10.8m	ADL Enviro 200 MMC	N40F	2023	
348	V	SK73CNJ	ADL E20D 10.8m	ADL Enviro 200 MMC	N40F	2023	
349	C	SK73CNU	ADL E20D 10.8m	ADL Enviro 200 MMC	N40F	2023	
350	C	YY73TGU	ADL E20D 10.8m	ADL Enviro 200 MMC	N40F	2024	
351	C	YY73TGV	ADL E20D 10.8m	ADL Enviro 200 MMC	N40F	2024	

352-371 ADL E20D 8.9m | ADL Enviro 200 MMC | N30F | 2024

352	V	YY73RGX	**357**	V	YY24HBA	**362**	V	YY24HBF	**367**	V	YY24HBL
353	C	YY73RGZ	**358**	V	YY24HBB	**363**	V	YY24HBG	**368**	V	YY24HBN
354	C	YY73RHA	**359**	V	YY24HBC	**364**	V	YY24HBH	**369**	V	YY24HBO
355	V	YY73RHE	**360**	V	YY24HBD	**365**	V	YY24HBJ	**370**	V	YY24HBP
356	V	YY73RHF	**361**	V	YY24HBE	**366**	V	YY24HBK	**371**	V	YY24HBU

402	V	YN04GPJ	Scania K114 EB4	Irizar Intercentury	C49FT	2004	Astons, Worcester
403	V	YR20VHT	Scania K360 EB4	Irizar PB	C53FT	2020	
410	V	W10VEC	Mercedes-Benz Tourismo	Mercedes-Benz	C48FT	2017	
411	V	W11VEC	Mercedes-Benz Tourismo	Mercedes-Benz	C48FT	2017	
412	V	W12VEC	Mercedes-Benz Tourismo	Mercedes-Benz	C48FT	2017	
413	V	W13VEC	Mercedes-Benz Tourismo	Mercedes-Benz	C48FT	2017	
414	V	W14VEC	Mercedes-Benz Tourismo	Mercedes-Benz	C48FT	2016	
415	V	W15VEC	Mercedes-Benz Tourismo	Mercedes-Benz	C48FT	2018	
416	V	W16VEC	Mercedes-Benz Tourismo	Mercedes-Benz	C48FT	2018	
417	V	W17VEC	Mercedes-Benz Tourismo	Mercedes-Benz	C48FT	2018	

501	C	CT21GAL	Optare Metrodekka	Optare	N51/25F	2021	
595	C	YP59OEM	Scania OmniCity CN230 UD	Scania	N41/22D	2010	RATP, 2019
597	C	YP59OES	Scania OmniCity CN230 UD	Scania	N41/22D	2010	RATP, 2019
599	C	YP59OEV	Scania OmniCity CN230 UD	Scania	N41/22D	2010	RATP, 2019
596	C	YP59OEO	Scania OmniCity CN230 UD	Scania	N41/22D	2010	RATP, 2019
598	C	YP59OET	Scania OmniCity CN230 UD	Scania	N41/22D	2010	RATP, 2019

Now numbered 328, CE21GAL, illustrates the colours latterly used by Central Connect. It was undertaking work in Harlow when seen. *Richard Godfrey*

903	C	YX22OGJ	ADL E20D 8.9m	ADL Enviro 200 MMC	N30F	2022	
912	C	LJ58AVE	ADL Dart 4	ADL Enviro 200	N29D	2008	Arriva London, 2021
913	C	LJ57USU	ADL Dart 4	ADL Enviro 200	N29D	2007	Arriva London, 2021
914	C	LX07BYA	ADL Dart 4	ADL Enviro 200	N29D	2007	Go-Ahead London, 2021
915	C	LX07BXV	ADL Dart 4	ADL Enviro 200	N29D	2007	Go-Ahead London, 2021
917	C	SN57DWZ	ADL Dart 4	ADL Enviro 200	N32D	2007	Go-Ahead London, 2021
918	C	LX09AZL	ADL Dart SLF	Optare Esteem	N29D	2009	Go-Ahead London, 2021
919	C	KX08HMF	ADL Dart 4 8.9m	ADL Enviro 200	N29F	2008	A2B Travel, Prenton, 2022
920	C	LK08DWA	ADL Dart 4 10.8m	ADL Enviro 200	N37F	2009	Arriva London, 2022
921	C	YX60DXY	ADL Dart 4 8.9m	ADL Enviro 200	N29F	2010	Tyrer, Bolton, 2022
922	C	YX12FPY	ADL Dart 4 8.9m	ADL Enviro 200	N29F	2012	Tyrer, Bolton, 2022
923	C	YX12DHM	ADL Dart 4 10.8m	ADL Enviro 200	N39F	2012	Newport Buses, 2022
924	C	YX12DHO	ADL Dart 4 10.8m	ADL Enviro 200	N39F	2012	Newport Buses, 2022
925	C	ML62OGY	ADL Dart 4 8.9m	ADL Enviro 200	N29F	2012	Tyrer, Bolton, 2022
926	C	MX12DZE	ADL Dart 4 8.9m	ADL Enviro 200	N29F	2012	CT Plus, Manchester
927	C	L8XEL	ADL Dart 4 10.8m	ADL Enviro 200	N29F	2011	Houstons, Lockerbie, 23
928	C	L9XEL	ADL Dart 4 10.8m	ADL Enviro 200	N29F	2011	Houstons, Lockerbie, 23
3000	G	DK64GAL	Irizar i6	Irizar	C57FT	2014	
3001	C	DK65GAL	VDL Futura FHD2-139.320	VDL	C53FT	2015	
3002	C	SS16GAL	VDL Futura FHD2-139.320	VDL	C44FT	2016	
3003	C	SS71GAL	Scania K410 EB6	Higer	C59F	2022	
3004	C	LX22GAL	Scania K410 EB6	Irizar i6	C59F	2022	
3005	C	JFZ7018	Scania K320	Irizar i4	C51F	2012	Ulsterbus
3006	C	LU22GAL	Scania K410 EB6	Irizar i6	C59F	2022	

Ancilliary vehicle:

TV	C	KP02PVO	ADL Dart SLF	Plaxton Pointer	tv	2002	Tower Transit, 2021

Flagfinders

Flagfinders (CTB) Ltd, Flagfinders CTB Ltd, 267 Coggeshall Road, Braintree, CM7 9EF

S190SLL	Mercedes-Benz Vario O810	Frank Guy	B24F	1998	
Y184NLK	Volvo B7TL	Plaxton President	N43/27F	2001	
LB02YXG	Volvo B7TL	Wrightbus Eclipse Gemini	N43/27F	2002	
LB02YXK	Volvo B7TL	Wrightbus Eclipse Gemini	N43/27F	2002	
LF52USV	Volvo B7TL	Wrightbus Eclipse Gemini	N44/22D	2002	
LF52ZSD	Volvo B7TL	Wrightbus Eclipse Gemini	N44/22D	2002	
LK03NHF	Volvo B7TL	Plaxton President	N43/27F	2003	
LK03NHG	Volvo B7TL	Plaxton President	N43/27F	2003	
LK03NHV	Volvo B7TL	Plaxton President	N43/27F	2003	
GK03JUC	Mercedes-Benz Sprinter 413 cdi	Stamford	M16	2003	
VU53FYR	Mercedes-Benz Sprinter 413 cdi	Excel	M16	2003	
NIL7251	Scania N94 UD	East Lancs Omnidekka	N43/32F	2003	
YN53RYD	Scania N94 UD	East Lancs Omnidekka	N43/32F	2003	
YN53RYR	Scania N94 UD	East Lancs Omnidekka	N43/32F	2003	
GB04FLG	VDL Futura FHD13-340	VDL Bova	C53FT	2004	
GB54FLG	VDL Futura FHD13-340	VDL Bova	C53FT	2004	
YN04PZY	Dennis Dart MPD	Plaxton Pointer	N29F	2004	
AE54FMG	Mercedes-Benz Vario O814	Eurocoach	C33F	2004	
PG04WHF	Volvo B7TL	East Lancs Viking	N47/32F	2004	
PO54OOD	Volvo B7TL	East Lancs Viking	N47/32F	2004	
YN05ASZ	Irisbus Euromidi CC95.18	Indcar Maxim 2	C33F	2005	
GB05FLG	VDL Futura FHD13-340	VDL Bova	C49FT	2005	
GB55FLG	VDL Futura FHD13-340	VDL Bova	C53FT	2005	
DC56PAN	ADL Dart 4	ADL Pointer	N29F	2006	
YN56FDD	Scania N94 UD	East Lancs Omnidekka	N45/31F	2006	
YN56FDX	Scania N94 UD	East Lancs Omnidekka	N45/31F	2006	
YN07EYP	Scania N94 UD	East Lancs Omnidekka	N51/35F	2007	
YN07EYT	Scania N94 UD	East Lancs Omnidekka	N51/35F	2007	
YN08MLY	Scania N94 UD	East Lancs Omnidekka	N51/35F	2008	
YL08FZS	Mercedes-Benz Sprinter 311 cdi	Malton Coachworks	M16	2008	
Y4FLG	Scania OmniExpress K340 EB4	Scania	C55FT	2009	Little, Ilkeston,
YX10BFO	ADL Dart 4	ADL Enviro 200	N36F	2010	
PO61LUW	Mercedes-Benz Sprinter 515 cdi	UNVI	M16	2011	
BT12AZN	Ford Transit	Ford	M8	2012	
Y2FLG	VDL Futura FHD2.129 VDL	VDL	C57FT	2015	
Y3FLG	Irizar i6	Irizar	C61FT	2015	

Depots: 267 Coggeshall Road, Braintree, CM7 9EF; Little Stubleys Farm, Sudbury Road, Halstead, CO9 2BB and Station Road Kelvedon, Colchester, CO5 9NP.

SIMONDS

Simonds of Botesdale Ltd, Roswald House, Oak Drive, Diss, IP22 4GX

4940VF	Volvo B10M	Van Hool T8 Alizée	C55F	1997	
XIL4072	Volvo B10M	Van Hool T9 Alizée	C49FT	1998	
X663VRL	Volvo B7TL	Alexander ALX400	N47/30F	2000	Dublin Bus
MSU917	Volvo B7TL	Alexander ALX400	N47/30F	2001	GHA, Wrexham
YVF158	Volvo B12M	Van Hool T9 Alizée	C57F	2002	Crawford, Neilston
KDX108	Volvo B10M	Van Hool T9 Alizée	C53F	2002	Wicksons, Walsall
LK53KVZ	Volvo B11B	Plaxton Panther	C49FT	2002	Go-Ahead London
8333UR	Volvo B11B	Van Hool T9 Alizée	C49FT	2002	Mayne's, Buckie
98TNO	Volvo B11B	Van Hool T9 Alizée	C53F	2002	Souls, Tamworth
WVE284	Scania N94 UD	East Lancs Omnidekka	N51/35F	2005	Go-Ahead London
378BNG	Volvo B11B	Van Hool T9 Alizée	C53F	2005	Mayne's, Buckie
TCF496	Volvo B12B	Van Hool T9 Alizée	C49F	2006	Mayne's, Buckie
7236PW	Volvo B12B	Van Hool T9 Alizée	C49FT	2006	
YK55ENL	Optare Solo M850	Optare	N28F	2006	Swift, Great Yarmouth
SN06BOV	ADL Enviro 300	ADL	N56F	2006	Suffolk CC
SN56AGV	Volvo B7TL	Wrightbus Eclipse Gemini	N44/29F	2006	Lothian Buses,
YJ56KCK	VDL DB250	East Lancs Lowlander	N51/34F	2006	Tyrer, Bolton
259JPA	Volvo B12B	Plaxton Panther	C57F	2006	Three-Star, Luton
YN56SGU	Volvo B12B	Plaxton Panther	C57F	2006	Classic Coaches
9383MX	ADL E20D 10.8m	ADL Enviro 200	N37F	2007	
224ENG	Volvo B12B	Van Hool T9 Alizée	C49FT	2008	Lochs & Glens
166EMB	Volvo B12B	Van Hool T9 Acron	C57FT	2009	Lochs & Glens

Vectare acquired Simonds of Botesdale in May 2024 after it had been operating in the Suffok village and later in Diss for over ninety-six years. Simonds MX60BXF joined the fleet from Cresswell and is one of eight Enviro 200s currently operated. Routes 112, 113 and 114 connect Ipswich with Diss, the route number changing at Eye. *John Birtwistle*

DSU116	ADL E20D 10.8m	ADL Enviro 200	N37F	2009	Webberbus, Bridgwate
UU59BOY	Mercedes-Benz Sprinter 515 cdi	Ferqui Soroco	C19F	2010	Golden Boy
JGV929	MAN 18.360	Plaxton Panther	C53F	2010	Mayne's, Buckie
MX60BXF	ADL E20D 10.8m	ADL Enviro 200	N37F	2010	Cresswell, Evesham
538ELX	Volvo B12B	Van Hool T9 Acron	C57FT	2010	
SIA488	Volvo B9R	Caetano Levanté	S70F	2011	National Express
SLK886	Volvo B9R	Caetano Levanté	S70F	2011	National Express
SN11PFM	ADL E20D 10.8m	ADL Enviro 200	N37F	2011	Ensignbus, Purfleet
MX62AWG	ADL E20D 10.8m	ADL Enviro 200	N37F	2012	Manchester CT
BT13YWE	Volvo B8RLE 11.3m	MCV eVoRa	N44F	2013	
BT13YWF	Volvo B8RLE 11.3m	MCV eVoRa	N44F	2013	
BT63UUP	Volvo B8RLE 11.3m	MCV eVoRa	N44F	2013	Webberbus, Bridgwater
BT63UUR	Volvo B8RLE 11.3m	MCV eVoRa	N44F	2013	Webberbus, Bridgwater
BT63UUX	Volvo B8RLE 11.3m	MCV eVoRa	N44F	2014	Webberbus, Bridgwater
BU14EHY	Volvo B8RLE 11.3m	MCV eVoRa	N44F	2014	
BN64CNY	Volvo B8RLE 11.3m	MCV eVoRa	N45F	2014	Volvo demonstrator
MT15UAE	Ford Transit	Ford	M16	2015	
BF65HVP	Mercedes-Benz Tourismo	Mercedes-Benz	C57FT	2015	
BU16GZB	Mercedes-Benz Tourismo	Mercedes-Benz	C57FT	2016	
BN17JJY	Mercedes-Benz Tourismo	Mercedes-Benz	C53FT	2017	
YN17MJF	Ford Tourneo	Ford	M8	2017	
YX17NDY	ADL E20D 10.8m	ADL Enviro 200	N37F	2017	Compass Bus
YX17NTU	ADL E20D 10.8m	ADL Enviro 200	N37F	2017	First
YY67HBH	ADL E20D 10.8m	ADL Enviro 200	N37F	2018	First
YX68UAC	Volvo B8R	Plaxton Panther	C57FT	2018	
YX68UCA	Volvo B8R	Plaxton Panther	C57FT	2018	
YX72OMY	ADL E20D 10.9m	ADL Enviro 200 MMC	N40F	2023	
BV73MSO	Volvo B8RLE 11.3m	MCV eVoRa	N46F	2023	

VISION

Vision Bus Ltd, Blackrod Interchange, Station Road, Blackrod, Bolton, BL6 5JE

LF55CYW	Volvo B7TL	Wrightbus Eclipse Gemini	N45/31F	2006	Abellio London, 2018
LX57CKC	ADL Trident 2	ADL Enviro 400	N39/24F	2007	Go-Ahead London, 2022
LX57CKD	ADL Trident 2	ADL Enviro 400	N39/24F	2007	Go-Ahead London, 2022
YN08HYY	Scania N230 UD	East Lancs Olympus	N51/28F	2008	Reading, 2018
FJ08BYX	Volvo B9TL	Wrightbus Eclipse Gemini	NC41/29F	2008	Transdev, 2017
YN08DHL	Scania OmniCity CN230 UD	Scania	N41/22D	2008	RATP, London, 2017
YN08MKX	Scania OmniCity CN270 UD	Scania	N47/30F	2008	Reading Buses, 2018
YN08MKZ	Scania OmniCity CN270 UD	Scania	N47/30F	2008	Reading Buses, 2018
LK58EDP	VDL DB300	Wrightbus Gemin 2	N41/24D	2009	RATP, 2023
LK58EDR	VDL DB300	Wrightbus Gemin 2	N41/24D	2009	RATP, 2023
LK09CZS	VDL DB300	Wrightbus Gemin 2	N41/24D	2009	RATP, 2023
BF10LSX	Volvo B9TL	Wrightbus Gemin 2	N41/24D	2009	Comfortdelgro, 2023
BF10LSY	Volvo B9TL	Wrightbus Gemin 2	N41/24D	2009	Comfortdelgro, 2023
BF10LTA	Volvo B9TL	Wrightbus Gemin 2	N41/24D	2009	Comfortdelgro, 2023
BK10MFJ	Volvo B9TL	Wrightbus Gemin 2	N41/24D	2009	Comfortdelgro, 2023
BV10WVS	Volvo B9TL	Wrightbus Gemin 2	N41/24D	2009	Comfortdelgro, 2023
BV10WVT	Volvo B9TL	Wrightbus Gemin 2	N41/24D	2009	Comfortdelgro, 2023
BV10WVW	Volvo B9TL	Wrightbus Gemin 2	N41/24D	2009	Comfortdelgro, 2023
	Scania OmniCity CN230 UD	Scania	N41/26F	2009	Stagecoach, 2019
LX09AFK	LX09AFV	LX09AGU			LX09AHC
LX09AFO					
	Scania OmniCity CN230 UD	Scania	N41/26F	2009	RATP, 2019
YP59OEA	YP59OEE	YP59OEH			YP59OEK
YP59OEC	YP59OEF	YP59OEJ			YP59OEL
YP59OED	YP59OEG				
LJ60AXH	VDL DB300	Wrightbus Gemin 2	N41/24D	2010	Arriva London, 2023
LJ60AXK	VDL DB300	Wrightbus Gemin 2	N41/24D	2010	Arriva London, 2023
LJ60AXM	VDL DB300	Wrightbus Gemin 2	N41/24D	2010	Arriva London, 2023
LJ60AXN	VDL DB300	Wrightbus Gemin 2	N41/24D	2010	Arriva London, 2023
LJ11AEO	VDL DB300	Wrightbus Gemin 2	N41/24D	2010	Arriva London, 2023
LJ11AEP	VDL DB300	Wrightbus Gemin 2	N41/24D	2010	Arriva London, 2023
LJ11AET	VDL DB300	Wrightbus Gemin 2	N41/24D	2010	Arriva London, 2023
LJ11AEU	VDL DB300	Wrightbus Gemin 2	N41/24D	2010	Arriva London, 2023
LJ11AEV	VDL DB300	Wrightbus Gemin 2	N41/24D	2010	Arriva London, 2023
HRZ6499	Wrightbus StreetLite WF	Wrightbus	N37F	2010	Wrightbus demonstrator, 21
	Volvo B9TL	Wrightbus Gemini 2	N43/30F	2011	Tower Transit, 2019
BJ11DRZ	BJ11DSY	BJ11DUV			BJ11DVM
BJ11DSE	BJ11DTF	BJ11DVF			BJ11DVP
BJ11DSU	BJ11DTV	BJ11DVL			BJ11DUU
LX11CVT	Volvo B9TL	Wrightbus Gemini 2	N43/30F	2011	Go-Ahead London, 2019
YX61FYG	ADL E20D	ADL Enviro 200	N29D	2012	Tower Transit, 2022
YX61FYN	ADL E20D	ADL Enviro 200	N29D	2012	Tower Transit, 2022
YX61FYO	ADL E20D	ADL Enviro 200	N29D	2012	Tower Transit, 2022
MX12JXU	Wrightbus StreetLite WF 9.6m	Wrightbus	N33F	2012	Roberts, Hugglescote, '20
	Wrightbus StreetLite DF 10.4m	Wrightbus	N36F	2013	Go-Ahead London, 2019
LJ13GLF	LJ13GLK	LJ13GKO			LJ13GKP
YY64GWA	ADL E20D	ADL Enviro 200	N29F	2014	iGo, Dudley, 2021
YY64GWC	ADL E20D	ADL Enviro 200	N29F	2014	iGo, Dudley, 2021
SN64CTU	Wrightbus StreetDeck	Wrightbus	N45/28F	2015	Wrightbus demonstrator, 22
SN64CTV	Wrightbus StreetDeck	Wrightbus	N41/21D	2015	Wrightbus demonstrator, 22
SL15ZGP	Wrightbus StreetDeck	Wrightbus	NC45/29F	2015	Wrightbus demonstrator, 19
SN65OKM	Wrightbus StreetLite WF	Wrightbus	N28F	2015	RATP, London, 2021
SN65ZGZ	ADL E20D	ADL Enviro 200 MMC	N30F	2016	West Coast Motors, 2024
SN65ZHA	ADL E20D	ADL Enviro 200 MMC	N30F	2016	West Coast Motors, 2024

Following the franchising of services in Greater Manchester, Vision have focused their efforts more towards Lancashire towns. Seen in Preston while operating route 113 for Leyland, once a Fishwick service, is Enviro 200 MMC YX23OXB. *Mark Lyons*

YX16ODJ	ADL E20D 10.8m	ADL Enviro 200	N37F	2016	Menzies, Heathrow, 2021
	ADL E40D	ADL Enviro 400 City	N45/29F	2016	Blackpool CT, 2023
SN16OVC	SN16OVF	SN16OVH			SN16OVK
SN16OVD	SN16OVG	SN16OVJ			SN16OVL
SN16WJY	ADL E20D 8.9m	ADL Enviro 200 MMC	N29F	2016	Evergreen, Birmingham, '21
SN66WJY	ADL E20D 8.9m	ADL Enviro 200 MMC	N29F	2016	Thandi, Smethwick, 2021
SN67XBH	ADL E20D 9.7m	ADL Enviro 200 MMC	N34F	2017	Cobra, Epsom, 2023
YX18KNR	ADL E20D 10.8m	ADL Enviro 200 MMC	N40F	2018	Evergreen, Birmingham, '21
YX18KNV	ADL E20D 10.8m	ADL Enviro 200 MMC	N40F	2018	Dawson Rentals, 2021
YX19ONU	ADL E40D	ADL Enviro 400 MMC	NC44/34F	2019	ADL demonstrator, 2021
YX20OCE	ADL E20D 8.9m	ADL Enviro 200 MMC	N34F	2020	Dawson Renatals, 2020
YX20ODA	ADL E20D 9.7m	ADL Enviro 200 MMC	N34F	2020	
YX20ODB	ADL E20D 9.7m	ADL Enviro 200 MMC	N34F	2020	
SK70BVT	ADL E40D	ADL Enviro 400 MMC	NC51/35F	2020	
SK70BVU	ADL E40D	ADL Enviro 400 MMC	NC51/35F	2020	
	ADL E20D 8.9m	ADL Enviro 200 MMC	N30F	2021	
YX21RNU	YX21RPV	YX21RSO			RX71OJJ
YX21RPU	YX21RRZ	YX21RSU			
YX23OSG	ADL E20D 8.9m	ADL Enviro 200 MMC	N30F	2023	
YX23OSW	ADL E20D 8.9m	ADL Enviro 200 MMC	N30F	2023	
YX23OSY	ADL E20D 8.9m	ADL Enviro 200 MMC	N30F	2023	
YX23OXA	ADL E20D 8.9m	ADL Enviro 200 MMC	N30F	2023	
YX23OXB	ADL E20D 8.9m	ADL Enviro 200 MMC	N30F	2023	
YX23OXC	ADL E20D 8.9m	ADL Enviro 200 MMC	N30F	2023	
MX73EPE	ADL E40D 8.9m	ADL Enviro 400 MMC	N51/34F	2023	

WARRINGTON

Warrington Borough Transport Ltd, Wilderspool Causeway, Warrington, WA4 6PT

Fleet No	Reg	Chassis	Body	Seating	Date	Notes
83-94		Volvo B7RLE	Wrightbus Eclipse Urban	NC45F	2009	

83	DK09ELU	**86**	DK09EMJ	**89**	DK09ELX	**92**	DK09EMV
84	DK09ELW	**87**	DK09ELO	**90**	DK09ELJ	**93**	DK09EMX
85	DK09ELV	**88**	DK09ELH	**91**	DK09EMM	**94**	DK09ENC

Fleet No	Reg	Chassis	Body	Seating	Date	Notes
95-100		Optare Versa V1080	Optare	N37F	2013	

95	YJ13HKB	**97**	YJ13HKD	**98**	YJ13HKE	**100**	YJ13HKA
96	YJ13HKC						

Fleet No	Reg	Chassis	Body	Seating	Date	Notes
186	CSZ7913	VDL DB250	Wrightbus Gemini	N43/29F	2004	Reading Buses, 2019
187	LK04HYY	Volvo B7TL 10.1m	Wrightbus Eclipse Gemini	N41/28F	2004	Tower Transit, 2018
188	BD51YCR	Volvo B7TL 10.1m	Wrightbus Eclipse Gemini	N41/28F	2001	RATP, London, 2012
189	BD51YCS	Volvo B7TL 10.1m	Wrightbus Eclipse Gemini	N41/28F	2001	RATP, London, 2012
191	LX53AZW	Volvo B7TL 10.1m	Wrightbus Eclipse Gemini	N41/28F	2003	Go-Ahead London, 2011
194	LJ04LGF	VDL DB250	Wrightbus Gemini	N43/27F	2004	Routemaster, Nantwich, '16
195	LJ04LGG	VDL DB250	Wrightbus Gemini	N43/27F	2004	Routemaster, Nantwich, '16
196	LJ04LGK	VDL DB250	Wrightbus Gemini	N43/27F	2004	Routemaster, Nantwich, '16
201-213		ADL E20D 10.8m	ADL Enviro 200 MMC	N35F	2018	

201	CH04CAT	**205**	CH57CAT	**208**	CH62CAT	**211**	YX18KTV
202	CH06CAT	**206**	CH58CAT	**209**	YX18KTP	**212**	YX18KUA
203	CH12CAT	**207**	CH59CAT	**210**	YX18KTT	**213**	YX18KUB
204	CH56CAT						

Fleet No	Reg	Chassis	Body	Seating	Date	Notes
214	CX65BUH	ADL E20D 8.9m	ADL Enviro 200	N29F	2015	Eifion's, Gwalchmai, 2020
215	CX65BUJ	ADL E20D 8.9m	ADL Enviro 200	N29F	2015	Eifion's, Gwalchmai, 2020
216-221		ADL Dennis Dart SLF	ADL Enviro 200	N39F	2010-11	Ensign Bus, 2020

216	SN11FFK	**218**	SN11FFP	**220**	SN11FFR	**221**	SN11FFL
217	SN11FFJ	**219**	YX10ECA				

Fleet No	Reg	Chassis	Body	Seating	Date	Notes
222	YY67USH	ADL E20D	ADL Enviro 200	N39F	2017	Yourbus, Heanor, 2020
223	YX09AFA	ADL E20D	ADL Enviro 200	N39F	2009	Panther, Parkeston, 2020
224	YX09AEV	ADL E20D	ADL Enviro 200	N36F	2009	Panther, Parkeston, 2020
225	YX10BCU	ADL E20D	ADL Enviro 200	N36F	2010	Metroline, 2020
227-236		Volvo B7RLE	Wrightbus Eclipse 2	N45F	2010-12	Transdev, 2020

227	BD12TEJ	**233**	BD12TEO	**235**	BU54JAR	**236**	HA10SRG
228	BD12TDX	**234**	BD12TEY				

Fleet No	Reg	Chassis	Body	Seating	Date	Notes
237	MM14DWU	ADL E20D 8.9m	ADL Enviro 200	N29F	2014	Jim Stones, Leigh, 2020
238	MM14DKX	ADL E20D 8.9m	ADL Enviro 200	N29F	2014	Jim Stones, Leigh, 2020
240	GX07HUJ	ADL E20D 10.8m	ADL Enviro 200	N38F	2007	Stagecoach, 2023
241	GX58GLY	ADL E20D 10.8m	ADL Enviro 200	N38F	2008	Stagecoach, 2023
242	GX58GLZ	ADL E20D 10.8m	ADL Enviro 200	N38F	2008	Stagecoach, 2023
243	YX65RHF	ADL E20D 8.9m	ADL Enviro 200	N29F	2015	CT Plus, 2023
244	YX15XMJ	ADL E20D 8.9m	ADL Enviro 200	N29F	2015	CT Plus, 2023
245	YY66PDX	ADL E20D 8.9m	ADL Enviro 200	N29F	2016	Xelabus, 2023
246	YY66PEO	ADL E20D 8.9m	ADL Enviro 200	N29F	2016	Xelabus, 2023
247	YY66PFA	ADL E20D 8.9m	ADL Enviro 200	N29F	2016	Xelabus, 2023
248	YY66PFO	ADL E20D 8.9m	ADL Enviro 200	N29F	2016	Xelabus, 2023
249	YY66PFU	ADL E20D 8.9m	ADL Enviro 200	N29F	2016	Xelabus, 2023
250	SK07CFV	Volvo B7RLE	Wrightbus Eclipse	N38F	2007	Hayfordian, 2023
300	LJ04LFG	VDL DB250	Wrightbus Pulsar Gemini	N43/27F	2004	Vision, Bolton, 2020
301	LJ04LGC	VDL DB250	Wrightbus Pulsar Gemini	N43/27F	2004	Vision, Bolton, 2020
303	PN16PAV	ADL E40D	ADL Enviro 400 City	N45/29F	2016	Blackpool Transport, 2020
304	SN16OVB	ADL E40D	ADL Enviro 400 City	N45/29F	2016	Blackpool Transport, 2020
305-311		ADL Trident 2	ADL Enviro 400	N41/29F	2009	Metroline, 2020

305	SN09CFM	**307**	SN09CDV	**309**	SN09CEK	**311**	SN09CDY
306	SN09CEX	**308**	SN09CDX	**310**	SN09CEF		

312	LK58CNV	ADL Trident 2	ADL Enviro 400	N43/31F	2008	Metroline, 2021
313	LK58KHU	ADL Trident 2	ADL Enviro 400	N43/31F	2008	Metroline, 2021
314	LK57AXF	ADL Trident 2	ADL Enviro 400	N43/31F	2007	Tower Transit, 2021
315	SN11BPZ	ADL E40D	ADL Enviro 400	N43/31F	2011	Tower Transit, 2021
316	SN11BRF	ADL E40D	ADL Enviro 400	N43/31F	2011	Tower Transit, 2021
317	LJ08CYP	ADL Trident 2	ADL Enviro 400	N43/31F	2008	Arriva London, 2021
319	PG04WGY	Volvo B7TL	East Lancs Viking	N45/29F	2004	Vision, Bolton, 2022
320	DK09NRN	Volvo B9TL	Wrightbus Gemini 2	N41/28F	2009	Selwyn, Runcorn, 2023
321	DK09NRNO	Volvo B9TL	Wrightbus Gemini 2	N41/28F	2009	Selwyn, Runcorn, 2023
322	DK09NRU	Volvo B9TL	Wrightbus Gemini 2	N41/28F	2009	Selwyn, Runcorn, 2023
323	DK09NSZ	Volvo B9TL	Wrightbus Gemini 2	N41/28F	2009	Selwyn, Runcorn, 2023
324	WU09BCZ	Volvo B9TL	Wrightbus Gemini 2	N41/28F	2009	Selwyn, Runcorn, 2023
325	LK08FMP	ADL E40D	ADL Enviro 400	N41/27F	2008	Metroline, 2023
326	LK08FMU	ADL E40D	ADL Enviro 400	N41/27F	2008	Metroline, 2023
327	LK08FMV	ADL E40D	ADL Enviro 400	N41/27F	2008	Metroline, 2023

1001-1049	Volvo BZL 10.8m	MCV	NC33F	2024

1001	BV24LPN	**1014**	BV24LUF	**1026**	-	**1038**	-
1002	BV24LPU	**1015**	-	**1027**	-	**1039**	-
1003	-	**1016**	BV24LUJ	**1028**	-	**1040**	-
1004	BV24LPZ	**1017**	BT24WRO	**1029**	-	**1041**	-
1005	BV24LRA	**1018**	-	**1030**	-	**1042**	-
1006	BV24LRE	**1019**	-	**1031**	-	**1043**	-
1007	-	**1020**	BT24WRU	**1032**	-	**1044**	-
1008	-	**1021**	BT24WRV	**1033**	-	**1045**	-
1009	BV24LRK	**1022**	-	**1034**	-	**1046**	-
1010	-	**1023**	-	**1035**	-	**1047**	-
1011	-	**1024**	-	**1036**	-	**1048**	-
1012	BV24LRO	**1025**	-	**1037**	-	**1049**	-
1013	-						

1201-1219	Volvo BZL 12.175m	MCV	NC37F	On order
2001-2033	Volvo BZL DD 10.9m	MCV	NC42/19F	On order
9001-9004	Volvo BZL 9.03m	MCV	NC29F	On order

Ancillary vehicle:

T225	BD12TEV	Volvo B7RLE	Wrightbus Eclipse 2	NC45F	2012

As we go to press the first of a whole fleet of Volvo BZL buses have started to arrive. Pictured on its first journey on its first day in service is 10.8 metre 1001, BV24LPN. *Andy Rigby*

WEARDALE

Weardale Motor Services Ltd, Shittlehope Burn Garage, Stanhope, Bishop Auckland, DL13 2YQ

	E13BUS	Dennis Trident	East Lancs Lolyne	N57/37F	2002	Lucketts, 2023
	F13BUS	Dennis Trident	East Lancs Lolyne	N57/37F	2002	Lucketts, 2023
w	LG52XZR	Dennis Trident	Alexander ALX400	N48/23F	2002	Abellio, London, 2018
w	PJ02RHF	TransBus Trident	TransBus President	N41/27F	2002	Go-Ahead London, 2011
w	(T66WMS)	Mercedes-Benz Vario 0814	Plaxton Beaver	B31F	2003	
	Y6WMS	Optare Solo M780	Optare	N25F	2004	
	Y14BUS	Volvo B9TL	East Lancs Olympus	N63/43F	2005	Lucketts, 2023
	OU05AVD	Volvo B9TL	East Lancs Olympus	N63/43F	2005	Lucketts, 2023
w	NIL9777	LDV Maxus	LDV	M11	2006	
	MX06XTA	LDV Maxus	LDV	M11	2006	
w	AG02WMS	MAN 18.36	Marcopolo Viggio	S70F	2006	Selwym, Runcorn, 2021
w	YN56FCJ	Scania OmniCity N94 UD	Scania	N45/27F	2006	RATP, London, 2022
w	D16WNS	Scania OmniCity CN94 UD	Scania	NC45/28F	2006	Lothian Buses, 2020
	P6WMS	Scania OmniCity CN94 UD	Scania	NC45/28F	2007	Lothian Buses, 2020
w	GO03WMS	Optare Solo M950	Optare	N33F	2007	
	GO05WMS	Optare Solo M880	Optare	N25F	2007	
	V6WMS	Mercedes-Benz Vario 0814	Unvi Riada	C29F	2007	
	LJ57NGF	LDV Maxus	LDV	M16	2007	
W	SV57FUM	LDV Maxus	LDV	M16	2008	
W	PO58SHJ	LDV Maxus	LDV	M8	2008	
	FJ08OEW	LDV Maxus	LDV	M8	2008	
	FJ08KLU	Scania K340 EB6	Caetano Levanté	S87F	2008	Go North East, 2020
	YN08DHG	Scania OmniCity N230 UD	Scania	N41/22D	2008	RATP, London, 2022
	YN08DHJ	Scania OmniCity N230 UD	Scania	N41/22D	2008	RATP, London, 2022
W	GIB6197	Irisbus Eurorider 397E.12.35A	Plaxton Panther	S61F	2008	Pearces, Oxford, 2020
	GIB1067	Dennis Javelin	Plaxton Profile	S70F	2008	Swanns, Chadderton, 2018
	W66WMS	Scania OmniCity N230 UD	Scania	N41/22D	2008	RATP, London, 2022
	GO59WMS	Scania OmniCity N230 UD	Scania	N41/22D	2008	RATP, London, 2022
	Y16WMS	Optare Solo M950 SL	Optare	N29F	2009	Marchants, Cheltenham
	Y66WMS	Optare Solo M880	Optare	N31F	2009	Webberbus, 2017
	E6WMS	Van Hool T916 Astron	Van Hool	C55FT	2010	Golden Boy, 2018
	YN61AXC	Volvo B7R	Plaxton Profile	C49F	2007	Cruisers, Redhill, 2024
	11WMS	Van Hool T917 Altano	Van Hool Altano	C61FT	2012	
	T66WMS	Optare Solo M960	Optare	N34F	2012	Tanat Valley, 2022
	YJ62FXO	Optare Solo M960	Optare	N34F	2012	Peter Hogg, Jedburgh, 2022

By 1921 Stanley Gibson was the proud owner of a Ford car and he started a taxi business and by 2029 Weardale Motor Services was established. Optare Solo GO05WMS is pictured in the Northumberland village of Blanchland.
John Young

	4WMS	Van Hool TX16 Alicron	Van Hool Alicron	C51FT	2013	
	YJ13HHS	Optare Solo M960	Optare	N34F	2013	Abbotts, Leeming, 2022
	YJ13HHT	Optare Solo M960	Optare	N34F	2013	Abbotts, Leeming, 2022
	M6WMS	Optare Solo M925H	Optare	N31F	2013	MCT, Manchester, 2021
	W6WMS	Optare Solo M925H	Optare	N31F	2013	MCT, Manchester, 2020
	X6WMS	Optare Solo M720 SE	Optare	N31F	2013	SPT, Glasgow, 2024
	V66VNS	Optare Solo M710 SE	Optare	N19F	2013	Gwynfor Coaches, 2023
	FN63PWU	Scania K440 EB6	Caetano Levanté II	S90F	2013	Bruce, Saisburgh, 2021
	YJ14BBK	Optare Solo M800 SL	Optare	N30F	2014	Shiel Buses, 2023
W	BX64AEU	King Long XMQ6130	King Long	S73F	2014	Hills, Telford, 2022
	C6BUS	Mercedes-Benz Atego	Unvi	C33F	2015	
	SO10WMS	Optare Solo M780 SE	Optare	N21F	2015	Craigs, Cumbernauld, 2023
	YJ65EUP	Optare Solo M9250 SR	Optare	N33F	2016	Gwynfor Coaches, 2023
	GO16WMS	Optare Metricity V1080	Optare	N38F	2016	Llew Jones, 2023
	OO16WMS	MAN 26.480	Beulas Glory	C64FT	2016	
	7WMS	Van Hool TX16 Alicron	Van Hool	C53FT	2016	
	NX66MOA	Ford Tourneo	Ford	M8	2016	
	8WMS	VDL Futura FHD2-129.365	VDL	C53FT	2018	
	9WMS	VDL Futura FHD2-129.366	VDL	C53FT	2018	
	10WKS	Irizar i6	Irizar	C54FT	2019	
	GO22WMS	Irizar i6	Irizar	C54FT	2022	
	BU22WMS	Van Hool EX17H	Van Hool	C53F	2022	
	OO22WMS	Volvo B8R	Plaxton Leopard	C59F	2022	
	SK22BTF	ADL E40D	ADL Enviro 400 MMC	NC59/26F	2022	
	YX22OJY	ADL E20D 9.7m	ADL Enviro 200 MMC	N34F	2022	
	OO23WMS	Volvo B8R	Plaxton Leopard	S72F	2023	
	GO23WMS	Volvo 9700	Volvo	C59FT	2023	
	GO72WMS	ADL E20D 9.7m	ADL Enviro 200 MMC	N34F	2023	
	WX24URF	Mercedes-Benz Sprinter 516 cdi	Illesbus i-City	N27F	2024	
	BU24WMS	ADL E40D	ADL Enviro 400 MMC	NC59/26F	2024	
	101WMS	Volvo B8RLE	MCV eVoRa	N38F	2024	
	OV24AWM	Neoplan Tourlliner N2216/3 SHDC	Neoplan	C53FT	2024	
	OV24AWN	Neoplan Tourlliner N2216/3 SHDC	Neoplan	C53FT	2024	
	GO24WMS	ADL E20D 8.9m	ADL Enviro 200 MMC	N30F	2024	
	OO24WMS	ADL E20D 10.3m	ADL Enviro 200 MMC	N40F	2024	

Special event vehicles:

YUP6	Leyland PD2/10	Roe	H37/28R	1958
WLT378	AEC Routemaster R2RH	Park Royal	H26/28R	1960
OGR625T	Leyland Leopard PSU3B/4R	Plaxton Supreme IV	C53F	1978
C666FMP	Volvo B10M-61	Plaxton Paramount 3200 II	S70F	1986

Depots: Stanhope, Bishop Auckland, DL13 2YQ and Copeland Lane, Crook.

In addition to the bus services, Weardale operates around ten front-line coaches. Representing them is OO16WMS, a Beulas-bodied MAN. *Steve Rice*

WHIPPET

Whippet Coaches Ltd, 2 Rowles Way, Swavesey, CB24 4UG

FX33	OU22ZWW	Neoplan Tourliner N2216/3	Neoplan	C53FT	2022	
FX34	OU22ZWX	Neoplan Tourliner N2216/3	Neoplan	C53FT	2022	

FX35-46		Neoplan Tourliner N2216/3		Neoplan		C53FT	2023
35	OY23CYF	**38**	OY23CYJ	**41**	OY23CYP	**44**	OY23CYW
36	OY23CYG	**39**	OY23CYK	**42**	OY23CYT	**45**	OY23CYX
37	OY23CYH	**40**	OY23CYL	**43**	OY23CYV	**46**	OY23CYZ

WG101	BG59FYB	Volvo B7RLE	Wrightbus Eclipse 2	N45F	2009	Volvo demonstrator 2013
WG102	BF63HFA	Volvo B7RLE	Wrightbus Eclipse 2	N45F	2013	
WG103	BF63HFB	Volvo B7RLE	Wrightbus Eclipse 2	N45F	2013	
WG104	BF63HFC	Volvo B7RLE	Wrightbus Eclipse 2	N45F	2013	

WG105-111		Volvo B8RLE		Wrightbus Eclipse 3		N45F	2016
105	BT66MVE	**107**	BT66MVH	**109**	BT66MVK	**111**	BT66MVL
106	BT66MVF	**108**	BT66MVG	**110**	BT66MVJ		

WG112-120		Mellor Sigma 12		Mellor		N44F	2023
112	UN14BUS	**115**	MX73GBY	**117**	MX73GDF	**119**	MX23LRZ
113	UN14CAM	**116**	MX23LRU	**118**	MX73GCK	**120**	MX73GCO
114	MX23LCW						

WS317	MX12CFA	ADL E20D 8.9m	ADL Enviro 200	N29F	2012	Impact, Perivale, 2018
WS318	MX12CFD	ADL E20D 8.9m	ADL Enviro 200	N29F	2012	Impact, Perivale, 2018
WD446	YN08DHM	Scania OmniCity CN230 UD	Scania	N41/22D	2008	RATP. London, 2022
WD451	YT10UWA	Scania OmniCity N230 UD	Scania	N41/22D	2010	RATP. London, 2023
WD452	YT10UWD	Scania OmniCity N230 UD	Scania	N41/22D	2010	RATP. London, 2023
WD453	YT10UWF	Scania OmniCity N230 UD	Scania	N41/22D	2010	RATP. London, 2023

Whippet Coaches is one of the operators that uses the Cambridge Busway. Liveried for the busway service is Volvo B7RLE WG103, BF63HFB, which was seen in Huntingdon. *Steve Rice*

WHITE BUS SERVICES

Baileys - Fernhill - White Bus

C E Jeatt & Sons Ltd, North Street Garage, North Street, Winkfield, Windsor, SL4 4TF

1	F	RO19ATE	Volvo B8R	Plaxton Panther	C61F	2019	
2	F	SPR124	MAN A91	Marcopolo Viale HF	S72D	2009	
3	F	YN05UUT	Irisbus 397E.12.35	Plaxton Paragon	C57F	2005	
4	F	BV66VHF	Volvo B11R	Sunsundegui SC7	C53FT	2016	
5	F	PE63OSX	MAN 19-360	Beulas Spica C	C57F	2014	
6	F	PE63OSZ	MAN 19-360	Beulas Spica C	C57F	2014	
8	F	YJ67TCK	Yutong TC9	Yutong	C37F	2017	
	F	BV24LNK	Volvo B8R	Sunsundegui SB4	S70F	2024	
	F	BV24LUR	Volvo B8R	Sunsundegui SB4	S70F	2024	
11	F	BU16OZF	Volvo B8R	Sunsundegui SB3	S60F	2016	
12	F	BV23NTU	Volvo B8R	Sunsundegui SB3	S72F	2023	
17	F	YJ67TCO	Yutong TC9	Yutong	C37F	2017	
18	F	YG68TJY	Yutong TC9	Yutong	C37F	2018	
19	F	YG68TJZ	Yutong TC9	Yutong	C37F	2018	
26	W	YX16NWB	Volvo B8R	Plaxton Leopard	C59F	2016	
27	W	YY65WUA	Volvo B8R	Plaxton Leopard	C59F	2015	
28	W	YX14SCZ	Volvo B9R	Plaxton Leopard	C59F	2015	Smartguide, Wembley, '16
29	W	RA15OBW	Volvo B8R	Plaxton Leopard	S70F	2015	Weaverway, 2018
30	W	YN61EOL	Volvo B7R	Plaxton Profile	S70F	2011	London Mini Coaches, '16
34	W	YN10ABK	Volvo B7R	Plaxton Profile	C57F	2010	Reays, Wigton, 2011
36	W	MX09GZL	ADL E300	ADL Enviro 300	N60F	2009	West Sussex CC, 2011
37	W	LJ58GCF	Volvo B9TL	Optare Olympus	NC61/39F	2008	Hilton, Newton-le-Willows
40	F	YD73FPE	Yutong GT12	Yutong	C53FT	2024	
41	F	YD73FPF	Yutong GT12	Yutong	C53FT	2024	
42	F	YD73FPG	Yutong GT12	Yutong	C53FT	2024	
43	F	YD73FPJ	Yutong GT12	Yutong	C53FT	2024	
44	F	YD24ERK	Yutong GT12	Yutong	C53FT	2024	
52	W	YX70OHP	ADL E20D 9.7m	ADL Enviro 200 MMC	N34F	2020	
53	W	YX70OHR	ADL E20D 9.7m	ADL Enviro 200 MMC	N34F	2020	
54	W	YX73RFZ	ADL E20D 9.7m	ADL Enviro 200 MMC	N34F	2023	
55	W	BN09FWR	Mercedes-Benz Citaro O530	Mercedes-Benz	N42F	2009	M&M, High Wycombe, '22
56	W	SK24XPJ	ADL E20D 8.9m	ADL Enviro 200 MMC	N30F	2024	
57	W	YX71OHY	ADL E20D 10.8m	ADL Enviro 200 MMC	N41F	2022	
58	W	YX71OHZ	ADL E20D 10.8m	ADL Enviro 200 MMC	N41F	2022	
59	W	SK24XPL	ADL E20D 8.9m	ADL Enviro 200 MMC	N30F	2024	
60	W	YY73RFX	ADL E20D 8.9m	ADL Enviro 200 MMC	N29F	2023	
61	W	YY73PKN	ADL E20D 8.9m	ADL Enviro 200 MMC	N29F	2023	
62	W	YJ14BBO	Optare Solo M890	Optare	N27F	2014	
63	W	YJ14BBN	Optare Solo M890	Optare	N27F	2014	
64	W	YY69TLV	ADL E20D 10.8m	ADL Enviro 200 MMC	N37F	2020	
65	W	YY69TLX	ADL E20D 10.8m	ADL Enviro 200 MMC	N37F	2020	
68	u	KFK941	Optare Solo M780 SL	Optare	N24F	2005	
70	W	YX17NTV	ADL E20D 10.8m	ADL Enviro 200	N37F	2017	Passenger Solutions, 2019
71	W	LF23DVW	Volvo B8RLE	MCV eVoRa	N38F	2023	
72	W	YX70OHT	ADL E20D 10.8m	ADL Enviro 200 MMC	N37F	2020	
73	W	YX70OHU	ADL E20D 10.8m	ADL Enviro 200 MMC	N37F	2020	
74	W	YX70OHV	ADL E20D 10.8m	ADL Enviro 200 MMC	N37F	2020	
75	W	YX71OJU	ADL E20D 8.9m	ADL Enviro 200 MMC	N30F	2022	
76	W	SJ16CRX	Volvo B8RLE	MCV eVoRa	N46F	2016	Robertson, Yell, 2022
77	W	SJ16CRZ	Volvo B8RLE	MCV eVoRa	N46F	2016	Robertson, Yell, 2022
78	W	BV73MKF	Volvo B8RLE	MCV eVoRa	N38F	2023	
79	W	BV73MKG	Volvo B8RLE	MCV eVoRa	N38F	2023	
80	W	BV73MKJ	Volvo B8RLE	MCV eVoRa	N38F	2023	
81	W	BV73MKK	Volvo B8RLE	MCV eVoRa	N38F	2023	
82	W	BV73MKL	Volvo B8RLE	MCV eVoRa	N38F	2023	
83	W	BV73MKM	Volvo B8RLE	MCV eVoRa	N38F	2023	
84	W	BV73MKN	Volvo B8RLE	MCV eVoRa	N38F	2023	
85	W	BV73MKO	Volvo B8RLE	MCV eVoRa	N38F	2023	

Established in 1921, C E Jeatt & Sons Ltd has continued trading as White Bus Services. A new route introduced in 1932 went through Windsor Great Park aimed to serve the numerous small settlements which ringed its southern boundary. To this day White Bus Services is the only operator to be allowed to run through the Great Park. Reflecting on the past, we illustrate the fleet with Volvo B8RLE 71, LF23DVW.
Mark Lyons

102	B	YG68TKA	Yutong TC9	Yutong	C37F	2018
103	B	YT68BYD	Irizar i4	Irizar	S70F	2018
104	B	YN66VYJ	Irizar i6	Irizar	C57F	2016
105	B	YN66VYH	Irizar i4	Irizar	S70F	2016
107	B	PO15GUE	MAN 19.290	Mobipeople Explorer	C59D	2015
108	B	PO64EXA	MAN 19.290	Mobipeople Explorer	S70D	2015
109	B	YN17CEO	Iveco Daily 70C17	Noone Turas 700	C29F	2017
110	B	PO64EXB	MAN 19.290	Mobipeople Explorer II	S70D	2015
111	B	PO64EXC	MAN 19.290	Mobipeople Explorer II	S70D	2015
	B	BV73MRX	Volvo B8R	Sunsundegui SC5	C41F	2023
	B	BV23NTT	Volvo B8R	Sunsundegui SB3	S72F	2023

Depots: Fernhill and White Bus: North Street, Windsor, SL4 4TF; Carthouse Lane, Woking, GU21 4YP and Longshot Lane, Bracknell, RG12 1RL. Baileys Coaches, Red Shute Hill Industrial Estate, Hermitage, Thatcham, RG18 9QL

WHITELAWS

Whitelaws Coaches Ltd, Lochpark Ind Est, Stonehouse, Lanark, ML9 3LR

SP54FML	Volvo B7R	Plaxton Profile	S70F	2005	Moffat & Williamson
5896WW	Volvo B7R	Plaxton Profile	C57F	2010	Woodstones, 2015
7062WW	Volvo B7R	Plaxton Profile	C57F	2010	Woodstones, 2015
KSL382	Volvo B11R	Plaxton Panther	C53F	2016	Logan, Dunloy, 2021
BD16YDJ	Volvo B8R	Sunsungedui SB3	S72F	2016	Diog, Glasgow, 2021
YX17OGF	Volvo B11R	Plaxton Panther	C48FT	2017	Logan, Dunloy, 2021
BV17CMO	Volvo B8RLE	MCV eVolution	N46F	2017	DeCoursey, Coventry, 2020
BV17CMU	Volvo B8RLE	MCV eVolution	N46F	2017	DeCoursey, Coventry, 2020
G1WHW	Volvo B8R	Sunsundegul SB3	S72F	2017	
G2WHW	Volvo B8R	Sunsundegul SB3	S72F	2017	
BU69XYS	Volvo B8R	Sunsundegul SB3	S72F	2020	Kiddles, Erith, 2023

	Volvo B8RLE 10.9m	MCV eVoRa	N37F	2021-22
G3WHW	G11WHW	G16WHW		G20WHW
G4WHW	G12WHW	G17WHW		W7WHW
G5WHW	G13WHW	G18WHW		W21WHW
G6WHW	G14WHW	G19WHW		W22WHW
G9WHW	G15WHW			

	Volvo B8R	Sunsundegul SB3	C72F	2022
191WHW	1716WW	7994WW		9396WW

Whitelaws was established in 1973 by George Whitelaw and the company remains owned by the Whitelaw family to this day. The current fleet is comprised entirely of Volvo products with B8RLE G20WHW shown.
Richard Godfrey

XELABUS

Sea View Coaches - Xelabus

Xelabus Limited, Unit 10 Barton Park, Eastleigh, SO50 6RR

301	HK21YSX	Ford Transit	Ford	M16	2021	
302	HG17UVL	Ford Transit	Ford	M16	2017	
620	GU73PKA	Isuzu AOS Grand Toro	AOS	C35F	2024	
432	YY66PFV	ADL E20D 8.9m	ADL Enviro 200	N29F	2017	
435	SN65OHH	ADL E20D 8.9m	ADL Enviro 200	N29F	2015	Britannia Parking, 2019
436	G7XEL	ADL E20D 10.8m	ADL Enviro 200	N39F	2018	Somerset PS, 2020
438	G5XEL	ADL E20D 10.8m	ADL Enviro 200	N39F	2018	Somerset PS, 2020
521	PA06AAU	Dennis Trident	East Lancs Lolyne	N47/27F	2006	Tyrer, Bolton, 2021
522	PA06AAV	Dennis Trident	East Lancs Lolyne	N47/27F	2006	Tyrer, Bolton, 2021
523	PA06AHL	Dennis Trident	East Lancs Lolyne	N47/27F	2006	Tyrer, Bolton, 2021
524	PA06AHO	Dennis Trident	East Lancs Lolyne	N47/27F	2006	Tyrer, Bolton, 2021
544	J16XEL	Volvo B5LH	Wrightbus Gemini 2	N41/27F	2011	Bakers, Biddulph, 2018
545	J18XEL	Volvo B5LH	Wrightbus Gemini 2	N41/27F	2011	Bakers, Biddulph, 2018
546	J20XEL	Volvo B5LH	Wrightbus Gemini 2	N41/27F	2011	Bakers, Biddulph, 2018
548-554		Scania N94 UD	East Lancs Omnidekka	N51/39F	2004	Nottingham Transport, '18
548 J17XEL	**549** J19XEL	**550** J7XEL	**551** L6XEL	**552** L7XEL	**553** J8XE	**554** N321KES
560	YN53RYF	Scania N94 UD	East Lancs Omnidekka	N45/29D	2003	Weardale MS, 2024
571	GB72XEL	ADL E40D	ADL Enviro 400 MMC	NC51/35F	2022	
572	PB72XEL	ADL E40D	ADL Enviro 400 MMC	NC51/35F	2022	
573	YX24OVZ	ADL E40D	ADL Enviro 400 MMC	NC51/35F	2024	
574	YX24OWA	ADL E40D	ADL Enviro 400 MMC	NC51/35F	2024	
575	-	ADL E40D	ADL Enviro 400 MMC	NC51/35F	on order	
576	-	ADL E40D	ADL Enviro 400 MMC	NC51/35F	on order	
607	YX67USP	Volvo B8R	Plaxton Panther	C53F	2018	Spencer Graham, Wigton
608	G5XCL	Mercedes-Benz Tourismo	Mercedes-Benz	C51FT	2016	
614	CB23XEL	Mercedes-Benz Tourismo	Mercedes-Benz	C53FT	2023	
615	GB23XCL	Mercedes-Benz Tourismo	Mercedes-Benz	C53FT	2023	
616	G12XEL	Mercedes-Benz Tourismo	Mercedes-Benz	C53FT	2023	
617	BF24AKO	Mercedes-Benz Tourismo	Mercedes-Benz	C53FT	2023	
619	G3XEL	Mercedes-Benz O510 Tourino	Mercedes-Benz	C53FT	20	
620	GJ73PKA	Isuzu AOS Grand Toro	AOS	C35F	2024	
621	GJ73PKC	Isuzu AOS Grand Toro	AOS	C35F	2024	
630	G13XEL	Scania K400 EB6	Irizar i6	C57FT	20	Taylor, Yeovil, 2024
631	G	Scania K400 EB6	Irizar i6	C35FT	2024	
801	KP51WAO	Volvo B7TL	Wrightbus Eclipse Gemini	N49/31F	2001	First, 2022

Southampton rail station is the starting point for Xelabus service to the science park. Now withdrawn Enviro 200 MMC G15SSP was seen there.
Steve Rice

YEOMANS

Yeomans - Lugg Valley

Yeomans Canyon Travel Ltd, Lugg Valley Travel Ltd; Lugg Valley Travel Ltd,
Old School Lane, Hereford, HR1 1EX

4	YO	YCV834	Scania K340 EB4	Caetano Levanté	C49FT	2007	
6	YO	YN53EKZ	Optare Solo M920	Optare	N31F	2003	
7	YO	FN03DXH	Volvo B12M	TransBus Paragon	C49FT	2003	
8	YO	YN08DDU	Scania OmniCity K270 UB	Scania	N53F	2008	Yarrington, Tetbury, 2018
9	YO	YT09FLM	Scania K340 EB4	Irizar PB	C49FT	2009	
11	YO	YJ58CCZ	Optare Solo M850	Optare	N31F	2008	
12	YO	YJ61JHF	Optare Versa V1110	Optare	N38F	2011	
15	YO	YJ54UBG	Optare Solo M990	Optare	N35F	2005	
17	YO	YT18YEO	Irizar i6	Irizar	C53FT	2018	
18	YO	YT15YTO	Irizar i6	Irizar	C53FT	2015	
19	YO	YT68YEO	Irizar i6	Irizar	C53FT	2019	
21	YO	YCT502	Volvo B12B	TransBus Paragon	C49FT	2003	
23	YO	YJ56WVW	Optare Solo M990	Optare	N35F	2006	
24	YO	YCT187	Scania K340 EB4	Irizar PB	C49FT	2007	
26	YO	YJ11EMK	Optare Solo M1020	Optare	N35F	2011	
28	LV	YN60BYZ	Dennis Javelin 12m	Plaxton Profile	S70F	2010	
30	YO	X185CHJ	Volvo B7TL	Alexander ALX400	N44/27F	2000	Applegates, Berkley, 2024

Hereford's free city bus service is currently undertaken by three Yutong E9s that joined Yeoman's fleet in 2023. Pictured in July 2024, Handsome Norman, YE73HZW, sets out on a another city circuit. *Bill Potter*

As well as National Express contracts, Yeomans operates a wide range of tours that are based at the Hereford premises. One of the three Irizar i6s is YN15YTO. *Bill Potter*

45	YO	FJ60EFZ	Volvo B9B	Caetano Levanté	C48FT	2010	
46	YO	FJ60HYG	Volvo B9B	Caetano Levanté	C48FT	2010	
47	YO	BK15AKJ	Scania K340 EB4	Caetano Levanté II	C48FT	2015	
48	YO	BK15AKN	Scania K340 EB4	Caetano Levanté II	C48FT	2015	
49	YO	BK15AKO	Scania K340 EB4	Caetano Levanté II	C48FT	2015	
50	YO	BV67JYG	Scania K410 EB6	Caetano Levanté II	C56FT	2017	
51	YO	BU18OSW	Scania K410 EB6	Caetano Levanté II	C56FT	2018	
52	YO	BV73ZTY	Scania K410 EB6	Caetano Levanté II	C56FT	2023	
53	YO	-	Scania K410 EB6	Caetano Levanté II	C56FT	2024	
54	YO	-	Scania K410 EB6	Caetano Levanté II	C56FT	2024	
55	YO	-	Scania K410 EB6	Caetano Levanté II	C56FT	2024	
71	YO	YE73HZW	Yutong ZK6890 BEVG	Yutong	N32D	2023	
72	YO	YE73HZX	Yutong ZK6890 BEVG	Yutong	N32D	2023	
73	YO	YE73HZZ	Yutong ZK6890 BEVG	Yutong	N32D	2023	
84	YO	YJ11EHB	Optare Solo M880 SL	Optare	N29F	2011	Coastal, Warton, 2015
85	YO	YJ11EHC	Optare Solo M880 SL	Optare	N29F	2011	Coastal, Warton, 2015
86	YO	YJ11EHD	Optare Solo M880 SL	Optare	N29F	2011	Coastal, Warton, 2015
87	YO	YJ11EHE	Optare Solo M880 SL	Optare	N29F	2011	Coastal, Warton, 2015
88	YO	YJ11EHF	Optare Solo M880 SL	Optare	N29F	2011	Coastal, Warton, 2015
89	YO	YJ17CVA	Optare Solo M9250 SR	Optare	N28F	2017	
90	YO	YJ17CVB	Optare Solo M9250 SR	Optare	N28F	2017	
91	YO	YJ17CVC	Optare Solo M9250 SR	Optare	N28F	2017	
92	YO	YJ17CVD	Optare Solo M9250 SR	Optare	N28F	2017	
93	YO	YJ68FVA	Optare Solo M9250 SR	Optare	N31F	2018	
94	YO	YJ68FVB	Optare Solo M9250 SR	Optare	N31F	2018	
95	YO	YJ68FVC	Optare Solo M9250 SR	Optare	N31F	2018	

Recent repaints at the Lugg Valley operation have been in a yellow and green scheme. Showing this is 117, YJ64DYF, one of five Optare Solo buses acquired from Scarlet Band in 2023. It was setting out from Leominster for the Shropshire town of Ludlow on route 490. *Bill Potter*

101	LV	YN11FUJ	Volvo B9R	Plaxton Panther	C53FT	2011	
102	LV	M22LVT	MercedesBenz Sprinter 616 cdi	UNVI Esker	C22F	2015	
104	u	MX61BCE	Wrightbus StreetLite WF	Wrightbus	N38F	2011	NIBS, Wickford, 2023
105	u	MX11CZR	Wrightbus StreetLite WF	Wrightbus	N38F	2011	NIBS, Wickford, 2023
106	LV	SF54ORA	Optare Solo M850	Optare	N28F	2004	Western Greyhound, 2015
109	LV	YK55ENU	Optare Solo M990	Optare	N35F	2005	
112	LV	BU51ADA	Optare Solo M920	Optare	N31F	2003	
117	LV	YJ64DYF	Optare Solo M900 SL	Optare	N32F	2014	Scarlet Band, 2023
118	LV	YJ64DYG	Optare Solo M900 SL	Optare	N32F	2014	Scarlet Band, 2023
119	LV	YJ64DYH	Optare Solo M900 SL	Optare	N32F	2014	Scarlet Band, 2023
120	LV	DJS203	Volvo B10M-62	Jonckheere Mistral 50	C53FT	2000	
122	LV	YJ58CCX	Optare Solo M950	Optare	N31F	2008	
123	LV	YJ57EHE	Optare Versa V1100	Optare	N38F	2007	Optare demonstrator, 2008
125	LV	YJ58CCY	Optare Solo M950	Optare	N31F	2008	
127	LV	YJ62FFN	Optare Solo M960	Optare	N33F	2012	
128	LV	YJ62FFO	Optare Solo M960	Optare	N33F	2012	
129	LV	L100LVT	Volvo B12M	Plaxton Paragon	C49FT	2013	
133	LV	YG52DGZ	Optare Solo M920	Optare	N35F	2002	
135	LV	YG52DGY	Optare Solo M920	Optare	N31F	2002	
182	LV	YJ64DXU	Optare Solo M900 SL	Optare	N32F	2014	Scarlet Band, 2023
183	LV	YJ64DXV	Optare Solo M900 SL	Optare	N32F	2014	Scarlet Band, 2023

Ancillary vehicle:

-	t	T414OUB	Optare Solo M920	Optare	Store	1999	Bakerbus, Biddulph, 2016

Depots: Old School Lane, Hereford, HR1 1EX (YO); Southern Avenue, Leominster, HR6 0QF (LV).

Vehicle Index

4WMS	Weardale
7WMS	Weardale
8WMS	Weardale
9WMS	Weardale
10WKS	Weardale
11WMS	Weardale
67UMN	Bus Vannin
98TNO	Vectare
101WMS	Weardale
1440PP	Eastern TH
166EMB	Vectare
191WHW	Whitelaws
200APB	Safeguard
2086PP	Eastern TH
219GRA	Beestons
221GRA	Beestons
224ENG	Vectare
226LRB	Beestons
229LRB	Beestons
247FCG	Safeguard
259JPA	Vectare
259VYC	Sanders Coaches
312YUK	Go-Coach
354TRT	Sanders Coaches
3680MN	Bus Vannin
378BNG	Vectare
3990ME	Sanders Coaches
410LMN	Bus Vannin
424DCD	Eastern TH
4940VF	Vectare
5048PP	Eastern TH
523FN	Beestons
524FN	Beestons
526FN	Beestons
536FN	Sanders Coaches
537FN	Sanders Coaches
538ELX	Vectare
538FN	Sanders Coaches
620DYE	Aintree Coachlines
638UYC	Connexions
644HAA	Safeguard
757FFR	Tanat Valley
789FAY	Connexions
808TYR	Tyrers
1482PP	Eastern TH
1642RH	Hornsby
1716WW	Whitelaws
1754PP	Eastern TH
1842PP	Eastern TH
2553RH	Hornsby
2732RH	Hornsby
3730RH	Hornsby
4078NU	Connexions
4092PP	Eastern TH
4178PP	Eastern TH
4312FM	Tyrers
5147UA	Connexions
5209UA	Connexions
5385WX	Connexions
5515LJ	Connexions
5611PP	Eastern TH
5896WW	Whitelaws
6053RH	Hornsby
6399PP	Eastern TH
6539FN	Connexions
6542FN	Sanders Coaches
6546FN	Sanders Coaches
7062WW	Whitelaws
7236PW	Vectare
7396LJ	Connexions
7419RH	Hornsby
7455RH	Hornsby
7994WW	Whitelaws
8333UR	Vectare
8548VF	Connexions
8955RH	Hornsby
9383MX	Vectare
9396WW	Whitelaws
9936UB	Connexions
A15TVC	Tanat Valley
A16TVC	Tanat Valley
A17SOE	Eastern TH
A132HLV	Aintree Coachlines
AA16FAR	Safeguard
AA16SAF	Safeguard
AA64SAF	Safeguard
AB60MTB	Newport
AC16FAR	Safeguard
AC73ACL	Aintree Coachlines
ACT540L	Delaine
AD03OCT	Delaine
AD04OCT	Delaine
AD05OCT	Delaine
AD07DBL	Delaine
AD08DBL	Delaine
AD09POF	Sanders Coaches
AD12DBL	Delaine
AD14DBL	Delaine
AD15DBL	Delaine
AD17DBL	Delaine
AD21DBL	Delaine
AD22DBL	Delaine
AD23DBL	Delaine
AD51DLD	Delaine
AD51DLE	Delaine
AD56DBL	Delaine
AD56DLD	Delaine
AD58DBL	Delaine
AD59DBL	Delaine
AD61DBL	Delaine
AD62DBL	Delaine
AD63DBL	Delaine
AD64DBL	Delaine
AD65DBL	Delaine
AD66DBL	Delaine
AD68DBL	Delaine
AD70DBL	Delaine
AD71DBL	Delaine
AD72DBL	Delaine
AD73DBL	Delaine
AD74DBL	Delaine
AE06GZR	Brylaine Travel
AE06TWU	Brylaine Travel
AE07DZB	Redline
AE07DZC	Redline
AE11FMF	Moffat & Williamson
AE12FGM	Reliance
AE54FMG	Vectare
AG02WMS	Weardale
AM05BUS	Faresaver
AP66ELV	Sanders Coaches
AT14NTC	Atlantic Travel
AT64KZT	Houston's
AU07DXS	Reliance
AU07DXT	Reliance
AU66JAK	Sanders Coaches
AUB170J	Connexions
AV62AUA	Sanders Coaches
AW53GBE	Townlynx
AX14GXS	Eastern TH
AY58CYJ	Travelmasters
B88BUS	JMB Travel
B144RWY	Connexions
BA15BXS	Reliance
BA58GHA	Compass Travel
BC05RVJ	Pilkingtons
BC05RVN	Pilkingtons
BC05RVO	Pilkingtons
BC05RVR	Pilkingtons
BC05RVU	Pilkingtons
BC24EHJ	Faresaver
BC24EHK	Faresaver
BC24EHL	Faresaver
BC24EHM	Faresaver
BC24EHN	Faresaver
BC24EKZ	Faresaver
BCF802	Beestons
BD12TDX	Warrington
BD12TEJ	Warrington
BD12TEO	Warrington
BD12TEY	Warrington
BD14KXR	UNO
BD14KXS	UNO
BD14KXT	UNO
BD14KXV	UNO
BD14KXW	UNO
BD16YDJ	Whitelaws
BD51YCR	Warrington
BD51YCS	Warrington
BF10LSX	Vision Bus
BF10LSY	Vision Bus
BF10LTA	Vision Bus
BF15KFJ	Faresaver
BF15KFL	Faresaver
BF16XPN	Newport
BF16XPO	Newport
BF16XPP	Newport
BF23CMK	Atlantic Travel
BF23CMO	Atlantic Travel
BF23CMU	Atlantic Travel
BF24AJU	Roberts Travel
BF24AJV	Roberts Travel
BF24AKJ	Roberts Travel
BF24AKK	Roberts Travel
BF24AKO	Xelabus
BF24AOA	Roberts Travel
BF59NHV	UNO
BF59NHX	UNO
BF59NHY	UNO
BF59NHZ	UNO
BF59NJJ	UNO
BF59NJK	UNO
BF59NJN	UNO
BF59NJO	UNO
BF62UYA	Tyrers
BF62UYB	Tyrers
BF62UYC	Tyrers
BF62UYD	Tyrers

A recent arrival with Beestons is partial open-top Scania BUS91R. *Mark Doggett*

Registration	Operator
BF62UYE	Tyrers
BF62UYG	Tyrers
BF62UYN	Atlantic Travel
BF62UYO	Reliance
BF62UYP	Atlantic Travel
BF63HEJ	Atlantic Travel
BF63HFA	Whippet
BF63HFB	Whippet
BF63HFC	Whippet
BF63ZRL	Travelmasters
BF65HTT	Landflight
BF65HTU	Landflight
BF65HVP	Vectare
BF65HVT	Ipswich Buses
BF65HVU	Ipswich Buses
BF65HVV	Ipswich Buses
BF65WHU	Travelmasters
BF67WFM	Landflight
BF68LCE	Eastern TH
BF68LCJ	Eastern TH
BF68LCK	Eastern TH
BF68LCM	Eastern TH
BF68LCN	Eastern TH
BF68ZHB	Cardiff Bus
BG14OOH	UNO
BG14OOX	UNO
BG14OOY	UNO
BG14OPA	UNO
BG14OPC	UNO
BG14OPD	UNO
BG14OPF	UNO
BG15BTY	Blackpool Transport
BG59FYB	Whippet
BG61SXK	Stotts Tours
BIG9781	Tyrers
BIG9782	Tyrers
BIG9783	Tyrers
BIG9784	Tyrers
BIL4710	Eastern TH
BIL7894	Eastern TH
BIL9406	Eastern TH
BJ11D2Z	Tyrers
BJ11DRZ	Vision Bus
BJ11DSE	Vision Bus
BJ11DSU	Vision Bus
BJ11DSV	Atlantic Travel
BJ11DSX	Tyrers
BJ11DSY	Vision Bus
BJ11DTF	Vision Bus
BJ11DTV	Vision Bus
BJ11DUA	Travelmasters
BJ11DUU	Vision Bus
BJ11DUV	Vision Bus
BJ11DVC	Travelmasters
BJ11DVF	Vision Bus
BJ11DVH	Atlantic Travel
BJ11DVL	Vision Bus
BJ11DVM	Vision Bus
BJ11DVN	Faresaver
BJ11DVO	Faresaver
BJ11DVP	Vision Bus
BJ11DVT	Faresaver
BJ11EAC	Faresaver
BJ11EAE	Reliance
BJ11EAO	Tyrers
BJ11EBL	Tyrers
BJ11EBM	Faresaver
BJ15AVX	Blackpool Transport
BJ15BEO	Blackpool Transport
BJ15BEU	Blackpool Transport
BJ15UVP	JMB Travel
BJ15UVV	JMB Travel
BJ15UVX	Blackpool Transport
BK10MFJ	Vision Bus
BK10MFU	Travelmasters
BK10MFV	Travelmasters
BK13NZM	Stotts Tours
BK13NZR	Stotts Tours
BK13NZS	Stotts Tours
BK13NZU	Stotts Tours
BK13XYF	Connexions
BK15AKJ	Yeomans
BK15AKN	Yeomans
BK15AKO	Yeomans
BL24FEG	Townlynx
BL24YFY	Tyrers
BL24YFZ	Tyrers
BN09FWR	White Bus
BN17JJY	Vectare
BN58BJJ	UNO
BN58BJK	UNO
BN58BJO	UNO
BN61MXC	Tyrers
BN61MXD	Atlantic Travel
BN61MXE	Tanat Valley
BN61MXF	Tyrers
BN61MXG	Tyrers
BN61MXH	Atlantic Travel
BN61MXJ	Stotts Tours

BN61MXL	Tyrers
BN61MXM	Stotts Tours
BN61MXR	Stotts Tours
BN61MXU	Stotts Tours
BN61MXY	Stotts Tours
BN61MYA	Stotts Tours
BN64CNY	Vectare
BP24GWW	Sanders Coaches
BP24GWX	Sanders Coaches
BR04AJV	Pilkingtons
BSK790	Moffat & Williamson
BT12AZN	Vectare
BT13LCT	Atlantic Travel
BT13YWE	Vectare
BT13YWF	Vectare
BT13ZCZ	Atlantic Travel
BT14DLX	Sanders Coaches
BT14DLZ	Sanders Coaches
BT63UUP	Vectare
BT63UUR	Vectare
BT63UUX	Vectare
BT66MVE	Whippet
BT66MVF	Whippet
BT66MVG	Whippet
BT66MVH	Whippet
BT66MVJ	Whippet
BT66MVK	Whippet
BT66MVL	Whippet
BT66UAP	JMB Travel
BT66UAR	JMB Travel
BT66UAS	JMB Travel
BU14EFV	Roberts Travel
BU14EGD	Minsterley Motors
BU14EHY	Vectare
BU16GZB	Vectare
BU16OZF	White Bus
BU16OZM	Minsterley Motors
BU16UYL	Lloyds
BU16UYM	Lloyds
BU18OSW	Yeomans
BU18YSM	Lloyds
BU18YSS	Lloyds
BU22WMS	Weardale
BU24WMS	Weardale
BU51ADA	Yeomans
BU51TOY	Faresaver
BU51WAY	Grant Palmer
BU52WAY	Grant Palmer
BU53WAY	Grant Palmer
BU54JAR	Warrington
BU54WAY	Grant Palmer
BU56WAY	Grant Palmer
BU57WAY	Grant Palmer
BU58WAY	Grant Palmer
BU59WAY	Grant Palmer
BU69XYS	Whitelaws
BUS91A	Beestons
BUS91C	Beestons
BUS91D	Beestons
BUS91E	Beestons
BUS91R	Beestons
BV10WVP	Faresaver
BV10WVS	Vision Bus
BV10WVT	Vision Bus
BV10WVW	Vision Bus
BV16YNJ	Newport
BV16YNK	Newport
BV17CMO	Whitelaws
BV17CMU	Whitelaws
BV19LPA	Newport
BV19LPC	Newport
BV19YHS	Roberts Travel
BV19YHT	Roberts Travel
BV20HOA	Roberts Travel
BV20UZK	Roberts Travel
BV21ONO	UNO
BV21ONU	UNO
BV21OOA	Sanders Coaches
BV21OOB	Sanders Coaches
BV21OOC	Sanders Coaches
BV21OOD	Sanders Coaches
BV21OOW	Lloyds
BV22HBG	Lloyds
BV22HBH	Reliance
BV22HBJ	Reliance
BV22HBN	Sanders Coaches
BV22HBO	Sanders Coaches
BV22WRJ	Atlantic Travel
BV22WRK	Atlantic Travel
BV22WRL	Atlantic Travel
BV23NNG	Newport
BV23NNH	Newport
BV23NNJ	Newport
BV23NNM	Newport
BV23NNO	Newport
BV23NNP	Newport
BV23NNR	Newport
BV23NNU	Newport
BV23NNZ	Sanders Coaches
BV23NUU	Sanders Coaches
BV23NUW	Sanders Coaches
BV23NTA	Tanat Valley
BV23NTT	White Bus
BV23NTU	White Bus
BV23NTX	Tanat Valley
BV23NUB	Connexions
BV23NUJ	Safeguard
BV23NUM	Safeguard
BV23NUP	Safeguard
BV23NVH	Go-Coach
BV24LME	Lloyds
BV24LMF	Lloyds
BV24LMJ	Lloyds
BV24LMK	Lloyds
BV24LML	Lloyds
BV24LMM	Lloyds
BV24LMO	Lloyds
BV24LMU	Lloyds
BV24LMX	Lloyds
BV24LNK	White Bus
BV24LPN	Warrington
BV24LPU	Warrington
BV24LPZ	Warrington
BV24LRA	Warrington
BV24LRE	Warrington
BV24LRK	Warrington
BV24LRO	Warrington
BV24LUF	Warrington
BV24LUJ	Warrington
BV24LUL	UNO
BV24LUO	UNO
BV24LUP	UNO
BV24LUR	White Bus
BV24LUT	UNO
BV24LUW	UNO
BV55UCT	Eastern TH
BV55UCW	Eastern TH
BV57VHE	UNO
BV57VHF	UNO
BV57VHH	UNO
BV57VHJ	UNO
BV66VHF	White Bus
BV67JYG	Yeomans
BV69LME	Roberts Travel
BV69LMJ	Roberts Travel
BV69LNW	Roberts Travel
BV69LNX	Roberts Travel
BV69LNY	Roberts Travel
BV69LNZ	Roberts Travel
BV69LTZ	Landflight
BV72KKA	Sanders Coaches
BV72KKB	Sanders Coaches
BV72KKC	Sanders Coaches
BV72KKD	Sanders Coaches
BV72KOD	Safeguard
BV73MHX	Tanat Valley
BV73MHY	Tanat Valley
BV73MJE	Faresaver
BV73MJF	Faresaver
BV73MJJ	Faresaver
BV73MJK	Faresaver
BV73MKF	White Bus
BV73MKG	White Bus
BV73MKJ	White Bus
BV73MKK	White Bus
BV73MKL	White Bus
BV73MKM	White Bus
BV73MKN	White Bus
BV73MKO	White Bus
BV73MLN	Lloyds
BV73MLO	Lloyds
BV73MLX	Redline
BV73MLY	Redline
BV73MLZ	Redline
BV73MME	Redline
BV73MRX	White Bus
BV73MSO	Vectare
BV73MTE	Redline
BV73MTF	Redline
BV73MTJ	Redline
BV73MTK	Redline
BV73MTZ	DRM
BV73MUY	Tanat Valley
BV73ZTY	Yeomans
BW67EVP	JMB Travel
BW67EVR	JMB Travel
BX07AZJ	Sanders Coaches
BX07OOH	Townlynx
BX07OPH	Townlynx
BX07OPW	Townlynx
BX11PTO	Compass Travel
BX12CVK	Faresaver
BX12CVL	Travelmasters
BX12CVM	Faresaver
BX12CVP	Travelmasters
BX55XMH	Moffat & Williamson
BX55XNO	Hornsby
BX55XNP	Moffat & Williamson
BX56VSJ	UNO
BX56VSL	UNO
BX56VSM	UNO
BX56VSN	UNO
BX64AEU	Weardale
BX64AEV	Globe
C3BCP	Roberts Travel
C6BCP	Roberts Travel
C6BUS	Weardale
C14UNO	UNO
C16UNO	UNO
C17UNO	UNO

Illustrating the colours for Cardiff routes 44 and 45 to St Mellons is Yutong 415, CE71YCN. It was pictured while heading out of the city along Kingsway. *Steve Rice*

Registration	Operator
C434HHL	Marshalls
C666FMP	Weardale
CA05GHA	Grant Palmer
CA52JJZ	Globe
CB23XEL	Xelabus
CC04GAL	Vectare
CC21GAL	Vectare
CC71GAL	Vectare
CE21GAL	Vectare
CE22WWH	Newport
CE22WWJ	Newport
CE22WWK	Newport
CE22WWL	Newport
CE22WWM	Newport
CE22WWN	Newport
CE22WWO	Newport
CE22WWP	Newport
CE22WWR	Newport
CE22WWT	Newport
CE22WXA	Newport
CE22WXB	Newport
CE22WXC	Newport
CE22WXD	Newport
CE22WXF	Newport
CE22WXG	Newport
CE23ZDJ	Newport
CE23ZDK	Newport
CE23ZDL	Newport
CE23ZDM	Newport
CE23ZGA	Newport
CE23ZGB	Newport
CE23ZGC	Newport
CE23ZGD	Newport
CE23ZGF	Newport
CE23ZGG	Newport
CE23ZGH	Newport
CE23ZGJ	Newport
CE23ZGK	Newport
CE23ZGL	Newport
CE23ZGM	Newport
CE23ZGN	Newport
CE63NYL	Cardiff Bus
CE63NYM	Cardiff Bus
CE63NYN	Cardiff Bus
CE63NYO	Cardiff Bus
CE63NYP	Cardiff Bus
CE63NYR	Cardiff Bus
CE63NYS	Cardiff Bus
CE63NYT	Cardiff Bus
CE63NYU	Cardiff Bus
CE63NYV	Cardiff Bus
CE63NYW	Cardiff Bus
CE63NYX	Cardiff Bus
CE63NYY	Cardiff Bus
CE63NYZ	Cardiff Bus
CE63NZA	Cardiff Bus
CE63NZB	Cardiff Bus
CE63NZC	Cardiff Bus
CE63NZD	Cardiff Bus
CE63NZF	Cardiff Bus
CE63NZG	Cardiff Bus
CE63NZH	Cardiff Bus
CE63NZJ	Cardiff Bus
CE63NZK	Cardiff Bus
CE63NZM	Cardiff Bus
CE63NZN	Cardiff Bus
CE63NZO	Cardiff Bus
CE63NZP	Cardiff Bus
CE63NZR	Cardiff Bus
CE63NZS	Cardiff Bus
CE63NZT	Cardiff Bus
CE71GAL	Vectare
CE71YCB	Cardiff Bus
CE71YCD	Cardiff Bus
CE71YCF	Cardiff Bus
CE71YCG	Cardiff Bus
CE71YCH	Cardiff Bus
CE71YCJ	Cardiff Bus
CE71YCK	Cardiff Bus
CE71YCL	Cardiff Bus
CE71YCM	Cardiff Bus
CE71YCN	Cardiff Bus
CE71YCO	Cardiff Bus
CE71YCP	Cardiff Bus
CE71YCR	Cardiff Bus
CE71YDA	Cardiff Bus
CE71YDB	Cardiff Bus
CE71YDC	Cardiff Bus
CE71YDD	Cardiff Bus
CE71YDF	Cardiff Bus
CE71YDG	Cardiff Bus
CE71YDH	Cardiff Bus
CE71YDJ	Cardiff Bus
CE71YXD	Cardiff Bus
CE71YXF	Cardiff Bus
CE71YXG	Cardiff Bus

The Scania Fencer f1 made its debut in 2021 and sold as a Scania product. Higer was founded in Suzhou, China, at the end of 1998 and builds the Fencer bodies in China. Cardiff took two in 2023 with 701, CN73AZX, pictured as is passes through Wenvoe on its way to Barry. *Richard Godfrey*

CE71YXH	Cardiff Bus	CK24AUW	Cardiff Bus	CN07KZM	Aintree Coachlines
CE71YXJ	Cardiff Bus	CK24AUX	Cardiff Bus	CN07KZM	Aintree Coachlines
CE71YXK	Cardiff Bus	CK24AUY	Newport	CN09EFJ	Cardiff Bus
CE71YXL	Cardiff Bus	CK24AVC	Cardiff Bus	CN09EFK	Cardiff Bus
CE71YXM	Cardiff Bus	CK24AVG	Cardiff Bus	CN09EFL	Cardiff Bus
CE71YXN	Cardiff Bus	CK24AVJ	Cardiff Bus	CN11EFX	Houston's
CE71YXO	Cardiff Bus	CK24AVL	Newport	CN11FBE	Eastern TH
CE71YXP	Cardiff Bus	CK24AVM	Newport	CN11KFY	Cardiff Bus
CE71YXR	Cardiff Bus	CK24AVN	Cardiff Bus	CN11KFZ	Cardiff Bus
CE71YXT	Cardiff Bus	CK24AVO	Cardiff Bus	CN17BGK	Cardiff Bus
CE71YXU	Cardiff Bus	CK24AVP	Newport	CN17BGO	Cardiff Bus
CE71YXV	Cardiff Bus	CK24AVT	Cardiff Bus	CN17EYL	Cardiff Bus
CE72YRL	Newport	CK24AVU	Cardiff Bus	CN17EYM	Cardiff Bus
CE72YRM	Newport	CK24AVV	Newport	CN17EYN	Cardiff Bus
CG15BUS	JMB Travel	CK24AVW	Newport	CN17EYO	Cardiff Bus
CH04CAT	Warrington	CK24AVX	Cardiff Bus	CN17EYP	Cardiff Bus
CH06CAT	Warrington	CK24AVZ	Cardiff Bus	CN17EYR	Cardiff Bus
CH12CAT	Warrington	CK24AWA	Newport	CN17EYS	Cardiff Bus
CH56CAT	Warrington	CK24AWF	Cardiff Bus	CN17EYU	Cardiff Bus
CH57CAT	Warrington	CK24AWG	Cardiff Bus	CN17EYV	Cardiff Bus
CH58CAT	Warrington	CK24AWH	Newport	CN17EYW	Cardiff Bus
CH59CAT	Warrington	CK24AWM	Cardiff Bus	CN17FZS	Cardiff Bus
CH62CAT	Warrington	CK24AWN	Cardiff Bus	CN17FZT	Cardiff Bus
CK24AUH	Newport	CK24AWO	Newport	CN17FZU	Cardiff Bus
CK24AUJ	Cardiff Bus	CK73ATY	Newport	CN17FZV	Cardiff Bus
CK24AUM	Cardiff Bus	CK73AVR	Newport	CN17FZW	Cardiff Bus
CK24AUN	Newport	CK73AVW	Newport	CN17FZX	Cardiff Bus
CK24AUO	Newport	CK73AWC	Newport	CN17FZY	Cardiff Bus
CK24AUP	Cardiff Bus	CK73AWJ	Newport	CN17FZZ	Cardiff Bus
CK24AUT	Cardiff Bus	CN04NLL	Townlynx	CN17GNX	Cardiff Bus
CK24AUU	Newport	CN06GFG	Connexions	CN17GNY	Cardiff Bus

CN57BJU	Cardiff Bus	D16WNS	Weardale	ET03WAE	Townlynx
CN58FFY	Cardiff Bus	D574LFX	Connexions	ET16ZVM	Falcon
CN58FFZ	Cardiff Bus	DC16OBY	Houston's	EU05ECV	Eastern TH
CN59CKU	Cardiff Bus	DC56PAN	Vectare	EU07FVN	Eastern TH
CN59CKV	Cardiff Bus	DJS203	Yeomans	EU08WNE	Stotts Tours
CN59CKX	Cardiff Bus	DK04NNB	Townlynx	EU09AUK	Eastern TH
CN59CKY	Cardiff Bus	DK09DZD	Sanders Coaches	EU09NYO	Eastern TH
CN59CLF	Cardiff Bus	DK09DZE	DRM	EU10NVP	Eastern TH
CN61FBB	Moffat & Williamson	DK09DZH	Sanders Coaches	EU10NVR	Eastern TH
CN61FBD	Moffat & Williamson	DK09ELH	Warrington	EU10NVS	Eastern TH
CN64FWJ	Cardiff Bus	DK09ELJ	Warrington	EU10NVT	Eastern TH
CN64FWK	Cardiff Bus	DK09ELO	Warrington	EU12HXW	Eastern TH
CN64FWL	Cardiff Bus	DK09ELU	Warrington	EU12HXY	Eastern TH
CN64FWM	Cardiff Bus	DK09ELV	Warrington	EU13EBK	Eastern TH
CN64FWO	Cardiff Bus	DK09ELW	Warrington	EU13EBL	Eastern TH
CN64FWP	Cardiff Bus	DK09ELX	Warrington	EU15AZT	Eastern TH
CN64FWR	Cardiff Bus	DK09EMJ	Warrington	EU23BZL	Eastern TH
CN64FWS	Cardiff Bus	DK09EMM	Warrington	EU24LWT	Eastern TH
CN64FWT	Cardiff Bus	DK09EMV	Warrington	EU24LWV	Eastern TH
CN64FWU	Cardiff Bus	DK09EMX	Warrington	EU58AXX	Eastern TH
CN65AAE	Cardiff Bus	DK09ENC	Warrington	EU58BLJ	Eastern TH
CN65AAF	Cardiff Bus	DK09NRN	Warrington	EU58BRX	Eastern TH
CN65AAJ	Cardiff Bus	DK09NRNO	Warrington	EU59BFK	Eastern TH
CN65AAK	Cardiff Bus	DK09NRU	Warrington	EU59BHX	Eastern TH
CN65AAO	Cardiff Bus	DK09NSZ	Warrington	EU60CAV	Eastern TH
CN65AAU	Cardiff Bus	DK12BXL	Moffat & Williamson	EU60CBF	Eastern TH
CN65AAV	Cardiff Bus	DK18AEL	Nottingham Community	EU62FBO	Eastern TH
CN65AAX	Cardiff Bus	DK18AHZ	Nottingham Community	EU62FDF	Eastern TH
CN65AAY	Cardiff Bus	DK19AWF	Nottingham Community	EU64CVP	Eastern TH
CN65AAZ	Cardiff Bus	DK57OPZ	Eastern TH	EU64CVR	Eastern TH
CN65ABF	Cardiff Bus	DK61DJD	Moffat & Williamson	EU65EOG	Eastern TH
CN65ABK	Cardiff Bus	DK62OSZ	Moffat & Williamson	EU65EOH	Eastern TH
CN65ABO	Cardiff Bus	DK64ETD	Moffat & Williamson	EU65EOJ	Eastern TH
CN65ABU	Cardiff Bus	DK64GAL	Vectare	EU65EOK	Eastern TH
CN65ABV	Cardiff Bus	DK65GAL	Vectare	EU65EOL	Eastern TH
CN65ABX	Cardiff Bus	DM09DRM	DRM	EU65EOM	Eastern TH
CN65ABZ	Cardiff Bus	DM10DRM	DRM	EU66AVB	Eastern TH
CN65ACF	Cardiff Bus	DM11OWD	Lloyds	EU66AVC	Eastern TH
CN65ACJ	Cardiff Bus	DM12DRM	DRM	EU66AVD	Eastern TH
CN65ACO	Cardiff Bus	DM56BUS	Connexions	EU66AVF	Eastern TH
CN71HFM	Tanat Valley	DM63DRM	DRM	EU66AVG	Eastern TH
CN71HFO	Tanat Valley	DM66DRM	DRM	EX63UZV	Eastern TH
CN71HFP	Tanat Valley	DMN16R	Bus Vannin	EX63UZW	Eastern TH
CN73AZX	Cardiff Bus	DRM195S	Beestons	EY07AXH	Travelmasters
CN73AZZ	Cardiff Bus	DRZ1305	JMB Travel	EY07AXJ	Travelmasters
CSZ7913	Warrington	DSU116	Vectare	EY07AXK	Travelmasters
CT19XCZ	Lloyds	DT17UHP	Houston's	EY07AXM	Travelmasters
CT21GAL	Vectare	DU12NCY	Tanat Valley	F13BUS	Weardale
CU12MDN	Cardiff Bus	DU60LOJ	Ipswich Buses	FA54VER	Faresaver
CU15PJO	Minsterley Motors	DU61DVY	Lynx	FB05KRE	Roberts Travel
CVE12V	Connexions	DX17EOS	Lloyds	FB05KRF	Roberts Travel
CX06EAK	Aintree Coachlines	DY61AXB	Lloyds	FB05KSK	Roberts Travel
CX11FZR	Cardiff Bus	DY61AXC	Lloyds	FB05KSN	Roberts Travel
CX11FZS	Cardiff Bus	E6WMS	Weardale	FC03VEM	Roberts Travel
CX11FZT	Cardiff Bus	E7ATD	Falcon	FC03VEY	Roberts Travel
CX12FLD	Cardiff Bus	E13BUS	Weardale	FC03VFM	Roberts Travel
CX12FLE	Cardiff Bus	E19SCL	Sanders Coaches	FC03VGN	Roberts Travel
CX12FLF	Cardiff Bus	E21AMX	Sanders Coaches	FC03VGT	Roberts Travel
CX12FNG	Cardiff Bus	E21APY	Sanders Coaches	FD54JYA	Lynx
CX12FNH	Cardiff Bus	E100AFW	Delaine	FD54JYB	Lynx
CX12FTT	Cardiff Bus	EA18NZZ	Lloyds	FD54JYC	Lynx
CX14EMS	Eastern TH	EB60MTB	Newport	FD54JYF	Lynx
CX55EAP	Aintree Coachlines	EC23SHA	Sanders Coaches	FF04JXS	Roberts Travel
CX55EAY	Aintree Coachlines	ED22WRD	Sanders Coaches	FF04JXV	Roberts Travel
CX55EBC	Aintree Coachlines	ED23SAN	Sanders Coaches	FHJ565	Beestons
CX55EBF	Aintree Coachlines	EDR793	Hornsby	FJ04SNV	Sargeant
CX65BUH	Warrington	EE08OXF	Minsterley Motors	FJ08BYX	Vision Bus
CX65BUJ	Warrington	EM09BUS	JMB Travel	FJ08FYK	Travelmasters
CY11GNK	Lloyds	EN16WKT	Vectare	FJ08KLU	Weardale
CY12EMS	Eastern TH	ESU912	Connexions	FJ08OEW	Weardale

New arrivals with Faresaver are a further six Volvo B8RLEs. Pictured in Dorchester Street in Bath on 30th July 2024 is BC24EHK. *Mark Lyons*

Registration	Operator
FJ54ZCL	Minsterley Motors
FJ55BZP	Connexions
FJ55DZL	Newport
FJ56PFG	DRM
FJ57CZM	Sanders Coaches
FJ57CZN	Sanders Coaches
FJ60FFZ	Yeomans
FJ60HYG	Yeomans
FJ61EYL	Travelmasters
FM55NVH	Pilkingtons
FN03DXH	Yeomans
FN06FLD	Globe
FN63PWU	Weardale
FSU375	Moffat & Williamson
FT11EBT	Globe
FW5696	Marshalls
FWA475V	Connexions
FX09YKF	Travelmasters
FX57GUF	Tyrers
FX57LKM	Tyrers
FY13FYE	Tanat Valley
G1WHW	Whitelaws
G2WHW	Whitelaws
G3WHW	Whitelaws
G3XEL	Xelabus
G4WHW	Whitelaws
G5WHW	Whitelaws
G5XCL	Xelabus
G5XEL	Xelabus
G6WHW	Whitelaws
G7XEL	Xelabus
G9WHW	Whitelaws
G11WHW	Whitelaws
G12WHW	Whitelaws
G12XEL	Xelabus
G13WHW	Whitelaws
G13XEL	Xelabus
G14WHW	Whitelaws
G15WHW	Whitelaws
G16WHW	Whitelaws
G17WHW	Whitelaws
G18WHW	Whitelaws
G19REL	Reliance
G19WHW	Whitelaws
G20WHW	Whitelaws
GB03ACL	Aintree Coachlines
GB04FLG	Vectare
GB05FLG	Vectare
GB23XCL	Xelabus
GB54FLG	Vectare
GB55FLG	Vectare
GB72XEL	Xelabus
GD09JHX	Travelmasters
GD10MVM	Ipswich Buses
GIB1067	Weardale
GIB6197	Weardale
GJ17FWA	Roberts Travel
GJ73PKA	Xelabus
GJ73PKC	Xelabus
GK03JUC	Vectare
GL19BES	Globe
GN59CDV	Moffat & Williamson
GN59FFM	Moffat & Williamson
GN59FFR	Moffat & Williamson
GO03WMS	Weardale
GO05WMS	Weardale
GO16WMS	Weardale
GO22WMS	Weardale
GO23WMS	Weardale
GO24WMS	Weardale
GO59WMS	Weardale
GO72WMS	Weardale
GP55BUS	Grant Palmer
GP56BUS	Grant Palmer
GT11EBT	Globe
GU64SAF	Safeguard
GU73PKA	Xelabus
GX07HUJ	Warrington
GX13FSN	Compass Travel
GX13FSO	Compass Travel
GX13FSP	Compass Travel
GX13FSS	Compass Travel
GX13FSU	Compass Travel
GX14NHL	Nottingham Community
GX23CZE	Houston's
GX23CZF	Houston's
GX57AFV	Compass Travel
GX58GLY	Warrington
GX58GLZ	Warrington
GX62CJO	Compass Travel
GX62CJU	Compass Travel
GX62CKP	Compass Travel
GX62CMY	Compass Travel
GX62CNN	Compass Travel
GX62COA	Compass Travel
GX62CSF	Compass Travel

Seen in its home town of Barnsley, Globe KX10DVH is one of four Enviro 300s operated. *John Young*

GX68LNE	Vectare
GX72BGK	UNO
GX73AYB	Houston's
GX73AYD	Houston's
GY66WYW	Minsterley Motors
HA10SRG	Warrington
HF54HFO	Sanders Coaches
HF54HFP	Sanders Coaches
HF54HHA	Sanders Coaches
HG17UVL	Xelabus
HIL2464	Houston's
HIL5657	Falcon
HK21YSX	Xelabus
HK22HKW	Falcon
HK22RVF	Falcon
HK69FYR	Falcon
HKF151	Aintree Coachlines
HM24SAN	Sanders Coaches
HMN689	Bus Vannin
HN15UZU	Tanat Valley
HN16XOB	Falcon
HN64DAO	Falcon
HRN249G	Aintree Coachlines
HRZ6499	Vision Bus
HV20HRV	Sanders Coaches
HV22HJN	Falcon
HV22HLX	Vectare
HV22HNG	Vectare
HY68AYS	Vectare
IUI6411	Connexions
J7XEL	Xelabus
J8XE	Xelabus
J16XEL	Xelabus
J17XEL	Xelabus
J18XEL	Xelabus
J19XEL	Xelabus
J20XEL	Xelabus
J200RTG	Roberts Travel
J300RTG	Roberts Travel
J800CXB	Connexions
JC72ACL	Aintree Coachlines
JCK892	Aintree Coachlines
JFZ7018	Vectare
JFZ9036	Aintree Coachlines
JGV929	Vectare
JJD472D	Go-Coach
JRZ3262	Tyrers
JRZ3263	Tyrers
JRZ3267	Tyrers
JRZ3268	Tyrers
JRZ3269	Tyrers
JRZ8513	Tyrers
JRZ8514	Tyrers
JSU721	Connexions
JW16BUS	Vectare
K10CTN	Nottingham Community
K11CTN	Nottingham Community
K12CTN	Nottingham Community
K13CTN	Nottingham Community
K14CTN	Nottingham Community
K16CTN	Nottingham Community
K18CTN	Nottingham Community
K19CTN	Nottingham Community
K20CTN	Nottingham Community
K25CTN	Nottingham Community
K26CTN	Nottingham Community
K30CTN	Nottingham Community
K33CTN	Nottingham Community
K40CTN	Nottingham Community
K44CTN	Nottingham Community
K66CTN	Nottingham Community
K100ACL	Aintree Coachlines
K200CXB	Connexions
KB07OXF	Redline
KBK750	Faresaver
KCK381H	Aintree Coachlines
KDX108	Vectare
KE12OEY	Atlantic Travel
KE66BVO	Moffat & Williamson
KF52NBN	Redline
KFK941	White Bus
KM21OXK	Nottingham Community
KM55KMH	Redline
KMN204L	Bus Vannin
KMN210L	Bus Vannin
KMN214U	Bus Vannin
KMN215U	Bus Vannin
KMN218U	Bus Vannin
KMN219U	Bus Vannin
KMN222U	Bus Vannin
KMN504	Bus Vannin
KN52NDG	Newport
KN52NDY	Newport
KN52NEO	Newport
KN52NEU	Newport
KN52NEY	Newport
KN52NFA	Newport
KP02PVO	Vectare
KP12BUS	Sanders Coaches

KP14ZDK	Lloyds
KP21OZT	Nottingham Community
KP21PCU	Nottingham Community
KP51WAO	Xelabus
KSL382	Whitelaws
KT17YKS	Travelmasters
KTL780	Delaine
KU02YBP	Townlynx
KV02URL	Newport
KV02URM	Newport
KV02URS	Newport
KV02URY	Townlynx
KV02USB	Newport
KV02USH	Newport
KV02USM	Newport
KV60WDF	DRM
KW68VWC	Moffat & Williamson
KX04RVJ	Brylaine Travel
KX07HDF	Globe
KX07HDU	Globe
KX07HEU	Globe
KX07HEV	Globe
KX07HFA	Globe
KX07HFC	Globe
KX08HLR	Globe
KX08HME	Grant Palmer
KX08HMF	Vectare
KX10DVF	Globe
KX10DVG	Globe
KX10DVH	Globe
KX10DVJ	Globe
KX10DVM	Globe
KX14FHJ	Falcon
KX14FHK	Falcon
KX14FJE	Houston's
KX15BLN	Stotts Tours
KX18NMM	Falcon
KX56TXZ	Moffat & Williamson
KX57BWD	Delaine
KX58GSZ	Globe
KX58GUW	Ipswich Buses
KX58GVE	Falcon
KX59CYW	Grant Palmer
KX59DLU	Newport
KX59GNY	Ipswich Buses
KX60DVO	Globe
KX60DVP	Globe
KX61GDU	Moffat & Williamson

KX61GDV	Moffat & Williamson
KX61GDY	Moffat & Williamson
KX61GEJ	Moffat & Williamson
KX61GEK	Moffat & Williamson
KX61GEU	Moffat & Williamson
KX61GFA	Moffat & Williamson
KX72CWO	Newport
KY63VTC	Houston's
KY63VTJ	Pilkingtons
L6XEL	Xelabus
L7XEL	Xelabus
L8XEL	Vectare
L9XEL	Vectare
L25WYN	Lloyds
L50LOW	Connexions
L100LVT	Yeomans
L600CKB	Connexions
LB02YXG	Vectare
LB02YXK	Vectare
LC06WYN	Lloyds
LC07WYN	Lloyds
LC08WYN	Lloyds
LC14WYN	Lloyds
LC18ZSL	Lloyds
LC61WYN	Lloyds
LC62WYN	Lloyds
LC66WYN	Lloyds
LC73WYN	Lloyds
LD72XZS	UNO
LF18AWH	UNO
LF18AWJ	UNO
LF18AWM	UNO
LF18AWN	UNO
LF18AWP	UNO
LF18AWR	UNO
LF23DVW	White Bus
LF52UPO	Redline
LF52USV	Vectare
LF52ZNZ	Travelmasters
LF52ZSD	Vectare
LF55CYW	Vision Bus
LF55CZB	Hornsby
LF69UXJ	UNO
LF72DUV	Safeguard
LFZ8051	Aintree Coachlines
LG02FCM	Pilkingtons
LG02FCU	Pilkingtons
LG02FEO	Pilkingtons

LG52XZR	Weardale
LJ04LDL	Lynx
LJ04LEU	Lynx
LJ04LFG	Warrington
LJ04LGC	Warrington
LJ04LGF	Warrington
LJ04LGG	Warrington
LJ04LGK	Warrington
LJ07ECX	Townlynx
LJ08CYP	Warrington
LJ09CCF	Delaine
LJ09CCK	Go-Coach
LJ09CCN	Delaine
LJ09CCO	Delaine
LJ09KPK	Go-Coach
LJ09KPL	Redline
LJ09KPZ	Redline
LJ09KRD	Go-Coach
LJ11AEO	Vision Bus
LJ11AEP	Vision Bus
LJ11AET	Vision Bus
LJ11AEU	Vision Bus
LJ11AEV	Vision Bus
LJ12BYW	UNO
LJ13GKO	Vision Bus
LJ13GKP	Vision Bus
LJ13GLF	Vision Bus
LJ13GLK	Vision Bus
LJ16EZN	UNO
LJ16EZP	UNO
LJ16EZR	UNO
LJ16LMK	Nottingham Community
LJ16LMM	Nottingham Community
LJ16LMO	Nottingham Community
LJ16LMU	Nottingham Community
LJ16LMV	Nottingham Community
LJ16LMX	Nottingham Community
LJ16LMY	Nottingham Community
LJ16LMZ	Nottingham Community
LJ16LNA	Nottingham Community
LJ16LNB	Nottingham Community
LJ16LNC	Nottingham Community
LJ16LNE	Nottingham Community
LJ16LNF	Nottingham Community
LJ53BFU	Lynx
LJ53BGU	Lynx
LJ56ONN	Grant Palmer
LJ56VTO	Newport

Tanat Valley operates just two double-decks. VDL DB300 501, LJ59LVX, is seen in Oswestry.
Chris Clegg

Registration	Operator
LJ57NGF	Weardale
LJ57USU	Vectare
LJ58AVE	Vectare
LJ58GCF	White Bus
LJ59LVX	Tanat Valley
LJ60AXH	Vision Bus
LJ60AXK	Vision Bus
LJ60AXM	Vision Bus
LJ60AXN	Vision Bus
LK03NHF	Vectare
LK03NHG	Vectare
LK03NHV	Vectare
LK03NLG	Eastern TH
LK04HYY	Warrington
LK06FLB	Redline
LK07BEV	Townlynx
LK07ELJ	Townlynx
LK08DWA	Vectare
LK08DWV	UNO
LK08FMP	Warrington
LK08FMU	Warrington
LK08FMV	Warrington
LK09CZS	Vision Bus
LK09EKP	Go-Coach
LK09EKU	Go-Coach
LK53KVZ	Vectare
LK55KKH	Redline
LK55KKO	Newport
LK55KKZ	Redline
LK57AXF	Warrington
LK57AXT	Go-Coach
LK57AYB	Go-Coach
LK58CNV	Warrington
LK58EDP	Vision Bus
LK58EDP	Vision Bus
LK58EDR	Vision Bus
LK58KHE	Aintree Coachlines
LK58KHO	Aintree Coachlines
LK58KHR	Aintree Coachlines
LK58KHU	Warrington
LK59DYY	Aintree Coachlines
LK59DZL	Aintree Coachlines
LK60AFY	UNO
LK60AGY	UNO
LL07WYN	Lloyds
LL09WYN	Lloyds
LL71SHA	Sanders Coaches
LM18DZA	Moffat & Williamson
LM18DZB	Moffat & Williamson
LM18DZC	Moffat & Williamson
LM18DZD	Moffat & Williamson
LM18DZE	Moffat & Williamson
LM18DZF	Moffat & Williamson
LM18DZG	Moffat & Williamson
LMN103J	Bus Vannin
LMN171K	Bus Vannin
LMN172K	Bus Vannin
LMN173K	Bus Vannin
LMN174K	Bus Vannin
LMN175K	Bus Vannin
LMN176K	Bus Vannin
LMN177N	Bus Vannin
LMN178N	Bus Vannin
LMN179N	Bus Vannin
LMN180N	Bus Vannin
LMN181N	Bus Vannin
LMN182N	Bus Vannin
LMN225D	Bus Vannin
LMN226H	Bus Vannin
LMN227H	Bus Vannin
LMN228H	Bus Vannin
LMN229H	Bus Vannin
LMN230H	Bus Vannin
LN19TXP	Moffat & Williamson
LN20PWF	Moffat & Williamson
LN51KXV	Newport
LNN353	Marshalls
LO69AKV	Moffat & Williamson
LR02BAU	Newport
LR02BBF	Newport
LR52KXJ	Go-Coach
LR52LWF	Newport
LR52LYC	Newport
LU22GAL	Vectare
LV73ZHT	Moffat & Williamson
LV73ZHU	Moffat & Williamson
LV73ZPE	Moffat & Williamson
LV73ZPH	Moffat & Williamson
LVR164	Faresaver
LW55AHF	Travelmasters
LW55AHZ	Travelmasters
LW55AJW	Travelmasters
LW55AJX	Travelmasters
LX03BTZ	Brylaine Travel
LX03BUA	Brylaine Travel
LX03BVG	Marshalls
LX03BVT	Brylaine Travel
LX03BVV	Brylaine Travel
LX03BWW	Brylaine Travel
LX03BWZ	Brylaine Travel
LX03OSD	Marshalls
LX03OSE	Marshalls
LX03OSV	Marshalls
LX03OSY	Townlynx
LX03OTB	Marshalls
LX03OTG	Townlynx
LX04FXM	Brylaine Travel
LX04FXZ	Brylaine Travel
LX04FYA	Brylaine Travel
LX04FYF	Brylaine Travel
LX04FYG	Brylaine Travel
LX04FYM	Brylaine Travel
LX04FYT	Brylaine Travel
LX05LLP	Marshalls
LX06DZJ	Moffat & Williamson
LX06DZK	Moffat & Williamson
LX06DZL	Moffat & Williamson
LX06DZM	Moffat & Williamson
LX06EZU	Pilkingtons
LX07BXV	Vectare
LX07BYA	Vectare
LX08ECD	Eastern TH
LX08ECE	Eastern TH
LX08ECF	Eastern TH
LX08ECJ	Eastern TH
LX08ECN	Eastern TH
LX08ECT	Eastern TH
LX08ECV	Eastern TH
LX08ECW	Eastern TH
LX09AFK	Vision Bus
LX09AFO	Vision Bus
LX09AFV	Vision Bus
LX09AGU	Vision Bus
LX09AHC	Vision Bus
LX09AZL	Vectare
LX11CVN	Tyrers
LX11CVO	Tyrers
LX11CVP	Tyrers
LX11CVT	Vision Bus
LX11CVU	Tyrers
LX11CVV	Tyrers
LX11CVZ	Tyrers
LX11CWC	Tyrers
LX11CWD	Tyrers
LX11CWE	Tyrers
LX11CWG	Tyrers
LX11CWJ	Tyrers
LX11CWK	Tyrers
LX11CWL	Tyrers
LX11CWM	Tyrers
LX11CWN	Tyrers
LX17DZB	Aintree Coachlines
LX17DZC	Aintree Coachlines
LX17GZL	Aintree Coachlines
LX19CXN	Go-Coach
LX22GAL	Vectare
LX51FJF	Brylaine Travel
LX51FJO	Brylaine Travel
LX51FKB	Brylaine Travel
LX51KXR	Newport
LX51KXW	Newport
LX53AZW	Warrington
LX53JYH	Marshalls
LX53JZL	Marshalls
LX53JZN	Marshalls
LX53JZR	Marshalls
LX53JZU	Marshalls
LX57CKC	Vision Bus
LX57CKD	Vision Bus
LX58CDY	Moffat & Williamson
LX58CHO	Go-Coach
LX58CHV	Go-Coach
LX58LML	Ipswich Buses
LX58LMM	Ipswich Buses
LX58LMO	Ipswich Buses
LX59CME	Tyrers
LX59CMF	Tyrers
LX59CMZ	Tyrers
LX59CNV	Tyrers
LX59CRF	Connexions
LX60DXD	Travelmasters
LX60DXE	Travelmasters
LX67DDU	Aintree Coachlines
LY73EHT	Moffat & Williamson
LY73EJG	Moffat & Williamson
M1OCT	Delaine
M6WMS	Weardale
M22LVT	Yeomans
M50RSW	Globe
M77GGT	Tanat Valley
M393VWX	Connexions
M500JJR	Connexions
MAN41H	Bus Vannin
MAN42H	Bus Vannin
MAN43H	Bus Vannin
MB71LUX	Sanders Coaches
MC16PYT	Tanat Valley
MH15LHR	Tyrers
MH17EGJ	Tyrers
MH17EGK	Tyrers
MIL8163	Globe
MJ65VVY	Nottingham Community
MJ65VWA	Nottingham Community
MJ65VWC	Nottingham Community
MJ65VWE	Nottingham Community
MJ65VWG	Nottingham Community
MJ65VWK	Nottingham Community
MK12DZJ	Grant Palmer
MK63WZY	Grant Palmer
MK63XAR	Redline

Registration	Operator
MK63XAS	Redline
MK63XAT	Redline
MK63XAU	Go-Coach
MK63XAW	Pilkingtons
ML62OGY	Vectare
ML68FCV	Tanat Valley
MM14DKX	Warrington
MM14DWU	Warrington
MM14DWX	Tyrers
MMN101L	Bus Vannin
MMN102L	Bus Vannin
MMN103L	Bus Vannin
MMN104L	Bus Vannin
MMN144G	Bus Vannin
MMN145G	Bus Vannin
MMN183U	Bus Vannin
MMN184U	Bus Vannin
MMN854L	Bus Vannin
MMN855L	Bus Vannin
MMN856L	Bus Vannin
MMN857L	Bus Vannin
MMN858L	Bus Vannin
MMN859L	Bus Vannin
MMN860L	Bus Vannin
MMN861L	Bus Vannin
MMN862T	Bus Vannin
MMN863T	Bus Vannin
MMN864T	Bus Vannin
MMN865T	Bus Vannin
MMN866T	Bus Vannin
MMN867T	Bus Vannin
MMN882B	Bus Vannin
MMN883B	Bus Vannin
MN1082	Bus Vannin
MN5105	Bus Vannin
MN5454	Bus Vannin
MP20BUS	Lloyds
MP21MPT	Tanat Valley
MSU917	Vectare
MT15UAE	Vectare
MT66MTE	Tyrers
MTL750	Delaine
MUN56N	Beestons
MUN59N	Beestons
MV07EFT	Houston's
MV12YYL	Aintree Coachlines
MV58FMY	Globe
MV62HTX	Aintree Coachlines
MW14BUS	Moffat & Williamson
MW15LUX	Moffat & Williamson
MW17BUS	Moffat & Williamson
MW18DEV	Moffat & Williamson
MW58HOW	Moffat & Williamson
MW59JAV	Moffat & Williamson
MX05CKJ	Connexions
MX05ELH	Lynx
MX06ACV	Moffat & Williamson
MX06ACZ	Moffat & Williamson
MX06ADO	Moffat & Williamson
MX06BPZ	Eastern TH
MX06XTA	Weardale
MX07BBK	Tanat Valley
MX07BVA	Brylaine Travel
MX07BVD	Brylaine Travel
MX07BVE	Travelmasters
MX07BVG	Brylaine Travel
MX07BVL	Brylaine Travel
MX08DHF	Brylaine Travel
MX08MYJ	Stotts Tours
MX09AOF	Go-Coach
MX09AOS	Marshalls
MX09CHK	Hornsby
MX09CHL	Hornsby
MX09GZL	White Bus
MX09HHL	Redline
MX09HHN	Redline
MX09HJN	Redline
MX09MKG	Pilkingtons
MX11CZM	Go-Coach
MX11CZR	Yeomans
MX12CFA	Whippet
MX12CFD	Whippet
MX12CFL	UNO
MX12CFM	UNO
MX12CFN	UNO
MX12CFO	UNO
MX12DZE	Vectare
MX12JXU	Vision Bus
MX13BCF	Redline
MX13BCK	Redline
MX13KUB	Faresaver
MX23LCW	Whippet
MX23LRU	Whippet
MX23LRZ	Whippet
MX55BXU	Sargeant
MX56ACF	Moffat & Williamson
MX57CDN	Tanat Valley
MX57KXR	Moffat & Williamson
MX57OEL	Moffat & Williamson
MX58ABF	Sargeant
MX59AVN	Eastern TH
MX60BWY	Stotts Tours
MX60BWZ	Stotts Tours
MX60BXF	Vectare
MX60GXJ	Redline
MX60GXK	Redline
MX61BAO	Redline
MX61BAU	Redline
MX61BCE	Yeomans
MX62AKY	Compass Travel
MX62AKZ	Compass Travel
MX62APK	Eastern TH
MX62APO	Eastern TH
MX62AWG	Vectare
MX67XWY	Eastern TH
MX73EPE	Vision Bus
MX73GBY	Whippet
MX73GCK	Whippet
MX73GCO	Whippet
MX73GDF	Whippet
MXZ3334	JMB Travel
MXZ3335	JMB Travel
MXZ3336	JMB Travel
MXZ3337	JMB Travel
MXZ3338	JMB Travel
MXZ3339	JMB Travel
N22HOU	Houston's
N33HOU	Houston's
N300MMS	Minsterley Motors
N321KES	Xelabus
NA52AWR	Travelmasters
NH04BUS	Hornsby
NH07BUS	Hornsby
NH09BUS	Hornsby
NH10BUS	Hornsby
NH11BUS	Hornsby
NH12BUS	Hornsby
NH13BUS	Hornsby
NH14BUS	Hornsby
NH15BUS	Hornsby
NH16BUS	Hornsby
NH17BUS	Hornsby
NHG541	Lloyds
NIL7251	Vectare
NIL8354	Falcon
NIL9777	Weardale
NJ11EXJ	Faresaver
NK04LBE	JMB Travel
NK04NPJ	JMB Travel
NK07KPT	Globe
NK09FVH	Nottingham Community
NK09FVJ	Nottingham Community
NK09FVL	Nottingham Community
NK56UCA	Pilkingtons
NK61DBZ	Connexions
NK61FMD	Connexions
NMN105K	Bus Vannin
NMN106K	Bus Vannin
NMN107K	Bus Vannin
NMN108K	Bus Vannin
NMN251M	Bus Vannin
NMN252M	Bus Vannin
NMN253M	Bus Vannin
NMN254M	Bus Vannin
NMN255M	Bus Vannin
NMN256M	Bus Vannin
NMN257M	Bus Vannin
NMN258M	Bus Vannin
NMN259X	Bus Vannin
NMN260X	Bus Vannin
NMN261X	Bus Vannin
NMN262X	Bus Vannin
NMN263X	Bus Vannin
NMN264X	Bus Vannin
NMN801A	Bus Vannin
NMN802A	Bus Vannin
NMN804A	Bus Vannin
NMN805V	Bus Vannin
NMN806V	Bus Vannin
NMN807V	Bus Vannin
NMN808V	Bus Vannin
NMN809V	Bus Vannin
NMN810V	Bus Vannin
NMN811V	Bus Vannin
NMN812V	Bus Vannin
NMN868B	Bus Vannin
NMN869B	Bus Vannin
NMN870B	Bus Vannin
NMN871B	Bus Vannin
NMN872B	Bus Vannin
NMN873B	Bus Vannin
NMN874B	Bus Vannin
NMN875B	Bus Vannin
NMN876H	Bus Vannin
NMN877H	Bus Vannin
NMN878H	Bus Vannin
NMN879H	Bus Vannin
NMN880H	Bus Vannin
NMN881H	Bus Vannin
NS17GAS	Sanders Coaches
NSV371	Beestons
NSV372	Beestons
NUH527	Faresaver
NX18NCZ	Sanders Coaches
NX18XYW	Sanders Coaches
NX66MOA	Weardale
OC21SAN	Sanders Coaches
OE16WHZ	JMB Travel
OE16WJD	JMB Travel
OE24SAN	Sanders Coaches

OGR625T	Weardale
OGR647	Sanders Coaches
OHF858S	Aintree Coachlines
OO05RTG	Roberts Travel
OO06RTG	Roberts Travel
OO07RTG	Roberts Travel
OO08RTG	Roberts Travel
OO09RTG	Roberts Travel
OO10RTG	Roberts Travel
OO16WMS	Weardale
OO22WMS	Weardale
OO23WMS	Weardale
OO24WMS	Weardale
OP14ARE	Sargeant
OU05AVD	Weardale
OU08AYF	Moffat & Williamson
OU10GYN	Moffat & Williamson
OU22ZWW	Whippet
OU22ZWX	Whippet
OV24AWM	Weardale
OV24AWN	Weardale
OX53ORU	Townlynx
OY23CYF	Whippet
OY23CYG	Whippet
OY23CYH	Whippet
OY23CYJ	Whippet
OY23CYK	Whippet
OY23CYL	Whippet
OY23CYP	Whippet
OY23CYT	Whippet
OY23CYV	Whippet
OY23CYW	Whippet
OY23CYX	Whippet
OY23CYZ	Whippet
OY73BJV	Tyrers
P3TYR	Tyrers
P6WMS	Weardale
P19 0WF	Newport
P24HOU	Houston's
P25HOU	Houston's
P700CXB	Connexions
PA06AAU	Xelabus
PA06AAV	Xelabus
PA06AHL	Xelabus
PA06AHO	Xelabus
PB72XEL	Xelabus
PC23SAN	Sanders Coaches
PDW484	Newport
PE63OSX	White Bus
PE63OSZ	White Bus
PF24SAN	Sanders Coaches
PG02YWA	Globe
PG04WGY	Warrington
PG04WHF	Vectare
PG17KMY	Tanat Valley
PG17KMZ	Tanat Valley
PJ02RDX	Reliance
PJ02RHF	Weardale
PJ53OLA	Ipswich Buses
PJ54YZT	Ipswich Buses
PJ54YZU	Ipswich Buses
PJ54YZV	Ipswich Buses
PK16BUS	Pilkingtons
PK20BUS	Pilkingtons
PK20BUZ	Pilkingtons
PK56AGO	Pilkingtons
PL06TFV	Minsterley Motors
PL08YLZ	Redline
PL08YMA	Redline
PM14JAM	Marshalls
PM16JAM	Marshalls
PM17JAM	Marshalls
PM19JAM	Marshalls
PM22JAM	Marshalls
PM23JAM	Marshalls
PM24JAM	Marshalls
PM64JAM	Marshalls
PM71JAM	Marshalls
PMN265D	Bus Vannin
PMN266D	Bus Vannin
PMN267D	Bus Vannin
PMN268D	Bus Vannin
PMN269D	Bus Vannin
PMN270D	Bus Vannin
PMN301E	Bus Vannin
PMN302E	Bus Vannin
PMN303E	Bus Vannin
PMN304E	Bus Vannin
PMN305E	Bus Vannin
PMN306E	Bus Vannin
PMN307E	Bus Vannin
PMN308E	Bus Vannin
PMN309E	Bus Vannin
PMN821G	Bus Vannin
PMN822G	Bus Vannin
PMN823G	Bus Vannin
PMN882G	Bus Vannin
PMN883G	Bus Vannin
PMN884G	Bus Vannin
PMN885G	Bus Vannin
PMN886G	Bus Vannin
PMN887G	Bus Vannin
PMN888G	Bus Vannin
PMN889G	Bus Vannin
PN08SWF	UNO
PN09EKT	Eastern TH
PN09ENH	Compass Travel
PN09ENK	Compass Travel
PN16PAV	Warrington
PN52XBO	Ipswich Buses
PN52XBP	Redline
PN52XBU	Ipswich Buses
PO12MXD	Atlantic Travel
PO15GUE	White Bus
PO54OOD	Vectare
PO58NPJ	Redline
PO58NPP	Redline
PO58SHJ	Weardale
PO61LUW	Vectare
PO64EXA	White Bus
PO64EXB	White Bus
PO64EXC	White Bus
PO71MXH	Roberts Travel
PO71MXM	Roberts Travel
PR06PET	Moffat & Williamson
PSV444	Faresaver
PVF377	Sanders Coaches
PX05ELH	JMB Travel
PX05ELO	JMB Travel
PX05ELU	JMB Travel
PX05ELV	JMB Travel
PX05ELW	JMB Travel
PX05EMJ	JMB Travel
PX05EMK	JMB Travel
PX07HBF	Moffat & Williamson
PX07HBH	Moffat & Williamson
PY66OSE	Houston's
R10PLK	Pilkingtons
R12PLK	Pilkingtons
R13TYB	Brylaine Travel
R14PLK	Pilkingtons
R18PLK	Pilkingtons
R19PLK	Pilkingtons
R20PLK	Pilkingtons
R366DJN	JMB Travel
R403EOS	Roberts Travel
R651MAN	Bus Vannin
R6PLK	Pilkingtons
RA15OBW	White Bus
RA65LZB	Landflight
RBZ1664	Roberts Travel
RBZ3430	Roberts Travel
RBZ494	Roberts Travel
RBZ5544	Roberts Travel
RBZ565	Roberts Travel
RBZ913	Roberts Travel
RBZ959	Roberts Travel
RBZ9595	Roberts Travel
RCT3	Delaine
RDV903	Sanders Coaches
RE15WAJ	Landflight
RE21LRJ	UNO
RE22ERJ	Vectare
RE22ETZ	Vectare
RE70EZU	Vectare
RE71OWP	Travelmasters
RF68FLN	Vectare
RF68FMA	Vectare
RF68FMC	Vectare
RF72ZFO	Tanat Valley
RG03BVU	JMB Travel
RJ21UYZ	Newport
RJ21XDB	UNO
RJ21YNL	UNO
RK68GWL	JMB Travel
RMN824E	Bus Vannin
RMN825E	Bus Vannin
RMN826E	Bus Vannin
RMN827E	Bus Vannin
RMN827E	Bus Vannin
RMN828E	Bus Vannin
RMN829G	Bus Vannin
RMN830E	Bus Vannin
RMN831E	Bus Vannin
RMN832E	Bus Vannin
RMN833E	Bus Vannin
RMN834E	Bus Vannin
RMN835E	Bus Vannin
RMN836E	Bus Vannin
RMN890G	Bus Vannin
RMN890J	Bus Vannin
RMN891J	Bus Vannin
RMN892J	Bus Vannin
RMN893J	Bus Vannin
RMN894J	Bus Vannin
RMN895J	Bus Vannin
RN52FPA	Travelmasters
RO15GJP	Landflight
RO19ATE	White Bus
RO21ODT	Newport
RO21TZF	Lloyds
RO21TZG	Lloyds
RO21VKU	Lloyds
RO21VKU	Newport
RO21WDN	Newport
RO23ODT	Pilkingtons
RO23OFP	Pilkingtons
ROC300R	Aintree Coachlines
RRN423	Aintree Coachlines
RRU345	Faresaver

Registration	Operator
RV68YLZ	Roberts Travel
RX18LNM	JMB Travel
RX18LNT	Vectare
RX20RDV	Vectare
RX20RJV	Vectare
RX22SKU	Sanders Coaches
RX23TFJ	Vectare
RX23TFK	Vectare
RX23TKV	Vectare
RX23TUU	Vectare
RX23TUV	Vectare
RX23TUW	Vectare
RX23TUY	Vectare
RX23TVD	Vectare
RX23TVE	Vectare
RX23TVF	Vectare
RX57MDZ	JMB Travel
RX68FLV	Vectare
RX70SKE	Vectare
RX71OJJ	Vision Bus
RX71SYW	Vectare
RX71TDV	Newport
RX71TDZ	Newport
RX71TGK	Vectare
RX72SZT	UNO
RX72TNV	Houston's
RX72TWP	Vectare
S4YRR	Marshalls
S190SLL	Vectare
S260KLG	Townlynx
S400SLT	Connexions
S519KFL	Go-Coach
S869HCG	Go-Coach
S900RGE	Connexions
SA14JHH	Tanat Valley
SA24SAF	Safeguard
SA71SAN	Sanders Coaches
SB09PEG	Lloyds
SB58BUS	Pilkingtons
SC23NJS	Sanders Coaches
SF04VTE	JMB Travel
SF07LCJ	Moffat & Williamson
SF07LCK	Moffat & Williamson
SF08GUU	Moffat & Williamson
SF08VTK	Houston's
SF09ACV	Moffat & Williamson
SF14UBE	Moffat & Williamson
SF14UBG	Moffat & Williamson
SF14UBH	Moffat & Williamson
SF54ORA	Yeomans
SF56FKX	JMB Travel
SF56FKY	JMB Travel
SF64VLH	Moffat & Williamson
SF64VLJ	Moffat & Williamson
SG24SAF	Safeguard
SGF965	Sanders Coaches
SGZ1001	Ipswich Buses
SGZ1002	Ipswich Buses
SGZ1003	Ipswich Buses
SGZ3346	Ipswich Buses
SGZ3347	Ipswich Buses
SGZ3348	Ipswich Buses
SGZ3349	Ipswich Buses
SGZ3350	Ipswich Buses
SGZ3351	Ipswich Buses
SGZ6664	Ipswich Buses
SHZ2712	Roberts Travel
SHZ3490	Roberts Travel
SHZ3492	Roberts Travel
SHZ3696	Roberts Travel
SHZ3698	Roberts Travel
SHZ8495	Tyrers
SHZ8496	Tyrers
SIA488	Vectare
SIL4054	Tyrers
SJ04VNP	Moffat & Williamson
SJ16CRX	White Bus
SJ16CRZ	White Bus
SJ16ZZV	Moffat & Williamson
SJ20KNL	Minsterley Motors
SJ22GZR	JMB Travel
SJ22GZS	JMB Travel
SJ22GZT	JMB Travel
SJ22GZU	JMB Travel
SJ22GZV	JMB Travel
SJ22GZW	JMB Travel
SJ22GZX	JMB Travel
SJ22GZY	JMB Travel
SJ22GZZ	JMB Travel
SJ24HWA	JMB Travel
SJ24HWB	JMB Travel
SJ57AAO	Moffat & Williamson
SJ57AAU	Moffat & Williamson
SJ57AAV	Moffat & Williamson
SJ69EYM	Houston's
SJ72HVT	JMB Travel
SJ72HVU	JMB Travel
SJ72HVV	JMB Travel
SJ72HVW	JMB Travel
SJ73HSV	Houston's
SJ73HSX	Houston's
SJ73HSY	Houston's
SJ73HVO	Houston's
SK07CFU	Aintree Coachlines
SK07CFV	Warrington
SK07CFX	Sanders Coaches
SK07CGG	Sanders Coaches
SK07DFP	Falcon
SK07DZA	Go-Coach
SK07DZB	Go-Coach
SK07DZC	Go-Coach
SK07DZD	Go-Coach
SK07DZE	Go-Coach
SK07DZF	Go-Coach
SK07DZG	Go-Coach
SK07DZJ	Go-Coach
SK07DZL	Go-Coach
SK07HLN	Eastern TH
SK07HLV	Eastern TH
SK10AFP	Houston's
SK10AJP	Houston's
SK15HBC	Compass Travel
SK15HBD	Compass Travel
SK15HBE	Compass Travel
SK15HBG	Lloyds
SK15HFP	Grant Palmer
SK20AUN	Blackpool Transport
SK20AUO	Blackpool Transport
SK20AUP	Blackpool Transport
SK20AUT	Blackpool Transport
SK21FHX	Falcon
SK21FKE	Globe
SK21FKF	Globe
SK21FNG	Lynx
SK21FNH	Lynx
SK22BTF	Weardale
SK22BVF	Cardiff Bus
SK22BVV	Faresaver
SK22BVW	Faresaver
SK22BVZ	Atlantic Travel
SK22BWA	Atlantic Travel
SK22BWB	Atlantic Travel
SK22BWC	Atlantic Travel
SK22BWD	Atlantic Travel
SK24CUH	Globe
SK24CUJ	Globe
SK24CWA	Newport
SK24CWC	Newport
SK24XPC	Falcon
SK24XPD	Falcon
SK24XPF	Falcon
SK24XPG	Falcon
SK24XPH	Falcon
SK24XPJ	White Bus
SK24XPL	White Bus
SK24XPN	Newport
SK52MPU	Redline
SK68LZF	Stotts Tours
SK68LZG	Stotts Tours
SK68LZN	Stotts Tours
SK68LZO	Stotts Tours
SK68TNL	UNO
SK68TNN	UNO
SK68TNO	UNO
SK68TNU	UNO
SK68TNV	UNO
SK70BUO	Newport
SK70BUP	Newport
SK70BVT	Vision Bus
SK70BVU	Vision Bus
SK71CKL	Newport
SK72CWE	UNO
SK72CWF	UNO
SK72CWG	UNO
SK73CNJ	Vectare
SK73CNO	Vectare
SK73CNU	Vectare
SL15ZGP	Vision Bus
SL17RSL	Marshalls
SLK886	Vectare
SM24MAR	Marshalls
SM63XAF	Atlantic Travel
SMK699F	Go-Coach
SMK725F	Travelmasters
SN04EGF	Moffat & Williamson
SN05HWX	Connexions
SN06BOV	Vectare
SN08BWM	Brylaine Travel
SN08BWO	Brylaine Travel
SN08BWP	Brylaine Travel
SN08BWU	Brylaine Travel
SN08BWV	Brylaine Travel
SN08BWW	Brylaine Travel
SN08BWX	Brylaine Travel
SN08BWZ	Brylaine Travel
SN08BXA	Brylaine Travel
SN08BXB	Brylaine Travel
SN08BXE	Brylaine Travel
SN08BXF	Brylaine Travel
SN08BXK	Brylaine Travel
SN08BYH	Brylaine Travel
SN09CDV	Warrington
SN09CDX	Warrington
SN09CDY	Warrington
SN09CEF	Warrington
SN09CEK	Warrington
SN09CEX	Warrington
SN09CFM	Warrington
SN09JUV	Safeguard
SN09JUX	Safeguard

SN11BPZ	Warrington	SN55BKV	Moffat & Williamson	SN66WJY	Vision Bus
SN11BRF	Warrington	SN55BKY	Moffat & Williamson	SN66WKD	Compass Travel
SN11FFJ	Warrington	SN55BKZ	Moffat & Williamson	SN66WKE	Compass Travel
SN11FFK	Warrington	SN55BOJ	Moffat & Williamson	SN66WKF	Eastern TH
SN11FFL	Warrington	SN55BPK	Moffat & Williamson	SN66WKG	Eastern TH
SN11FFP	Warrington	SN55HSF	Tanat Valley	SN66WLL	Eastern TH
SN11FFR	Warrington	SN55HSU	Globe	SN66WLO	Eastern TH
SN11FFT	Faresaver	SN55OUF	DRM	SN66WPJ	Grant Palmer
SN11PFM	Vectare	SN56ABO	Moffat & Williamson	SN67WZA	Blackpool Transport
SN12ARU	UNO	SN56ACF	Moffat & Williamson	SN67WZB	Blackpool Transport
SN12ASO	UNO	SN56ACU	Moffat & Williamson	SN67WZC	Blackpool Transport
SN13CHJ	Compass Travel	SN56ACV	Moffat & Williamson	SN67WZD	Blackpool Transport
SN15CCE	Houston's	SN56ADO	Moffat & Williamson	SN67WZE	Blackpool Transport
SN15ETD	Eastern TH	SN56ADX	Moffat & Williamson	SN67WZF	Blackpool Transport
SN15ETE	Eastern TH	SN56AEU	Moffat & Williamson	SN67WZG	Blackpool Transport
SN15ETF	Eastern TH	SN56AEV	Moffat & Williamson	SN67WZH	Blackpool Transport
SN15LRY	Houston's	SN56AEW	Moffat & Williamson	SN67WZJ	Blackpool Transport
SN16BRV	Atlantic Travel	SN56AEX	Moffat & Williamson	SN67WZK	Blackpool Transport
SN16OGG	Ipswich Buses	SN56AEY	Moffat & Williamson	SN67WZL	Blackpool Transport
SN16OGH	Ipswich Buses	SN56AEZ	Moffat & Williamson	SN67WZM	Blackpool Transport
SN16OGJ	Ipswich Buses	SN56AFA	Moffat & Williamson	SN67WZO	Blackpool Transport
SN16OGK	Ipswich Buses	SN56AGV	Vectare	SN67WZP	Blackpool Transport
SN16OGP	Aintree Coachlines	SN56AXA	Travelmasters	SN67WZR	Blackpool Transport
SN16OGS	Compass Travel	SN56AXU	Moffat & Williamson	SN67WZS	Blackpool Transport
SN16ORS	Eastern TH	SN57DAU	Connexions	SN67WZT	Blackpool Transport
SN16ORU	Eastern TH	SN57DCX	Ipswich Buses	SN67WZU	Blackpool Transport
SN16OSA	JMB Travel	SN57DWZ	Vectare	SN67WZV	Blackpool Transport
SN16OSB	JMB Travel	SN57GNO	Reliance	SN67WZW	Blackpool Transport
SN16OSV	Compass Travel	SN58ENU	Travelmasters	SN67XBH	Vision Bus
SN16OVB	Warrington	SN59AVT	Go-Coach	SN67XBJ	Stotts Tours
SN16OVC	Vision Bus	SN59AWA	Go-Coach	SN67XBL	Stotts Tours
SN16OVD	Vision Bus	SN59AWC	Go-Coach	SO10WMS	Weardale
SN16OVF	Vision Bus	SN59AWF	Go-Coach	SP05EOH	Moffat & Williamson
SN16OVG	Vision Bus	SN59AWJ	Go-Coach	SP06FVA	Moffat & Williamson
SN16OVH	Vision Bus	SN59BFZ	Reliance	SP06FVB	Moffat & Williamson
SN16OVJ	Vision Bus	SN60DJF	Moffat & Williamson	SP06FVD	Moffat & Williamson
SN16OVK	Vision Bus	SN60FMO	Safeguard	SP07HHO	Moffat & Williamson
SN16OVL	Vision Bus	SN61CYY	Compass Travel	SP07HHT	JMB Travel
SN16OVM	Vectare	SN62AOH	Newport	SP07HHV	Moffat & Williamson
SN16OVO	Vectare	SN62AOO	Newport	SP07HHW	Moffat & Williamson
SN16OVP	Vectare	SN62AOP	Newport	SP54FML	Whitelaws
SN16OVR	Vectare	SN62AOW	Newport	SP55CXJ	JMB Travel
SN16WJY	Vision Bus	SN62AOX	Newport	SP55CXK	Moffat & Williamson
SN17MFJ	Blackpool Transport	SN64CTU	Vision Bus	SP55EEA	Moffat & Williamson
SN17MFK	Blackpool Transport	SN64CTV	Vision Bus	SP56CXF	Moffat & Williamson
SN17MFO	Blackpool Transport	SN64CVA	UNO	SP58DPE	Tanat Valley
SN17MFP	Blackpool Transport	SN65OEW	Compass Travel	SP58DPF	Tanat Valley
SN17MFU	Blackpool Transport	SN65OEX	Compass Travel	SP59BSX	Moffat & Williamson
SN17MFV	Blackpool Transport	SN65OFO	Faresaver	SP59DCE	Moffat & Williamson
SN17MFX	Blackpool Transport	SN65OFP	Faresaver	SPO6FVC	JMB Travel
SN17MFY	Blackpool Transport	SN65OHH	Xelabus	SPO6FVE	JMB Travel
SN17MFZ	Blackpool Transport	SN65OHZ	Cardiff Bus	SPR124	White Bus
SN17MGE	Blackpool Transport	SN65OHZ	Ipswich Buses	SS16GAL	Vectare
SN17MGJ	Blackpool Transport	SN65OJA	Ipswich Buses	SS71GAL	Vectare
SN17MGO	Blackpool Transport	SN65OJB	Ipswich Buses	SUG588M	Connexions
SN17MGU	Blackpool Transport	SN65OKM	Vision Bus	SV05DKO	Moffat & Williamson
SN17MGV	Blackpool Transport	SN65ZGO	UNO	SV11FFT	Moffat & Williamson
SN17MGX	Blackpool Transport	SN65ZGU	UNO	SV11FFX	Moffat & Williamson
SN17MGY	Blackpool Transport	SN65ZGV	UNO	SV12CJU	Moffat & Williamson
SN17MGZ	Blackpool Transport	SN65ZGW	UNO	SV55BZL	JMB Travel
SN17MHA	Blackpool Transport	SN65ZGX	UNO	SV55BZM	JMB Travel
SN17MHE	Blackpool Transport	SN65ZGY	UNO	SV55BZR	Moffat & Williamson
SN17MHF	Blackpool Transport	SN65ZGZ	Vision Bus	SV55BZX	Moffat & Williamson
SN17MHJ	Blackpool Transport	SN65ZHA	Vision Bus	SV55CCD	Moffat & Williamson
SN17MHK	Blackpool Transport	SN66WHH	Moffat & Williamson	SV55CCN	JMB Travel
SN17MHL	Blackpool Transport	SN66WHJ	Moffat & Williamson	SV55FJP	Townlynx
SN17MHM	Blackpool Transport	SN66WHK	Moffat & Williamson	SV56BVR	JMB Travel
SN17MHO	Blackpool Transport	SN66WHL	Moffat & Williamson	SV56BVZ	JMB Travel
SN51AYL	JMB Travel	SN66WHM	Moffat & Williamson	SV56BWA	JMB Travel
SN53EUW	Brylaine Travel	SN66WHR	Moffat & Williamson	SV57BYW	Moffat & Williamson

One of three Optare Versa buses new to Smith Coaches of Woodside, Blairgowrie, SP58DPF is now with Tanat Valley as its 262. *Chris Clegg*

Registration	Operator
SV57FUM	Weardale
SV59CHL	Newport
SV61CTY	Moffat & Williamson
SV61CUA	Moffat & Williamson
SV61CUC	Moffat & Williamson
SV61CUG	Moffat & Williamson
SV61CUJ	Moffat & Williamson
SW16BUS	Vectare
SW16LOW	Travelmasters
SW63TAV	Sanders Coaches
SW64SAR	Go-Coach
SW65GSW	Falcon
T3YRR	Marshalls
T10MAN	Bus Vannin
T10MCL	Reliance
T10TVC	Tanat Valley
T11TVC	Tanat Valley
T12TVC	Tanat Valley
T21UNO	UNO
T22UNO	UNO
T23UNO	UNO
T24UNO	UNO
T25RRT	Redline
T28KLN	Lynx
T29KLN	Lynx
T66WMS	Weardale
T414OUB	Yeomans
T900NTS	Sargeant
TC02TVC	Tanat Valley
TC03TVC	Tanat Valley
TC06TVC	Tanat Valley
TC08TVC	Tanat Valley
TC09TVC	Tanat Valley
TC10TVC	Tanat Valley
TCF496	Vectare
TJ24TJH	Sanders Coaches
TJ69XWG	Tyrers
TUB250R	Aintree Coachlines
TUI1438	Falcon
TUI1440	Falcon
TUI4762	Falcon
TUI4763	Falcon
TYR10R	Tyrers
TYR11R	Tyrers
TYR12R	Tyrers
TYR14R	Tyrers
TYR15R	Tyrers
TYR16R	Tyrers
TYR17R	Tyrers
TYR18R	Tyrers
TYR19R	Tyrers
TYR20R	Tyrers
TYR21R	Tyrers
TYR22R	Tyrers
TYR23R	Tyrers
TYR24R	Tyrers
TYR25R	Tyrers
TYR26R	Tyrers
TYR27R	Tyrers
TYR28R	Tyrers
TYR29R	Tyrers
TYR2R	Tyrers
TYR30R	Tyrers
TYR311R	Tyrers
TYR31R	Tyrers
TYR4R	Tyrers
TYR5R	Tyrers
TYR6R	Tyrers
TYR7R	Tyrers
TYR8R	Tyrers
UK23ACL	Aintree Coachlines
UK66ACL	Aintree Coachlines
UN14BUS	Whippet
UN14CAM	Whippet
UNZ9109	JMB Travel
UNZ9141	JMB Travel
UNZ9789	JMB Travel
UP63RWL	Nottingham Community
URH806	Connexions
UU59BOY	Vectare
UUG384	Connexions
UWW2X	Lynx
V112LGC	Redline
V119LGC	Redline
V185OOE	Redline
V524ESC	Cardiff Bus
V66VNS	Weardale
V6WMS	Weardale
VA61BFN	Compass Travel
VE58XKX	Travelmasters
VHZ3765	JMB Travel
VNZ1742	JMB Travel
VNZ2901	JMB Travel
VNZ7605	JMB Travel
VNZ7647	JMB Travel
VR24VAR	Sanders Coaches

Hulleys of Baslow' fleet is listed under the Go-Coach name. A quiet Derbyshire road through Stanton-in-the-Peak and Hulleys 21, Y100HOB, head towards Bakewell. The Volvo B8RLE joins a similar one delivered in 2023. *John Young*

VU02TTJ	Safeguard
VU19WNP	Newport
VU53FYR	Vectare
W6WMS	Weardale
W7WHW	Whitelaws
W10VEC	Vectare
W11VEC	Vectare
W12VEC	Vectare
W13VEC	Vectare
W14VEC	Vectare
W15VEC	Vectare
W161EAX	Cardiff Bus
W16VEC	Vectare
W17VEC	Vectare
W21WHW	Whitelaws
W22WHW	Whitelaws
W25RRT	Redline
W648RCG	Newport
W66WMS	Weardale
W100ACL	Aintree Coachlines
WA07KXX	Safeguard
WA14NWW	Lloyds
WA18DDY	Sanders Coaches
WA57CYY	Safeguard
WA58EOO	Safeguard
WA66DVN	Lloyds
WF20ENX	Go-Coach
WF20EOA	Go-Coach
WF20EOO	Go-Coach
WF20KJK	Go-Coach
WF63LVH	Sanders Coaches
WH11CHR	Sanders Coaches
WH66BUS	Vectare
WK11APV	Brylaine Travel
WK11APX	Brylaine Travel
WK11APY	Go-Coach
WLT378	Weardale
WN21UJO	Moffat & Williamson
WN69FYL	Vectare
WOA521	Sanders Coaches
WP20LDO	Vectare
WP21XFB	Lloyds
WSV503	Sanders Coaches
WT54JAC	Newport
WU09BCZ	Warrington
WV20VDO	Vectare
WVE284	Vectare
WW65GSW	Falcon
WX06JXT	Cardiff Bus
WX06JYA	Sanders Coaches
WX09TCK	Travelmasters
WX24URF	Weardale
WX57TLU	Cardiff Bus
WX57TLV	Cardiff Bus
WX57TLY	Cardiff Bus
WX58BVV	Houston's
WX6025	Connexions
WX66EGE	Sanders Coaches
WXG316	Go-Coach
X6WMS	Weardale
X7OCT	Delaine
X111ACL	Aintree Coachlines
X154FBB	Redline
X185CHJ	Yeomans
X211HBT	Roberts Travel
X400MTT	Eastern TH
X663VRL	Vectare
X929YCC	Roberts Travel
XER134T	Connexions
XHK234X	Eastern TH
XIL4072	Vectare
XL66ACL	Aintree Coachlines
XMN346	Bus Vannin
XNT421	Connexions
XOI2520	Aintree Coachlines
Y2FLG	Vectare
Y3FLG	Vectare
Y4FLG	Vectare
Y6WMS	Weardale
Y8OCT	Delaine
Y14BUS	Weardale
Y16WMS	Weardale
Y66WMS	Weardale
Y20CXB	Connexions
Y24COM	Compass Travel
Y25COM	Compass Travel
Y26COM	Compass Travel
Y100HOB	Go-Coach
Y184NLK	Vectare
Y445CUB	Reliance
Y703TGH	Redline
Y734TGH	Redline
YCT187	Yeomans

YCT502	Yeomans
YCV834	Yeomans
YD02PXM	JMB Travel
YD19HGE	Landflight
YD19HGF	Landflight
YD19HHR	Roberts Travel
YD21NFF	Roberts Travel
YD21NFG	Roberts Travel
YD21NFH	Roberts Travel
YD21NFJ	Roberts Travel
YD21NFK	Roberts Travel
YD21NFL	Roberts Travel
YD21NFM	Roberts Travel
YD21NFN	Roberts Travel
YD21NFO	Roberts Travel
YD21NFP	Roberts Travel
YD21NFR	Roberts Travel
YD23FLX	Landflight
YD23FNJ	Landflight
YD23FNK	Landflight
YD23FNL	Landflight
YD24ERK	White Bus
YD24ERV	Nottingham Community
YD24ESG	Nottingham Community
YD24ETR	Roberts Travel
YD63UZB	Tanat Valley
YD63UZJ	Safeguard
YD63UZL	Go-Coach
YD63UZV	Brylaine Travel
YD63UZW	Brylaine Travel
YD63UZX	Brylaine Travel
YD63VDZ	Sargeant
YD63VEU	Minsterley Motors
YD63VFG	Minsterley Motors
YD70CFE	Newport
YD70CFF	Newport
YD70CFG	Newport
YD70CFJ	Newport
YD70CFK	Newport
YD70CFL	Newport
YD70CFM	Newport
YD70CHG	Newport
YD70CHH	Newport
YD70CHJ	Newport
YD70CHK	Newport
YD70CHL	Newport
YD70CHN	Newport
YD70CHO	Newport
YD73FPE	White Bus
YD73FPF	White Bus
YD73FPG	White Bus
YD73FPJ	White Bus
YD73FRL	Roberts Travel
YD73FRN	Roberts Travel
YD73FSC	Nottingham City T
YD73FSE	Nottingham City T
YD73FSF	Nottingham City T
YD73FSG	Nottingham City T
YD73FSJ	Nottingham City T
YD73FSK	Nottingham City T
YD73FSL	Nottingham City T
YD73FSO	Nottingham City T
YD73FSP	Nottingham City T
YD73FSS	Nottingham City T
YD73FSU	Nottingham City T
YD73FSV	Nottingham City T
YE73HZW	Yeomans
YE73HZX	Yeomans
YE73HZZ	Yeomans
YE73PYG	UNO
YE73PZZ	UNO
YG16LGF	Travelmasters
YG18CVS	Newport
YG52DGY	Yeomans
YG52DGZ	Yeomans
YG68TJY	White Bus
YG68TJZ	White Bus
YG68TKA	White Bus
YG73PGY	Falcon
YH24MFA	Nottingham City T
YH24MFE	Nottingham City T
YH24MFF	Nottingham City T
YH24MFJ	Nottingham City T
YH24MFK	Nottingham City T
YH24MFN	Nottingham City T
YH24MFO	Nottingham City T
YH24MFP	Nottingham City T
YH24MFU	Nottingham City T
YH24MFV	Nottingham City T
YH24MFX	Nottingham City T
YH24MFY	Nottingham City T
YH63CXE	Sanders Coaches
YH63CXF	Sanders Coaches
YJ05JXD	Brylaine Travel
YJ05JXE	Brylaine Travel
YJ05JXF	Brylaine Travel
YJ05JXG	Brylaine Travel
YJ05JXH	Brylaine Travel
YJ05JXK	Brylaine Travel
YJ05JXL	Brylaine Travel
YJ05UKR	Reliance
YJ05WCF	Brylaine Travel
YJ05WDC	Grant Palmer
YJ06FXM	Safeguard
YJ06FYO	Sargeant
YJ06FYU	Sargeant
YJ06LFW	Hornsby
YJ06XLM	Brylaine Travel
YJ06YRU	Aintree Coachlines
YJ06YSP	Brylaine Travel
YJ07VSK	Lynx
YJ07VSL	Lynx
YJ07VSM	Lynx
YJ07VSN	Lynx
YJ08PHV	Brylaine Travel
YJ08PHX	Brylaine Travel
YJ08PHY	Brylaine Travel
YJ09CVF	Tanat Valley
YJ09CXD	Aintree Coachlines
YJ09MHN	Go-Coach
YJ09MHY	Brylaine Travel
YJ09MHZ	Brylaine Travel
YJ09MMK	Go-Coach
YJ09MMO	Go-Coach
YJ09MMU	Go-Coach
YJ09OTH	Go-Coach
YJ09OTP	Lloyds
YJ09ZCL	Newport
YJ10DJV	Sanders Coaches
YJ10DJX	Minsterley Motors
YJ10EZL	Nottingham Community
YJ10EZM	Nottingham Community
YJ10EZO	Nottingham Community
YJ10EZT	Safeguard
YJ10MDE	Brylaine Travel
YJ10MDU	Brylaine Travel
YJ10MGX	Faresaver
YJ10MHU	Sargeant
YJ11EHB	Yeomans
YJ11EHC	Yeomans
YJ11EHD	Yeomans
YJ11EHE	Yeomans
YJ11EHF	Yeomans
YJ11EHN	Go-Coach
YJ11EHR	Go-Coach
YJ11EHX	Go-Coach
YJ11EJA	Go-Coach
YJ11EJD	Go-Coach
YJ11EJN	JMB Travel
YJ11EKA	Go-Coach
YJ11EKB	Go-Coach
YJ11EKD	Go-Coach
YJ11EKY	Marshalls
YJ11EMK	Yeomans
YJ11OHA	Nottingham City T
YJ12GSV	Houston's
YJ12GSZ	Houston's
YJ12GTF	Houston's
YJ12GVF	Sargeant
YJ12GVG	Sargeant
YJ12GWA	Ipswich Buses
YJ12GWC	Ipswich Buses
YJ12GWD	Ipswich Buses
YJ12GWE	Ipswich Buses
YJ12GWF	Ipswich Buses
YJ12GWG	Ipswich Buses
YJ12GWK	Ipswich Buses
YJ12GWL	Ipswich Buses
YJ12GWM	Ipswich Buses
YJ12GWN	Ipswich Buses
YJ12GWO	Ipswich Buses
YJ12GWP	Ipswich Buses
YJ12GWU	Ipswich Buses
YJ12GXU	Tyrers
YJ12GXV	Tyrers
YJ12GXW	Tyrers
YJ12GXZ	Tyrers
YJ12GYN	Nottingham City T
YJ12GYO	Nottingham City T
YJ12GYP	Nottingham City T
YJ12GYR	Nottingham City T
YJ12GYS	Nottingham City T
YJ12GYT	Nottingham City T
YJ12GYU	Nottingham City T
YJ12GYV	Nottingham City T
YJ12GYW	Nottingham City T
YJ12GYX	Nottingham City T
YJ12GYY	Nottingham City T
YJ12GYZ	Nottingham City T
YJ12PMY	Minsterley Motors
YJ13HHS	Weardale
YJ13HHT	Weardale
YJ13HKA	Warrington
YJ13HKB	Warrington
YJ13HKC	Warrington
YJ13HKD	Warrington
YJ13HKE	Warrington
YJ13HKX	Faresaver
YJ13HNN	JMB Travel
YJ13HTN	Roberts Travel
YJ14BBK	Weardale
YJ14BBN	White Bus
YJ14BBO	White Bus
YJ14BBU	Minsterley Motors
YJ14BBV	Minsterley Motors
YJ14BCO	Lloyds
YJ14BCU	Lloyds
YJ14BCV	Lloyds
YJ14BCX	Lloyds
YJ14BCY	Lloyds

YJ14BCZ	Lloyds	YJ59PKN	Go-Coach	YJ64DYF	Yeomans
YJ14BEU	Lloyds	YJ59PKV	Go-Coach	YJ64DYG	Yeomans
YJ14BFY	Go-Coach	YJ59SFK	Newport	YJ64DYH	Yeomans
YJ14BGK	Sargeant	YJ59SFV	Newport	YJ64DYX	Tyrers
YJ14BGO	Sargeant	YJ59SGO	Newport	YJ64DZS	Townlynx
YJ14BGZ	Stotts Tours	YJ59SGU	Newport	YJ64FWF	Sanders Coaches
YJ15ANX	JMB Travel	YJ60GDO	Tanat Valley	YJ65ERY	Marshalls
YJ15AOB	JMB Travel	YJ60GFA	Tanat Valley	YJ65EUM	Lloyds
YJ15APF	Houston's	YJ60GPZ	Moffat & Williamson	YJ65EUN	Lloyds
YJ15APU	Houston's	YJ60KAA	Lynx	YJ65EUP	Weardale
YJ15AYE	Faresaver	YJ60KAE	Lynx	YJ65EVT	Minsterley Motors
YJ15AYF	Faresaver	YJ60KAK	Lynx	YJ65EVU	Minsterley Motors
YJ15AYG	Faresaver	YJ60KAO	Lynx	YJ65EVV	Minsterley Motors
YJ15AYH	Faresaver	YJ60KAU	Lynx	YJ65EVW	Minsterley Motors
YJ16DDA	Sargeant	YJ60KAX	Lynx	YJ65EVX	Minsterley Motors
YJ16DFG	Sargeant	YJ60KBF	Lynx	YJ66ANU	Faresaver
YJ16DXR	Faresaver	YJ60KBO	Marshalls	YJ66ANV	Faresaver
YJ16UTR	Roberts Travel	YJ60KFP	Pilkingtons	YJ66ANX	Faresaver
YJ17CPV	JMB Travel	YJ60KFU	Lloyds	YJ66AOA	Faresaver
YJ17CVA	Yeomans	YJ60KGE	Brylaine Travel	YJ66AOO	Sargeant
YJ17CVB	Yeomans	YJ60KHE	Houston's	YJ66AOS	Faresaver
YJ17CVC	Yeomans	YJ60LRO	Safeguard	YJ66AOT	Faresaver
YJ17CVD	Yeomans	YJ60LRX	Marshalls	YJ66APZ	Sargeant
YJ17FYY	Lloyds	YJ61CFZ	Nottingham City T	YJ67FYV	Sargeant
YJ17FYZ	Lloyds	YJ61CGF	Nottingham City T	YJ67FYX	Safeguard
YJ17FZE	Safeguard	YJ61CGG	Nottingham City T	YJ67FZL	Lloyds
YJ18CZG	Sargeant	YJ61CGK	Nottingham City T	YJ67FZM	Lloyds
YJ18CZL	Sargeant	YJ61CGO	Nottingham City T	YJ67FZN	Lloyds
YJ18DHC	Houston's	YJ61CGU	Nottingham City T	YJ67FZO	Lloyds
YJ18DHD	Houston's	YJ61CGX	Nottingham City T	YJ67FZP	Lloyds
YJ18DKX	Go-Coach	YJ61CGY	Nottingham City T	YJ67GEK	Sargeant
YJ18DKY	Sargeant	YJ61CGZ	Nottingham City T	YJ67TCK	White Bus
YJ19BBX	Globe	YJ61CHC	Nottingham City T	YJ67TCO	White Bus
YJ22AYL	Houston's	YJ61CKA	Tyrers	YJ68FTO	Sargeant
YJ23CWS	UNO	YJ61CKC	Tyrers	YJ68FVA	Yeomans
YJ53VDV	Travelmasters	YJ61JDO	Tyrers	YJ68FVB	Yeomans
YJ54UBG	Yeomans	YJ61JGZ	Marshalls	YJ68FVC	Yeomans
YJ54UBY	Brylaine Travel	YJ61JHF	Yeomans	YJ71GSY	Sargeant
YJ55BJE	Lynx	YJ61JHL	Tyrers	YJ72ETZ	Sargeant
YJ55BKG	Lynx	YJ61JHO	Tyrers	YJ72EUM	Sargeant
YJ55BKO	Brylaine Travel	YJ62AEC	Marshalls	YJ72EUN	Sargeant
YJ55KZR	Travelmasters	YJ62FCD	Marshalls	YK05CAO	Go-Coach
YJ56ATU	Brylaine Travel	YJ62FDK	Faresaver	YK05CDE	Moffat & Williamson
YJ56KCK	Vectare	YJ62FEH	Stotts Tours	YK05CDF	Moffat & Williamson
YJ56WVA	Lynx	YJ62FET	Stotts Tours	YK06DTZ	JMB Travel
YJ56WVW	Yeomans	YJ62FEU	Stotts Tours	YK10WBM	Nottingham Community
YJ57BTX	Globe	YJ62FFB	Nottingham Community	YK54ENN	Reliance
YJ57EGY	Brylaine Travel	YJ62FFN	Yeomans	YK55ENL	Vectare
YJ57EHE	Yeomans	YJ62FFO	Yeomans	YK55ENU	Yeomans
YJ57EHX	Brylaine Travel	YJ62FLD	Nottingham Community	YK57FHM	Brylaine Travel
YJ57XVO	Marshalls	YJ62FMZ	Globe	YK66CBC	Newport
YJ57YCB	Tanat Valley	YJ62FUD	Go-Coach	YL08FZS	Vectare
YJ57ZWP	Go-Coach	YJ62FUG	Go-Coach	YL23FSA	Houston's
YJ58CCX	Yeomans	YJ62FVN	Go-Coach	YL23FUG	Houston's
YJ58CCY	Yeomans	YJ62FVT	Sargeant	YM51WGG	Townlynx
YJ58CCZ	Yeomans	YJ62FXK	Sargeant	YM51WGU	Townlynx
YJ58CEK	Tanat Valley	YJ62FXO	Weardale	YN04GPJ	Vectare
YJ58CEY	Safeguard	YJ62FYB	Stotts Tours	YN04PZY	Vectare
YJ58PHO	Eastern TH	YJ62FYN	Lloyds	YN04UJL	Connexions
YJ58PHW	Eastern TH	YJ62FZO	Sargeant	YN04UJY	Connexions
YJ58VBX	Go-Coach	YJ62FZR	Sargeant	YN04YJR	Eastern TH
YJ58VCE	Aintree Coachlines	YJ62JZT	Tanat Valley	YN05ASZ	Vectare
YJ59AYY	Sanders Coaches	YJ64DBV	Faresaver	YN05GXA	Connexions
YJ59AZA	Tanat Valley	YJ64DSE	Pilkingtons	YN05GXB	Connexions
YJ59AZN	Sanders Coaches	YJ64DVY	Safeguard	YN05GXB	Connexions
YJ59GFG	Go-Coach	YJ64DVZ	Faresaver	YN05GXC	Connexions
YJ59GFK	Go-Coach	YJ64DXU	Yeomans	YN05GXD	Globe
YJ59GFO	Go-Coach	YJ64DXV	Yeomans	YN05GXD	Globe
YJ59GGK	Faresaver	YJ64DXZ	Tyrers	YN05GXX	Sanders Coaches
YJ59NNZ	Brylaine Travel	YJ64DYA	Tyrers	YN05UUT	White Bus

YN05VSG	Sanders Coaches	YN14MUB	Nottingham City T	YN19EEX	Nottingham City T
YN05WKF	Connexions	YN14MUC	Nottingham City T	YN19EEY	Nottingham City T
YN05WKJ	Connexions	YN14MUE	Nottingham City T	YN19EEZ	Nottingham City T
YN06JWC	Sanders Coaches	YN14MUO	Nottingham City T	YN19EFA	Nottingham City T
YN06JWF	Sanders Coaches	YN14MUP	Nottingham City T	YN19EFB	Nottingham City T
YN06JWP	Sanders Coaches	YN14MUU	Nottingham City T	YN19EFC	Nottingham City T
YN06MXP	Lloyds	YN14MUV	Nottingham City T	YN19EFD	Nottingham City T
YN06MXR	DRM	YN14MUW	Nottingham City T	YN19EFE	Nottingham City T
YN06MXU	Newport	YN14MUY	Nottingham City T	YN19EFF	Nottingham City T
YN06MXV	Newport	YN14MVA	Nottingham City T	YN19EFG	Nottingham City T
YN06NXR	Sanders Coaches	YN14MVC	Nottingham City T	YN19EFJ	Nottingham City T
YN06NXS	Sanders Coaches	YN14MVD	Nottingham City T	YN19EFK	Nottingham City T
YN06PFF	Globe	YN14MVE	Nottingham City T	YN19EFL	Nottingham City T
YN06TFZ	Ipswich Buses	YN14MVF	Nottingham City T	YN19EFM	Nottingham City T
YN06UGP	Moffat & Williamson	YN14MVG	Nottingham City T	YN19EFN	Nottingham City T
YN06WMT	Connexions	YN14MVH	Nottingham City T	YN19EFP	Nottingham City T
YN07DSU	JMB Travel	YN14MVK	Nottingham City T	YN19EFR	Nottingham City T
YN07DUU	Sanders Coaches	YN14MVL	Nottingham City T	YN19EFS	Nottingham City T
YN07EAX	Tanat Valley	YN14MVM	Nottingham City T	YN19EFT	Nottingham City T
YN07EYK	Redline	YN14MVO	Nottingham City T	YN19EFU	Nottingham City T
YN07EYM	Connexions	YN15EJA	Nottingham City T	YN19EFV	Nottingham City T
YN07EYP	Vectare	YN15EJC	Nottingham City T	YN19EFW	Nottingham City T
YN07EYT	Vectare	YN15EJD	Nottingham City T	YN19EFX	Nottingham City T
YN07EYX	Sanders Coaches	YN15EJE	Nottingham City T	YN19EFY	Nottingham City T
YN07EYY	Sanders Coaches	YN15EJF	Nottingham City T	YN19EFZ	Nottingham City T
YN07LDY	DRM	YN15EJJ	Nottingham City T	YN19EGC	Nottingham City T
YN07LHD	Eastern TH	YN15EJK	Nottingham City T	YN19EGD	Nottingham City T
YN07LHP	Eastern TH	YN16BNO	Minsterley Motors	YN19EGE	Nottingham City T
YN07LHU	Eastern TH	YN16WTX	Lloyds	YN19EGF	Nottingham City T
YN07LHX	Eastern TH	YN16WTY	Lloyds	YN19EGJ	Nottingham City T
YN07OPG	Globe	YN16WTZ	Lloyds	YN19EGK	Nottingham City T
YN08CXA	Minsterley Motors	YN17CEO	White Bus	YN19EGX	Nottingham City T
YN08DDU	Yeomans	YN17MJF	Vectare	YN19EGY	Nottingham City T
YN08DFK	Connexions	YN17ONJ	Cardiff Bus	YN19EHB	Nottingham City T
YN08DFL	Connexions	YN17ONK	Cardiff Bus	YN19EHC	Nottingham City T
YN08DHG	Weardale	YN17ONL	Cardiff Bus	YN19EHD	Nottingham City T
YN08DHJ	Weardale	YN18SVA	Nottingham City T	YN19EHE	Nottingham City T
YN08DHL	Vision Bus	YN18SVC	Nottingham City T	YN22BLX	Nottingham City T
YN08DHM	Whippet	YN18SVD	Nottingham City T	YN22BLZ	Nottingham City T
YN08HYY	Vision Bus	YN18SVE	Nottingham City T	YN22BMO	Nottingham City T
YN08MKX	Vision Bus	YN18SVF	Nottingham City T	YN22BMU	Nottingham City T
YN08MKZ	Vision Bus	YN18SVU	Nottingham City T	YN22BMV	Nottingham City T
YN08MLY	Vectare	YN18SVV	Nottingham City T	YN22BMY	Nottingham City T
YN08OAM	Eastern TH	YN18SVW	Nottingham City T	YN22BMZ	Nottingham City T
YN08OAO	Eastern TH	YN18SVX	Nottingham City T	YN22BNA	Nottingham City T
YN08OAP	Eastern TH	YN18SVY	Nottingham City T	YN22BNB	Nottingham City T
YN08OCR	Eastern TH	YN18SVZ	Nottingham City T	YN22BND	Nottingham City T
YN10ABK	White Bus	YN18SXA	Nottingham City T	YN22BNE	Nottingham City T
YN10ABX	Moffat & Williamson	YN18SXB	Nottingham City T	YN22BNF	Nottingham City T
YN10ABZ	Moffat & Williamson	YN18SXC	Nottingham City T	YN22BNJ	Nottingham City T
YN10FZT	Newport	YN18SXD	Nottingham City T	YN22BNK	Nottingham City T
YN10GBO	Tyrers	YN18SXE	Nottingham City T	YN22BNL	Nottingham City T
YN11FBG	Hornsby	YN18SXF	Nottingham City T	YN22BNO	Nottingham City T
YN11FUA	Lloyds	YN18SXG	Nottingham City T	YN22BNU	Nottingham City T
YN11FUJ	Yeomans	YN18SXJ	Nottingham City T	YN22BNV	Nottingham City T
YN12CRX	Minsterley Motors	YN18SXK	Nottingham City T	YN22BNX	Nottingham City T
YN12CRZ	Minsterley Motors	YN18SXL	Nottingham City T	YN22BNY	Nottingham City T
YN12CSO	Globe	YN18SXM	Nottingham City T	YN22BNZ	Nottingham City T
YN13AVX	Sanders Coaches	YN18SXO	Nottingham City T	YN22BOF	Nottingham City T
YN13GBY	Compass Travel	YN18ZPB	Falcon	YN53CFF	Sanders Coaches
YN13GDY	Compass Travel	YN19EEJ	Nottingham City T	YN53CFP	Eastern TH
YN14MTJ	Nottingham City T	YN19EEM	Nottingham City T	YN53CFU	Eastern TH
YN14MTK	Nottingham City T	YN19EEO	Nottingham City T	YN53CFV	Eastern TH
YN14MTO	Nottingham City T	YN19EEP	Nottingham City T	YN53CFX	Eastern TH
YN14MTU	Nottingham City T	YN19EER	Nottingham City T	YN53CFY	Eastern TH
YN14MTV	Nottingham City T	YN19EES	Nottingham City T	YN53CFZ	Sanders Coaches
YN14MTX	Nottingham City T	YN19EET	Nottingham City T	YN53EKZ	Yeomans
YN14MTY	Nottingham City T	YN19EEU	Nottingham City T	YN53GGU	Newport
YN14MTZ	Nottingham City T	YN19EEV	Nottingham City T	YN53PZR	Newport
YN14MUA	Nottingham City T	YN19EEW	Nottingham City T	YN53RYD	Vectare

YN53RYF Xelabus
YN53RYR Vectare
YN54AFF Eastern TH
YN54AFJ Eastern TH
YN54AFU Sanders Coaches
YN54AFV Sanders Coaches
YN54AJX Hornsby
YN54AOC Newport
YN54NXL Beestons
YN54OCE Newport
YN55KME Moffat & Williamson
YN55NDY Beestons
YN55NHA Eastern TH
YN55NHB Eastern TH
YN55NHF Eastern TH
YN55NHP Eastern TH
YN55NHV Eastern TH
YN55NJE Eastern TH
YN55NJF Eastern TH
YN55NJK Eastern TH
YN55NJV Eastern TH
YN55NKA Eastern TH
YN55NKC Eastern TH
YN55NKE Eastern TH
YN55NKH Eastern TH
YN55NKJ Eastern TH
YN55NKK Eastern TH
YN55NKL Eastern TH
YN56FAK Tyrers
YN56FAM Tyrers
YN56FAO Tyrers
YN56FAU Tyrers
YN56FBK Cardiff Bus
YN56FBY Connexions
YN56FCJ Weardale
YN56FDD Vectare
YN56FDX Vectare
YN56FEV Newport
YN56FEX Newport
YN56NVF Connexions
YN56NVG Connexions
YN56SGU Vectare
YN57FWH Sanders Coaches
YN57FWJ Sanders Coaches
YN57FYV DRM
YN57FYW DRM
YN57FYX DRM
YN57FZT Newport
YN57FZU Newport
YN57FZV Newport
YN57FZY Newport
YN58FXH Brylaine Travel
YN60BYZ Yeomans
YN60FMF Minsterley Motors
YN61AXC Weardale
YN61EOL White Bus
YN62AAE Sanders Coaches
YN63WEC Nottingham City T
YN64CAV Landflight
YN65XFG Nottingham City T
YN65XFH Nottingham City T
YN65XFJ Nottingham City T
YN65XFK Nottingham City T
YN65XFL Nottingham City T
YN65XFM Nottingham City T
YN65XFO Nottingham City T
YN65XFP Nottingham City T
YN65XFR Nottingham City T
YN65XFS Nottingham City T
YN65XFT Nottingham City T
YN65XFU Nottingham City T
YN65XFV Nottingham City T
YN65XFW Nottingham City T
YN65XFX Nottingham City T
YN66VYH White Bus
YN66VYJ White Bus
YN67CFE Marshalls
YN69DOH Nottingham City T
YN69DOJ Nottingham City T
YN69DOU Nottingham City T
YN69DPE Nottingham City T
YN69DPF Nottingham City T
YN69DPK Nottingham City T
YN69DPO Nottingham City T
YN69DPU Nottingham City T
YN69DPV Nottingham City T
YN69DPX Nottingham City T
YN69DPY Nottingham City T
YN69DPZ Nottingham City T
YN69DRO Nottingham City T
YN69DRV Nottingham City T
YN69DRX Nottingham City T
YN69DRZ Nottingham City T
YN69DSE Nottingham City T
YN69DSO Nottingham City T
YN69DSU Nottingham City T
YN69XVC Falcon
YN71CYK Nottingham City T
YO02PCV Townlynx
YO52FHD Townlynx
YP11SPV Nottingham Community
YP17UFA Nottingham City T
YP17UFB Nottingham City T
YP17UFC Nottingham City T
YP17UFD Nottingham City T
YP17UFE Nottingham City T
YP17UFH Nottingham City T
YP17UFJ Nottingham City T
YP17UFK Nottingham City T
YP17UFL Nottingham City T
YP17UFM Nottingham City T
YP17UFN Nottingham City T
YP17UFO Nottingham City T
YP17UFR Nottingham City T
YP17UFS Nottingham City T
YP17UGA Nottingham City T
YP17UGB Nottingham City T
YP17UGC Nottingham City T
YP17UGD Nottingham City T
YP17UGE Nottingham City T
YP17UGF Nottingham City T
YP17UGG Nottingham City T
YP17UGH Nottingham City T
YP17UGJ Nottingham City T
YP17UGK Nottingham City T
YP17UGL Nottingham City T
YP17UGM Nottingham City T
YP17UGN Nottingham City T
YP17UGO Nottingham City T
YP17UGR Nottingham City T
YP17UGT Nottingham City T
YP59ODU Tyrers
YP59ODV Tyrers
YP59ODW Tyrers
YP59OEA Vision Bus
YP59OEC Vision Bus
YP59OED Vision Bus
YP59OEE Vision Bus
YP59OEF Vision Bus
YP59OEG Vision Bus
YP59OEH Vision Bus
YP59OEJ Vision Bus
YP59OEK Vision Bus
YP59OEL Vision Bus
YP59OEM Vectare
YP59OEO Vectare
YP59OES Vectare
YP59OET Vectare
YP59OEV Vectare
YP63WFA Nottingham City T
YP63WFB Nottingham City T
YP63WFC Nottingham City T
YP63WFD Nottingham City T
YP63WFE Nottingham City T
YP63WFF Nottingham City T
YP63WFG Nottingham City T
YP63WFH Nottingham City T
YP63WFJ Nottingham City T
YP63WFK Nottingham City T
YR10BDV Hornsby
YR10FFX UNO
YR10FGC UNO
YR10FGF UNO
YR10FGM UNO
YR17ATU Landflight
YR20VHT Vectare
YR59FYP Eastern TH
YR59FYT Ipswich Buses
YR59FYU Eastern TH
YR59FZB Cardiff Bus
YR59FZD Cardiff Bus
YR61RPV Ipswich Buses
YR61RPY Ipswich Buses
YR61RRU Ipswich Buses
YR61RRV Ipswich Buses
YR61RRZ Ipswich Buses
YR61RSV Ipswich Buses
YR61RTV Ipswich Buses
YR61RUC Ipswich Buses
YR61RUH Ipswich Buses
YR61RUJ Ipswich Buses
YR61RUL Ipswich Buses
YR61RUU Ipswich Buses
YR61RUV Ipswich Buses
YR61RUW Ipswich Buses
YR61RVE Ipswich Buses
YR61RVF Ipswich Buses
YR63OKB Minsterley Motors
YRC194 Tanat Valley
YRW194 Connexions
YS03ZLN Globe
YS21JUT Newport
YS21JUX Newport
YS21JVA Newport
YS21JVD Newport
YS21JVE Newport
YS21JVF Newport
YS21JVG Newport
YS21JVH Newport
YS21JVJ Newport
YS21JVK Newport
YS21OFA Newport
YS66YFA Lloyds
YS66YFB Lloyds
YS66YFC Lloyds
YS66YFD Lloyds
YT09FLM Yeomans
YT09FLZ DRM
YT09ZCE Hornsby
YT09ZCF Eastern TH

YT10UWA	Whippet
YT10UWD	Whippet
YT10UWF	Whippet
YT10UWJ	Cardiff Bus
YT10UWK	Cardiff Bus
YT10UWL	Cardiff Bus
YT10UWM	Cardiff Bus
YT10UWN	Cardiff Bus
YT10UWO	Cardiff Bus
YT10UWP	Cardiff Bus
YT10UWR	Cardiff Bus
YT11LTF	Ipswich Buses
YT11LUF	Newport
YT11LUH	Newport
YT11LUJ	Newport
YT11LUL	Newport
YT11LUO	Newport
YT11LUP	Newport
YT13HKZ	Falcon
YT15AWC	Minsterley Motors
YT15YTO	Yeomans
YT18PHX	Lloyds
YT18PHZ	Lloyds
YT18YEO	Yeomans
YT19DWY	Falcon
YT19DWZ	Falcon
YT19EBU	Minsterley Motors
YT19EBV	Minsterley Motors
YT59DXZ	Eastern TH
YT59DYS	Compass Travel
YT59DYU	Compass Travel
YT59DYV	Compass Travel
YT59DYW	Compass Travel
YT59NZM	Eastern TH
YT59PBV	Cardiff Bus
YT59PBY	Cardiff Bus
YT59PBZ	Cardiff Bus
YT59PCO	Cardiff Bus
YT59SFF	Hornsby
YT59SFY	Eastern TH
YT61FFM	Nottingham City T
YT61FFN	Nottingham City T
YT61FFO	Nottingham City T
YT61FFP	Nottingham City T
YT61FFR	Nottingham City T
YT61FFS	Nottingham City T
YT61FFU	Nottingham City T
YT61FFV	Nottingham City T
YT61GOJ	Ipswich Buses
YT61GOP	Nottingham City T
YT61GOX	Atlantic Travel
YT61GPF	Nottingham City T
YT61GPJ	Nottingham City T
YT61GPK	Nottingham City T
YT61GPO	Nottingham City T
YT61GPU	Nottingham City T
YT61GPV	Nottingham City T
YT61GPZ	Atlantic Travel
YT66HCJ	Tanat Valley
YT66NPG	Tanat Valley
YT68BYD	White Bus
YT68YEO	Yeomans
YT73BVB	Atlantic Travel
YT73BVC	Atlantic Travel
YUP6	Weardale
YVF158	Vectare
YVJ677	Sanders Coaches
YW68PFA	Landflight
YW68PFD	Landflight
YW68PFE	Landflight
YW68PFF	Landflight
YW68PFG	Landflight
YW68PFJ	Landflight
YW68PFK	Landflight
YX08MDY	Redline
YX09AEV	Warrington
YX09AFA	Warrington
YX09ETA	Moffat & Williamson
YX09FKT	Compass Travel
YX09FMD	Redline
YX09FMJ	Grant Palmer
YX09FNJ	Compass Travel
YX09HYV	Hornsby
YX09HYV	Hornsby
YX09HZF	Grant Palmer
YX09HZJ	Go-Coach
YX10BCU	Warrington
YX10BFO	Vectare
YX10BFZ	Redline
YX10ECA	Warrington
YX10FEF	Redline
YX10FEH	Eastern TH
YX10FEU	Eastern TH
YX10FEV	Eastern TH
YX10FFA	Eastern TH
YX10FFE	Eastern TH
YX10FFG	Eastern TH
YX10FFJ	Redline
YX10FFK	Eastern TH
YX10FFL	Eastern TH
YX10FFM	Eastern TH
YX10FFN	Eastern TH
YX11AEN	Go-Coach
YX11AGK	Newport
YX11AGY	Newport
YX11AGZ	Newport
YX11AHV	Newport
YX11CRK	Newport
YX11CRU	Newport
YX11CSY	Go-Coach
YX11CTO	Eastern TH
YX11CTU	Eastern TH
YX11HPU	Grant Palmer
YX12AEW	Redline
YX12AGY	Redline
YX12AXU	Redline
YX12AZN	Redline
YX12DHG	Grant Palmer
YX12DHJ	Grant Palmer
YX12DHM	Vectare
YX12DHN	Go-Coach
YX12DHO	Vectare
YX12DKA	Redline
YX12DME	Newport
YX12DMF	Newport
YX12FPY	Vectare
YX12FRC	Compass Travel
YX12TAT	Faresaver
YX13AEU	Nottingham City T
YX13BNO	Nottingham City T
YX13BNV	Redline
YX13EGC	Newport
YX13EGD	Newport
YX14EFM	Minsterley Motors
YX14RWL	Ipswich Buses
YX14SCZ	White Bus
YX15OVT	Safeguard
YX15XMJ	Warrington
YX16NWB	White Bus
YX16OBO	Vectare
YX16OBP	Eastern TH
YX16OBR	Eastern TH
YX16OBS	Vectare
YX16OCV	Compass Travel
YX16OCZ	Landflight
YX16ODJ	Vision Bus
YX16OHT	Grant Palmer
YX16OHU	Grant Palmer
YX17NDY	Vectare
YX17NJN	Faresaver
YX17NJO	Aintree Coachlines
YX17NPY	UNO
YX17NPZ	UNO
YX17NRE	UNO
YX17NRF	UNO
YX17NRJ	UNO
YX17NRK	UNO
YX17NRO	Faresaver
YX17NSJ	Faresaver
YX17NTN	Faresaver
YX17NTU	Vectare
YX17NTV	White Bus
YX17NYW	Eastern TH
YX17NYZ	Eastern TH
YX17NZA	Falcon
YX17NZB	Townlynx
YX17OGF	Whitelaws
YX17OGR	Tanat Valley
YX17OGS	Tanat Valley
YX18KND	Grant Palmer
YX18KNE	Grant Palmer
YX18KNN	Falcon
YX18KNR	Vision Bus
YX18KNV	Vision Bus
YX18KNW	Ipswich Buses
YX18KNY	Compass Travel
YX18KOD	Safeguard
YX18KTP	Warrington
YX18KTT	Warrington
YX18KTV	Warrington
YX18KUA	Warrington
YX18KUB	Warrington
YX18KUD	Faresaver
YX18KUE	Compass Travel
YX18KUH	Lloyds
YX18KUK	Compass Travel
YX18KUN	Compass Travel
YX18KUT	Falcon
YX18KUY	Globe
YX18KUY	Lloyds
YX18KWA	Blackpool Transport
YX18KWB	Blackpool Transport
YX18KWC	Blackpool Transport
YX18KWD	Blackpool Transport
YX18KWE	Blackpool Transport
YX18KWF	Blackpool Transport
YX18KWG	Blackpool Transport
YX18KWH	Blackpool Transport
YX18KWJ	Blackpool Transport
YX18KWK	Blackpool Transport
YX18KWL	Blackpool Transport
YX18KWM	Blackpool Transport
YX18KWN	Blackpool Transport
YX18KWO	Blackpool Transport
YX18KWP	Blackpool Transport
YX18KWR	Blackpool Transport
YX18KWS	Blackpool Transport
YX18KWT	Blackpool Transport
YX18KWU	Landflight
YX18KYE	Lloyds

YX18LHD	Safeguard	YX22OGP	Globe	YX63GXV	Eastern TH
YX19MKE	Globe	YX22OGR	Vectare	YX63GXW	Eastern TH
YX19MKN	Houston's	YX22OGS	Vectare	YX63GXY	Ipswich Buses
YX19MLY	Globe	YX22OGT	Vectare	YX63KFG	Eastern TH
YX19MLZ	Globe	YX22OGU	Vectare	YX63KFJ	Eastern TH
YX19ONK	Falcon	YX22OGV	Vectare	YX63KFK	Eastern TH
YX19ONL	Falcon	YX22OGW	Vectare	YX63LGE	Ipswich Buses
YX19ONM	Falcon	YX22OGY	Vectare	YX63LGF	Ipswich Buses
YX19ONN	Falcon	YX22OGZ	Vectare	YX63LHU	Eastern TH
YX19ONO	Falcon	YX22OHA	Vectare	YX63LJA	Sanders Coaches
YX19ONP	Falcon	YX22OHB	Vectare	YX63LJC	Sanders Coaches
YX19ONU	Vision Bus	YX22OHD	Landflight	YX63LJE	Redline
YX19ONV	Reliance	YX22OHE	Landflight	YX63ZVP	Faresaver
YX19OOU	Blackpool Transport	YX22OHZ	Falcon	YX63ZVS	Faresaver
YX19OOV	Blackpool Transport	YX22OJB	Cardiff Bus	YX63ZVV	Ipswich Buses
YX19OOW	Blackpool Transport	YX22OJC	Cardiff Bus	YX63ZVW	Ipswich Buses
YX19OOY	Blackpool Transport	YX22OJJ	Vectare	YX64VPR	Travelmasters
YX19OPA	Blackpool Transport	YX22OJY	Weardale	YX65RFN	Aintree Coachlines
YX19OPB	Blackpool Transport	YX22OLN	Lynx	YX65RGV	Redline
YX19OPC	Blackpool Transport	YX22OLO	Lynx	YX65RHA	Globe
YX19OPD	Blackpool Transport	YX22OLP	Lynx	YX65RHA	Globe
YX19OPE	Blackpool Transport	YX23ORV	Falcon	YX65RHF	Warrington
YX19OPF	Blackpool Transport	YX23OSE	Lynx	YX66WCJ	Ipswich Buses
YX19OPH	Blackpool Transport	YX23OSG	Vision Bus	YX66WCK	Ipswich Buses
YX19OPJ	Blackpool Transport	YX23OSK	Roberts Travel	YX66WCL	Ipswich Buses
YX19OPK	Blackpool Transport	YX23OSW	Vision Bus	YX66WCM	Ipswich Buses
YX19OPL	Blackpool Transport	YX23OSY	Vision Bus	YX66WFD	Go-Coach
YX19OUU	Stotts Tours	YX23OSZ	Falcon	YX66WFE	Go-Coach
YX19OUV	Stotts Tours	YX23OUM	Compass Travel	YX66WFF	Go-Coach
YX19OWA	Reliance	YX23OUN	Compass Travel	YX66WFG	Go-Coach
YX20OCE	Vision Bus	YX23OUO	Compass Travel	YX66WFH	Go-Coach
YX20OCO	Stotts Tours	YX23OUP	Compass Travel	YX67USP	Xelabus
YX20OCP	Stotts Tours	YX23OXA	Vision Bus	YX67UYD	Compass Travel
YX20OCY	Falcon	YX23OXB	Vision Bus	YX67UYE	Compass Travel
YX20OCZ	Falcon	YX23OXC	Vision Bus	YX67UYF	Compass Travel
YX20ODA	Vision Bus	YX23OXD	Tanat Valley	YX67UYG	Travelmasters
YX20ODB	Vision Bus	YX23OYH	Falcon	YX67UYK	Travelmasters
YX20OFA	Blackpool Transport	YX24MBF	Roberts Travel	YX67VFR	UNO
YX20OFB	Blackpool Transport	YX24OVZ	Xelabus	YX67VFS	UNO
YX20OFD	Blackpool Transport	YX24OWA	Xelabus	YX67VFT	UNO
YX20OFE	Blackpool Transport	YX24OWM	Compass Travel	YX67VFU	UNO
YX20OFG	Blackpool Transport	YX24OXE	Compass Travel	YX67VFV	UNO
YX20OFH	Blackpool Transport	YX24OXF	Compass Travel	YX67VFW	UNO
YX20OFJ	Blackpool Transport	YX24OXG	Compass Travel	YX67VFY	UNO
YX20OFK	Blackpool Transport	YX24OXH	Compass Travel	YX67VGJ	Falcon
YX20OFL	Blackpool Transport	YX24PLJ	Tanat Valley	YX67VGK	Falcon
YX20OFM	Blackpool Transport	YX58EEY	Moffat & Williamson	YX68UAC	Vectare
YX20OFN	Blackpool Transport	YX59CAA	Hornsby	YX68UCA	Vectare
YX20OFO	Blackpool Transport	YX60DXY	Vectare	YX68UJO	Lloyds
YX20OFP	Blackpool Transport	YX60FUD	Grant Palmer	YX68UJP	Falcon
YX20OFR	Blackpool Transport	YX60FUH	Grant Palmer	YX68UJR	Falcon
YX20OGW	Travelmasters	YX61DVT	Newport	YX68UJU	Compass Travel
YX21RNU	Vision Bus	YX61DVU	Newport	YX68UJV	Compass Travel
YX21RPO	Falcon	YX61DVV	Newport	YX68UJW	Compass Travel
YX21RPU	Vision Bus	YX61FYG	Vision Bus	YX68ULP	Falcon
YX21RPV	Vision Bus	YX61FYN	Vision Bus	YX68ULR	Falcon
YX21RRZ	Vision Bus	YX61FYO	Vision Bus	YX68ULS	Falcon
YX21RSO	Vision Bus	YX62BHD	UNO	YX68ULT	Falcon
YX21RSU	Vision Bus	YX62BHW	UNO	YX68ULU	Falcon
YX21RSV	Globe	YX62BJF	UNO	YX68URM	Reliance
YX21RTO	Compass Travel	YX62BJU	UNO	YX69KZD	Landflight
YX21RTU	Compass Travel	YX62BUA	UNO	YX69NPJ	Nottingham City T
YX21RTV	Compass Travel	YX62BUE	UNO	YX69NRE	Nottingham City T
YX21RTZ	Globe	YX62ECT	Faresaver	YX69NRF	Nottingham City T
YX21RYH	Globe	YX62EDO	Faresaver	YX69NRJ	Nottingham City T
YX22BVB	Stotts Tours	YX62EDP	Faresaver	YX69NRK	Nottingham City T
YX22BVC	Stotts Tours	YX62FET	Faresaver	YX69NRL	Nottingham City T
YX22BVD	Stotts Tours	YX63GXP	Compass Travel	YX69NRN	Nottingham City T
YX22OGJ	Globe	YX63GXR	Compass Travel	YX69NRO	Nottingham City T
YX22OGJ	Vectare	YX63GXS	Ipswich Buses	YX69NRU	Nottingham City T

Illustrating the Go-Coach colours is Enviro 200 MMC, one of five currently on loan. Numbered 8345, YX66WFF was seen on Star Hill Road while heading for Lockbottom. *Richard Godfrey*

YX69NRV	Nottingham City T	YX71OHE	Atlantic Travel	YX73OVM	Vectare
YX69NUC	Landflight	YX71OHF	Atlantic Travel	YX73OVN	Vectare
YX69NUE	Landflight	YX71OHU	Globe	YX73OVO	Vectare
YX69NUF	Landflight	YX71OHU	Globe	YX73OVP	Vectare
YX69NWB	Vectare	YX71OHY	White Bus	YX73OYP	Falcon
YX69NXK	Grant Palmer	YX71OHZ	White Bus	YX73OYR	Falcon
YX70OHP	White Bus	YX71OJF	Grant Palmer	YX73PJJ	Compass Travel
YX70OHR	White Bus	YX71OJG	Grant Palmer	YX73PJO	Compass Travel
YX70OHS	Go-Coach	YX71OJH	Falcon	YX73PJU	Compass Travel
YX70OHT	White Bus	YX71OJN	Falcon	YX73PJV	Compass Travel
YX70OHU	White Bus	YX71OJU	White Bus	YX73PJY	Compass Travel
YX70OHV	White Bus	YX72OJE	Globe	YX73PNJ	Lynx
YX70OKG	Grant Palmer	YX72OJF	Globe	YX73RFZ	White Bus
YX70OKH	Grant Palmer	YX72OJY	Falcon	YY15CMX	Faresaver
YX70OKR	Globe	YX72OJZ	Falcon	YY15CNA	Faresaver
YX70OKT	Globe	YX72OKS	Grant Palmer	YY15CNC	Faresaver
YX70OKU	Falcon	YX72OKT	Grant Palmer	YY15CNE	Faresaver
YX70OKV	Falcon	YX72OLJ	Cardiff Bus	YY15FZC	Eastern TH
YX70OKW	Falcon	YX72OLK	Cardiff Bus	YY15FZD	Eastern TH
YX70OKZ	Falcon	YX72OLL	Cardiff Bus	YY15JNJ	Lloyds
YX70OLA	Newport	YX72OLM	Cardiff Bus	YY15NHK	Compass Travel
YX71LTN	Safeguard	YX72OMV	Tanat Valley	YY15NHL	Compass Travel
YX71LTO	Safeguard	YX72OMY	Vectare	YY15NHM	Compass Travel
YX71LVD	Roberts Travel	YX72ONB	Vectare	YY15NHN	Compass Travel
YX71LVE	Roberts Travel	YX72OND	Vectare	YY15NHU	JMB Travel
YX71OGZ	Falcon	YX72ONE	Vectare	YY15NJO	Eastern TH
YX71OHA	Atlantic Travel	YX72ONR	Newport	YY15NKA	UNO
YX71OHB	Atlantic Travel	YX72ONU	Newport	YY15NKC	UNO
YX71OHC	Atlantic Travel	YX73OMJ	Tanat Valley	YY15NKD	UNO
YX71OHD	Atlantic Travel	YX73OTY	Falcon	YY15NKE	UNO

YY17GPF	Compass Travel	YY64GWC	Vision Bus	YY67HBH	Vectare
YY17GPJ	Compass Travel	YY64GXG	UNO	YY67USC	Eastern TH
YY17GPK	Compass Travel	YY64TZX	Compass Travel	YY67USD	Eastern TH
YY17GPO	Compass Travel	YY64YKJ	Faresaver	YY67USH	Warrington
YY17GPU	Compass Travel	YY65WUA	White Bus	YY67USP	Aintree Coachlines
YY17GPX	Faresaver	YY66OFE	Grant Palmer	YY69TLV	White Bus
YY17GRZ	Minsterley Motors	YY66PDX	Warrington	YY69TLX	White Bus
YY24EKZ	Lynx	YY66PEO	Warrington	YY69TMZ	Falcon
YY24ELC	Lynx	YY66PFA	Warrington	YY73PKN	White Bus
YY24ELH	Lynx	YY66PFO	Warrington	YY73RFX	White Bus
YY24ELJ	Lynx	YY66PFU	Warrington	YY73RGX	Vectare
YY24HBG	Vectare	YY66PFV	Xelabus	YY73RGZ	Vectare
YY24HBH	Vectare	YY66PFZ	Compass Travel	YY73RHA	Vectare
YY24HBP	Vectare	YY66PGE	Compass Travel	YY73RHE	Vectare
YY24HBU	Vectare	YY66PGF	Compass Travel	YY73RHF	Vectare
YY24HCV	Roberts Travel	YY66PGK	Compass Travel	YY73TGU	Vectare
YY64GWA	Vision Bus	YY67HBG	Houston's	YY73TGV	Vectare

Warrington's new Volvo BZLs will displace most of the older fleet. Illustrating the current Cheshire Cat scheme is Enviro 200 MMC 201, CH04CAT. *Mark Lyons*

ISBN978-1-912063-67-3 © Published by British Bus Publishing Ltd, August 2024

British Bus Publishing Ltd, 16 St Margaret's Drive, Telford, TF1 3PH

Telephone: 01952 255669

web; www.britishbuspublishing.co.uk
e-mail: sales@britishbuspublishing.co.uk